Guide to the Essentials of
WORLD HISTORY

PEARSON
Prentice
Hall

Upper Saddle River, New Jersey
Glenview, Illinois
Needham, Massachusetts

TO THE TEACHER

The *Guide to the Essentials of World History* is designed to provide students with the most essential content in their world history course in an easy-to-follow format. The text summaries and graphic organizers will help students organize key information. Vocabulary terms are highlighted and defined in the text narrative, as well as in the glossary. A chapter test at the end of each chapter checks students' understanding of the basic content.

You may wish to use the *Guide to the Essentials* as a preview or review of textbook chapters covered in the course, or as a summary of textbook chapters that cannot be studied in detail because of time considerations.

SPECIAL CONSULTANT

Michael Sells
Professor of Religion
Haverford College
Haverford, Pennsylvania

ISBN 0-13-063109-4

4 5 6 7 8 9 10   07 06 05 04 03

Contents

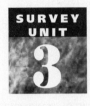

SURVEY UNIT 8
MODERN ERA UNIT 5

The World Today

SURVEY   MODERN ERA

Toward Civilization (Prehistory–3000 B.C.)

SECTION 1 — UNDERSTANDING OUR PAST

■ TEXT SUMMARY

Human beings have always been interested in learning about the past. We know that the first people lived more than two million years ago in prehistoric times. **Prehistory** is the time before people invented writing. Prehistoric people had no cities, countries, or organized governments. About 5,000 years ago, some people in different parts of the world invented writing. This event marked the beginning of history.

Archaeology is a science that helps us learn about our past. It is the study of how early people lived. Archaeologists are scientists who study **artifacts.** Artifacts are things, such as tools, weapons, and clothing, that early people left behind. By studying artifacts, archaeologists learn about the beliefs and actions of our ancestors.

Historians also study how people lived in the past. Like archaeologists, they study things that early people left behind. However, historians pay more attention to written artifacts such as letters and diaries. They use records to explain how events happened.

Geography is the study of Earth and its people. Geography and history are linked because geography shows how places influence the way people live. Geographers study what happens when groups of people move from one place to another. They also study the movement of goods and ideas.

> ### THE **BIG** IDEA
>
> Scientists and historians study the past to see how early people lived.

■ GRAPHIC SUMMARY: *Learning About the Past*

	ARCHAEOLOGY	HISTORY	GEOGRAPHY
What is it?	Study of early people by examining things they left behind	Study of what happened and how people lived in the past	Study of Earth, its people and its resources
Who does it?	Archaeologist	Historian	Geographer
What do they do?	Study artifacts, such as tools, weapons, clothing, pottery	Study artifacts, especially written documents	Study where people lived and why they lived there
Why do they do it?	To learn about the beliefs and activities of a group of people	To learn how events happened	To learn how places affect the way people live and how people move from place to place

Archaeologists, geographers, and historians all contribute to our knowledge of the past.

■ REVIEW QUESTIONS

1. Give an example of how geography affects the way people live.

2. **Chart Skills** What do archaeologists learn from studying artifacts?

SECTION 2 THE DAWN OF HISTORY

TEXT SUMMARY

The earliest people lived during the Old Stone Age. This period is also called the Paleolithic Age. The Old Stone Age began more than two million years ago. Paleolithic people were **nomads.** Nomads moved from place to place, hunting and gathering food. They made simple tools and weapons from stone, bone, or wood. As time passed, they developed a spoken language.

Paleolithic people developed religious beliefs. They thought that the world was filled with spirits. They also believed in life after death. Old Stone Age people buried tools and weapons with their dead so that they had what they needed in the afterlife.

Around 10,000 B.C., people made two very important discoveries. They learned to plant seeds to grow food. They also learned to tame animals. These discoveries allowed people to stay in one place and to farm. This change marked the beginning of the New Stone Age, or Neolithic Age. Historians call these discoveries the Neolithic agricultural revolution because they changed the way people lived.

After the Neolithic agricultural revolution, there was more food to eat. With more food, the population increased. People lived together in villages. These villages later led to the development of advanced societies called **civilizations.**

THE BIG IDEA

Old Stone Age people made tools and learned skills to survive. The New Stone Age brought farming and settled communities.

GRAPHIC SUMMARY: *The First People*

Old Stone Age or Paleolithic Period (2,500,000 B.C.)

- Very small population
- Nomads
- Hunters and gatherers
- Simple tools and weapons
- First spoken languages
- Discovery of fire
- Cave paintings
- Belief in afterlife
- Women important

New Stone Age or Neolithic Period (10,000 B.C.)

- Increasing population
- Villages
- Farmers
- Domestic animals
- Calendar and technology
- Personal possessions
- Village headman and council of elders
- Women less important

People of the Old Stone Age and the New Stone Age made many important discoveries.

REVIEW QUESTIONS

1. What two discoveries were made during the Neolithic agricultural revolution?
2. **Graph Skills** When did people discover fire?

SECTION 3

BEGINNINGS OF CIVILIZATION

◼ TEXT SUMMARY

By about 5,000 years ago, the first civilizations began to develop. Historians have found basic features common to most early civilizations. Some of these features are cities, organized governments, and social classes. (See chart below.)

The most important feature of early civilizations was the rise of cities. The first cities developed as people began to farm along river valleys in the Middle East, Africa, and Asia. These river valleys provided water, **fertile** (rich) soil, and transportation. Farmers could produce extra food. More food helped the population to grow. As a result, villages slowly grew into cities.

All civilizations change as time passes. Civilizations change when the environment changes. For example, when all the wood in a forest has been cut, people must find new building materials. Civilizations also change through **cultural diffusion**. Cultural diffusion is the sharing of ideas and technology. Cultural diffusion results from war, trade, and the migration of people.

> ### THE **BIG** IDEA
>
> **Civilizations share basic features. Contacts between civilizations brought cultural change.**

◼ GRAPHIC SUMMARY: *What Makes a Civilization?*

CENTRAL GOVERNMENTS

ORGANIZED RELIGION

DIFFERENT JOBS

SOCIAL CLASSES

What Makes A Civilization?

SYSTEM OF WRITING

ART AND ARCHITECTURE

ROADS, BRIDGES, TEMPLES, AND OTHER PUBLIC WORKS

CITIES

There are eight basic features common to most early civilizations.

◼ REVIEW QUESTIONS

1. When does cultural diffusion happen?

2. Diagram Skills Name three features of a civilization.

CHAPTER 1 *Test*

◪ IDENTIFYING MAIN IDEAS

Write the letter of the correct answer in the blank provided. (10 points each)

____ 1. Archaeologists refer to the period of time before people invented writing systems as
A. geography.
B. technology.
C. prehistory.
D. archaeology.

____ 2. Which of the following is the study of how early people lived?
A. prehistory
B. archaeology
C. geography
D. technology

____ 3. Historians are like archaeologists in that they both study how people lived by examining
A. longitude and latitude.
B. artifacts.
C. plants and animals.
D. regions.

____ 4. When did early people first begin to use stone tools?
A. in the Old Stone Age
B. in the New Stone Age
C. in the Neolithic Age
D. at the beginning of civilization

____ 5. What evidence suggests that early people believed in life after death?
A. They painted angels on cave walls.
B. They held elaborate funeral services.
C. They buried their dead with great care.
D. They kept track of their good deeds in books.

____ 6. What was the Neolithic revolution?
A. the change from hunting and food-gathering to farming
B. a war for independence
C. a rejection of Paleolithic values by Neolithic people
D. the movement of people to North America

____ 7. Which of the following changes characterized the New Stone Age?
A. People moved from villages to cities.
B. People began living in caves.
C. People established farming villages.
D. People migrated to North America.

____ 8. Which was a key feature of early civilizations?
A. cities
B. social equality
C. steel-making
D. a system of exchanging goods for money

____ 9. Where did the first cities emerge?
A. along trade routes
B. in river valleys
C. along the Mediterranean coast
D. in the Americas

____ 10. Which of the following aided cultural diffusion among ancient peoples?
A. trade
B. new technology
C. poor leaders
D. farming

First Civilizations: Africa and Asia (3200 B.C.–500 B.C.)

SECTION 1 ANCIENT KINGDOMS OF THE NILE

■ TEXT SUMMARY

One of the earliest civilizations arose in Egypt about 5,000 years ago. Since most of Egypt is desert, people settled along the Nile River. The fertile soil of the Nile Valley produced good crops. Yearly floods soaked the land and deposited rich soil. The river also served as a highway for travel by boat.

The Egyptian ruler was called a **pharaoh.** After the death of a pharaoh, power usually passed to another member of his family. These ruling families were called **dynasties.** The three periods of Egyptian history are the Old Kingdom, the Middle Kingdom, and the New Kingdom. (See chart below.)

During the Old Kingdom, the pharaohs created a strong government. They also built giant **pyramids.** These burial tombs took many years and millions of stone blocks to build.

The Middle Kingdom was a troubled period. The Nile did not flood regularly, so in many years crops did not grow. Although Egypt conquered other lands, rebellions were common. Then invaders, called the Hyksos, defeated the pharaoh's army and gained control of Egypt.

The New Kingdom began over a hundred years later when the Egyptians drove out the Hyksos. Powerful pharaohs created a large empire that reached the Euphrates River. Egypt traded with Asia and Africa. Trade and warfare spread Egyptian culture to other countries. In return, those places gave Egyptians new ideas.

> ### THE **BIG** IDEA
>
> Historians split ancient Egyptian history into three periods—the Old Kingdom, the Middle Kingdom, and the New Kingdom.

■ GRAPHIC SUMMARY: *Ancient Egyptian Civilization*

OLD KINGDOM
(2700 B.C.–2200 B.C.)

- Pharaohs organize strong government
- Egyptians believe pharaoh is a god
- Old Kingdom also known as Pyramid Age
- Egyptians build giant pyramids at Giza

MIDDLE KINGDOM
(2050 B.C.–1800 B.C.)

- Egyptians suffer food shortages
- People rebel
- Pharaohs drain land for farming
- Hyksos conquer Egypt

NEW KINGDOM
(1550 B.C.–1100 B.C.)

- Powerful pharaohs build large empire
- Queen Hatshepsut becomes Pharaoh; encourages trade
- Ramses II conquers Palestine and Syria
- Egyptian power begins to decline

A rich, long-lasting civilization developed in the Nile Valley.

■ REVIEW QUESTIONS

1. Why did Egyptian civilization emerge along the Nile River?

2. Chart Skills When did Queen Hatshepsut rule Egypt?

EGYPTIAN CIVILIZATION

TEXT SUMMARY

Religion was an important part of everyday life in ancient Egypt. Egyptians believed in many gods and goddesses. They also believed in life after death. They prepared their dead for the afterlife through a preservation process called **mummification.** The mummies of some pharaohs were buried in pyramids. (See Section 1.)

Egyptian society had its own class system. Egyptians believed that the pharaoh was both a god and a king. He had the highest position in society. Next were the priests, who served the gods and goddesses. Near the bottom was the biggest group, the peasant farmers. Beneath the peasants were the slaves. (See diagram at right.) Women in Egyptian society had more freedom than in any other ancient civilization.

The Egyptians made many advances in learning and art. In medicine, they learned to cure many illnesses and to perform surgery. Egyptians developed a calendar very similar to the one we use today. They also created picture writing called **hieroglyphics.** Their temples and monuments have survived thousands of years. Egyptian statues and paintings show daily life, ceremonies, and military victories.

THE BIG IDEA

Ancient Egypt was an advanced society where people were divided into classes.

GRAPHIC SUMMARY:

Egyptian Society

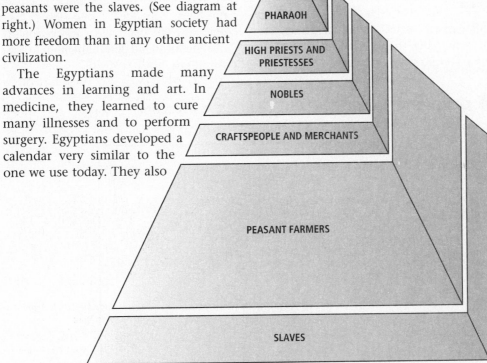

PHARAOH

HIGH PRIESTS AND PRIESTESSES

NOBLES

CRAFTSPEOPLE AND MERCHANTS

PEASANT FARMERS

SLAVES

Egyptian society was organized into classes.

REVIEW QUESTIONS

1. What were three achievements of Egyptian civilization?

2. **Diagram Skills** What were the top three classes of people in Egyptian society?

CITY-STATES OF ANCIENT SUMER

◼ TEXT SUMMARY

Geography helps explain the rise of civilization in the Middle East. Like the Nile River in Egypt, the Tigris and Euphrates rivers made the land around them fertile. This region was called the **Fertile Crescent** because the good farm land curved in the shape of a crescent. (See map below.) The land between the rivers was called Mesopotamia.

> ### THE **BIG** IDEA
>
> The fertile land between the Tigris and Euphrates rivers supported the development of Sumerian civilization.

By 5,000 years ago, villages along the Tigris and the Euphrates rivers had grown into busy cities. These city-states made up the civilization of Sumer. Different city-states fought each other for land and water. During the fighting, people turned to powerful war leaders to protect them. Over time, leadership passed down within the war leaders' families, and social classes developed.

Like the Egyptians, the Sumerians made important contributions to the world. They built the first wheeled vehicles. Systems of dikes and canals provided flood protection and water for crops. The Sumerians were the first people to write. They used wedge-shaped writing called **cuneiform** to record information as early as 3200 B.C. They developed algebra and geometry. By studying the sun and the moon, the Sumerians invented an accurate calendar. Later on, invaders conquered the Sumerians. The conquerors adopted many Sumerian ideas and passed them on to later civilizations.

◼ GRAPHIC SUMMARY: *The Fertile Crescent*

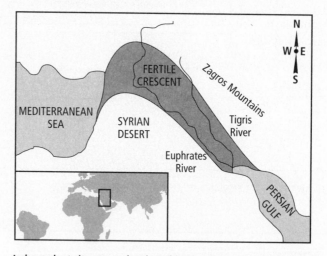

Independent city-states developed in Mesopotamia, the part of the Fertile Crescent between the Tigris and Euphrates rivers.

◼ REVIEW QUESTIONS

1. What were two achievements of the Sumerians?

2. Map Skills What are the two major rivers in the Fertile Crescent?

INVADERS, TRADERS, AND EMPIRE BUILDERS

■ TEXT SUMMARY

Many groups invaded and conquered the civilizations of the Fertile Crescent. Some invaders destroyed the city-states. Others stayed to rule. Some of these rulers created large, well-organized **empires.** An empire is a group of territories under the control of one ruler or government.

One powerful ruler was King Hammurabi of Babylon. Around 1790 B.C., Hammurabi put together a set of laws, called the Code of Hammurabi. The Code of Hammurabi was the first major collection of laws in history. Another important ruler was Darius of Persia. In 522 B.C., Darius controlled an empire that stretched from Asia Minor to India. Darius divided his empire into **provinces,** or locally controlled regions. Later rulers used his ideas about government.

Different groups of people met in the crossroads of the Fertile Crescent. Many groups made advances in technology and ideas. For example, Phoenicians developed the first real alphabet to record their trades. (See chart below.) Through warfare and trade, ideas and technology spread. As time passed, the contributions of people who lived in the Fertile Crescent reached all the way to India and Europe.

> **THE BIG IDEA**
>
> Strong rulers united the lands of the Fertile Crescent into well-organized empires.

■ GRAPHIC SUMMARY: *Civilizations of the Fertile Crescent*

CIVILIZATION	DATES	ACHIEVEMENTS
Babylonians	1790 B.C.	Created Code of Hammurabi Studied astronomy, especially sun, moon, and planets
Hittites	1400 B.C.	Forged iron tools and weapons
Assyrians	1100 B.C.	Set up one of the first libraries Maintained a well-organized society
Persians	539 B.C.	Conquered large empire from Asia Minor to India Improved trade by using coins and standard measures Zoroaster taught new religion
Phoenicians	600 B.C.	Gained fame as great sailors and traders Created alphabet similar to the one we use today

The people of the Fertile Crescent made advances in government, technology, science, and writing.

■ REVIEW QUESTIONS

1. Why was the Code of Hammurabi important?

2. Chart Skills Which civilization used coins?

THE ROOTS OF JUDAISM

◼ TEXT SUMMARY

The Hebrews were one of the groups that lived in the Fertile Crescent. The Hebrews recorded their history in a sacred book called the Torah. According to the Torah, God made a **covenant,** or binding agreement, with Abraham to be the God of the Hebrews. Later, the Egyptian pharaoh made slaves of the Hebrews. Moses helped the Hebrews escape. For 40 years, they wandered in the desert. Finally, they set up the kingdom of Israel, with Jerusalem as its capital. The Hebrews believed that God had promised them this land. Later, the kingdom split apart, and both sections were conquered.

In time, Hebrew beliefs evolved into the religion we know today as Judaism. Judaism was different from the other ancient religions. Other religions believed in many gods. Judaism was **monotheistic,** teaching a belief in one God. The Hebrews also believed that God had chosen them as His people. The laws of Judaism are called the Ten Commandments. They describe how people should behave toward God and toward each other.

Often in Jewish history, there were **prophets,** or spiritual leaders, who explained God's will. The prophets taught about moral standards and justice. For example, powerful people should protect the weak. Prophets also taught that all people were equal before God.

> ### THE **BIG** IDEA
>
> **The Jewish religion was unique in the ancient world because it was monotheistic.**

◼ GRAPHIC SUMMARY: *Judaism: The Religion of the Hebrews*

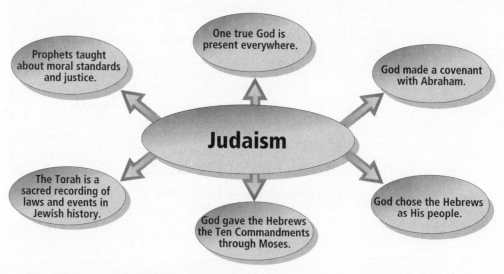

Judaism evolved from the religion of the Hebrews.

◼ REVIEW QUESTIONS

1. What were two lessons taught by the prophets?

2. Diagram Skills What were three beliefs of Judaism?

Name _____ Class _____ Date _____

CHAPTER 2 *Test*

◼ IDENTIFYING MAIN IDEAS

Write the letter of the correct answer in the blank provided. (10 points each)

____ 1. Why did Egyptians look forward to the annual flooding of the Nile River?
  A. Egyptians could travel faster on the flooded waters.
  B. Flooding allowed other groups to use the Nile as a trade route.
  C. The flood produced farmland by depositing a rich layer of soil called silt.
  D. The floods allowed the Egyptians to test the strength of their dikes.

____ 2. Why did the Egyptians of the Old Kingdom design and build the pyramids?
  A. The pyramids were built to serve as temples where all Egyptians came to pray.
  B. The pyramids were built as tombs and were filled with the objects people would need in life after death.
  C. The pyramids were built to show the wealth and strength of the Egyptians.
  D. The pyramids were built to use up surplus supplies of limestone blocks.

____ 3. How did ancient Egyptians view their pharaohs?
  A. as gods
  B. as cruel rulers
  C. as father figures
  D. as equals

____ 4. What social class contained the majority of Egyptians?
  A. high priests and priestesses
  B. nobles
  C. peasant farmers
  D. merchants, scribes, and artisans

____ 5. The Fertile Crescent is the arc of land that
  A. lies between the Tigris and Euphrates rivers.
  B. curves from the Persian Gulf to the eastern Mediterranean coast.
  C. lies along the banks of the Nile River.
  D. reaches down to the African kingdom of Nubia.

____ 6. Sumer was made up of
  A. provinces.
  B. independent city-states.
  C. hieroglyphics.
  D. two kingdoms.

____ 7. What was the significance of the Code of Hammurabi?
  A. It was the first set of laws all written by one person.
  B. It was the first major collection of laws in history.
  C. It was the first system of laws that allowed for unrestricted personal vengeance.
  D. It was the first set of laws to deal exclusively with criminal laws.

____ 8. What new technology did the Hittites bring to Mesopotamia?
  A. a writing system
  B. land irrigation
  C. iron making
  D. a code of laws

____ 9. A covenant is
  A. a recorded history of the Hebrews.
  B. the belief in one god.
  C. a spiritual leader.
  D. a binding agreement.

____ 10. How did the Jewish view of God differ from the beliefs of most people in the ancient world?
  A. Jews believed in many gods who shared equal power.
  B. Jews believed in one main God with several minor gods and goddesses.
  C. Jews believed in only one God.
  D. Jews believed in no God.

Early Civilizations in India and China

(2500 B.C.–256 B.C.)

 **SECTION 1** *CITIES OF THE INDUS VALLEY*

TEXT SUMMARY

The Indus Valley is located on the subcontinent of India in South Asia. High mountain ranges separate India from other lands. Three major regions in India include a well-watered northern plain, a dry central plateau, and coastal plains. (See chart below.) Its huge size and varied geography have made India hard to unite.

Winds called **monsoons** bring rain every summer. When there is not enough rain, people cannot grow crops. When there is too much, rivers such as the Ganges rise in deadly floods.

The first Indian civilization arose in the Indus River valley about 2500 B.C., but archaeologists did not uncover it until 1922. Many of its cities remain undiscovered. Scientists have found writing samples, but they do not yet understand them. As a result, we do not know much about this civilization. We do know that the Indus Valley civilization was larger than any other at that time. Its cities were very well planned. Most Indus Valley people were farmers. They were the first to grow cotton and weave it into cloth. Valley merchants traveled far and traded with the cities of Sumer. (See Chapter 2, Section 3.)

Around 1750 B.C., Indus Valley civilization began to **decline,** or become weaker. We do not know exactly why this happened. In the end, nomadic warriors called Aryans conquered the Indus Valley.

> **THE BIG IDEA**
>
> Archaeologists uncovered the remains of India's first civilization in the Indus River valley.

GRAPHIC SUMMARY: *The Regions of the Indian Subcontinent*

THE NORTHERN PLAIN	THE DECCAN PLATEAU	THE COASTAL PLAINS
• Himalaya mountains in northeast	• Triangular shape	• Eastern Ghats and Western Ghats
• Hindu Kush mountains in northwest	• No major rivers	• Flat land along coasts
• Two sacred rivers: Indus River and Ganges River	• Land too dry for farming	• Fishing and trading
• Fertile land	• Small population	• Rain and rivers provide water for farming

The subcontinent of India has three major geographic regions.

REVIEW QUESTIONS

1. Why are there many things we do not know about the Indus Valley civilization?

2. **Chart Skills** If you wished to start farming in the Indian subcontinent, which region would be your *last* choice for a location? Why?

KINGDOMS OF THE GANGES

◼ TEXT SUMMARY

The Aryans were a warrior group that moved across Asia. Early Aryans did not build cities and left few artifacts. Around 1500 B.C., they conquered the Indus Valley civilization. The Aryans gradually mixed with the people they conquered and learned new ways. They settled in villages to farm and raise cattle. About 800 B.C., the Aryans learned to make tools and weapons out of iron. With these, the Aryans carved out more territory in the Ganges River basin. Soon cities ruled by chiefs called **rajahs** arose. By 500 B.C., the Aryans had built a new Indian civilization.

Most of what we know about the Aryans comes from a collection of writings called the **Vedas.** The period from 1500 B.C. to 500 B.C., the Vedic Age, is named for those writings. According to the Vedas, the Aryans were warriors who loved food, music, and chariot racing. They organized people into social classes by **occupation** or job type. This was the beginning of the **caste system.** (See chart below.) Under this system, people stayed in the social class into which they were born.

Like the Vedas, stories called **epics** have been told and retold over thousands of years. The epics also give us information about the lives and the beliefs of the early Aryans. They tell stories of families, wars, and love. The Aryans used epics to teach values and lessons about how people should behave.

> ### THE **BIG** IDEA
>
> **Aryan warriors invaded India and developed a new civilization.**

◼ GRAPHIC SUMMARY: *Early Class System in Aryan Society*

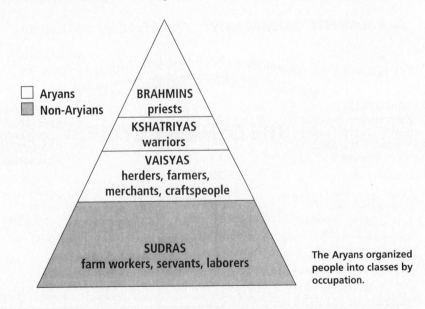

☐ Aryans
▨ Non-Aryians

BRAHMINS
priests

KSHATRIYAS
warriors

VAISYAS
herders, farmers,
merchants, craftspeople

SUDRAS
farm workers, servants, laborers

The Aryans organized people into classes by occupation.

◼ REVIEW QUESTIONS

1. Why are the Vedas and epics important to historians?

2. Diagram Skills To which class did non-Aryans belong?

EARLY CIVILIZATION IN CHINA

■ TEXT SUMMARY

China covers a huge area, but until recent times most people lived only along the east coast or in the river valleys. China is surrounded by mountains, jungles, deserts, and an ocean. Therefore, China was more **isolated**, or cut off, from the rest of the world than other early civilizations were.

Chinese civilization arose around the Huang He and Yangzi river valleys. About 1650 B.C., a Chinese people called the Shang gained control of part of northern China. During the Shang dynasty, kings controlled only a small amount of land. Groups of families called **clans** controlled most of the land. Merchants and craftspeople earned a living in cities. However, most people were peasants who lived in farming villages.

In 1027 B.C., the Zhou people overthrew the Shang and set up their own dynasty. The Zhou told the people that the gods had become angry with the Shang and now had chosen the Zhou to rule. The right to rule was called the **Mandate of Heaven,** or the divine right to rule. From that time on, each new dynasty would claim the Mandate of Heaven. (See diagram below.)

The Chinese made progress in many areas during the Shang and Zhou periods. They developed a complex religion. The Chinese created a system of writing and made the first books. They learned to produce bronze and made detailed figures. They discovered how to make silk thread from the cocoons of silkworms. The Chinese also studied astronomy, recording eclipses of the sun and inventing an accurate calendar.

> ### THE **BIG** IDEA
>
> Early Chinese people developed a complex civilization. They made many advances in learning and in the arts.

■ GRAPHIC SUMMARY: *The Mandate of Heaven*

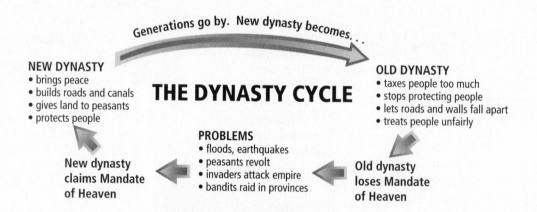

Generations go by. New dynasty becomes...

NEW DYNASTY
• brings peace
• builds roads and canals
• gives land to peasants
• protects people

THE DYNASTY CYCLE

OLD DYNASTY
• taxes people too much
• stops protecting people
• lets roads and walls fall apart
• treats people unfairly

New dynasty claims Mandate of Heaven

PROBLEMS
• floods, earthquakes
• peasants revolt
• invaders attack empire
• bandits raid in provinces

Old dynasty loses Mandate of Heaven

The Mandate of Heaven helped explain the rise and fall of dynasties.

■ REVIEW QUESTIONS

1. Why was China isolated from the rest of the world?

2. **Diagram Skills** What were two reasons why an old dynasty might lose the Mandate of Heaven?

CHAPTER 3 *Test*

▊ IDENTIFYING MAIN IDEAS

Write the letter of the correct answer in the blank provided. (10 points each)

____ 1. The summer monsoon is a defining feature of life in India because
A. the hot, dry air destroys crops.
B. it does not come every year.
C. people harness its winds to produce energy.
D. it brings rains that water the crops.

____ 2. What evidence suggests that the Indus Valley cities had a well-organized government?
A. well-planned cities
B. writings on stone seals
C. records left by kings
D. statues of goddesses

____ 3. Which of the following is a true statement about the Indus Valley civilization?
A. It lasted for thousands of years.
B. It spread to other parts of Asia.
C. It thrived until modern times.
D. It disappeared without a trace and was only rediscovered in 1922.

____ 4. Aryan settlers established cities
A. in the low coastal areas.
B. in the jungles of the Ganges basin.
C. guarding the high mountain passes.
D. on the dry, barren plateau.

____ 5. The Aryans divided people into classes by
A. age.
B. race.
C. occupation.
D. sex.

____ 6. Priest-poets told stories called epics to
A. entertain children.
B. teach different lessons about good behavior.
C. keep people informed.
D. explain the caste system.

____ 7. China was more isolated from the rest of the world than other early civilizations because
A. it is an island.
B. it is surrounded by mountains, jungles, deserts, and an ocean.
C. Chinese rulers forbade travel.
D. no one wanted to trade with China.

____ 8. Which statement best describes what government was like under the Shang?
A. Shang kings maintained control over vast areas of land.
B. Clans controlled most of the land.
C. Women dominated the government during the Shang dynasty.
D. Individual city-states, led by merchants, controlled the government.

____ 9. The Mandate of Heaven is the idea behind which of the following?
A. the feudal system
B. the dynastic cycle
C. ancestor worship
D. the Shang social order

____ 10. Which of the following was first achieved by the Chinese?
A. ironworking
B. the horse-drawn chariot
C. a writing system based on the alphabet
D. silkmaking

Empires of India and China (600 B.C.–A.D. 550)

SECTION 1 HINDUISM AND BUDDHISM

◼ TEXT SUMMARY

Hinduism and Buddhism were two very important religions that developed in ancient India. They both influenced Indian civilization.

Hinduism is one of the most complex religions in the world. Unlike most major religions, Hinduism has no single founder. It also has many sacred texts, instead of just one. Hinduism developed and changed over 3,500 years. Many different groups added their own beliefs and gods. To a Hindu, different gods are forms of an all-powerful spiritual force. The goal of life is to become one with this force. Hindus believe that because it is hard to achieve this goal in one lifetime, people are **reincarnated** many times. Reincarnation

is the rebirth of the soul in another bodily form. Hinduism is still an important religion in India today.

The founder of Buddhism, Siddhartha Gautama, or Buddha, was born about 566 B.C. After studying and reflecting, he believed that he had found the cure for human suffering. Buddha taught that individuals must free themselves from desires. He urged people to live a moral life and avoid evil words and actions. Through meditation, a person might achieve **enlightenment,** or understanding. Buddha attracted many followers. After his death, missionaries spread his teachings across many parts of Asia. Although Buddhism took root in other parts of Asia, it slowly declined in India.

> ### THE **BIG** IDEA
>
> India was the birthplace of two major religions—Hinduism and Buddhism.

◼ GRAPHIC SUMMARY: *Hinduism and Buddhism*

HINDUISM
- No one founder, developed over 3,500 years
- Supported caste system
- Had many priests and religious rituals
- Important in India today

- Told people to live moral lives
- Many followers avoided violence
- Accepted reincarnation
- Goal was union with an all-powerful spiritual force

BUDDHISM
- Buddha was founder in late 500s B.C.
- Rejected caste system
- Focused on individuals
- Important throughout Asia, but few followers in India today

Although there are important differences, Hinduism and Buddhism share many of the same beliefs.

◼ REVIEW QUESTIONS

1. Which religion is still widely practiced in India today?

2. **Diagram Skills** What two beliefs do Hinduism and Buddhism share?

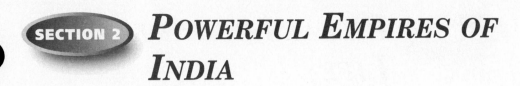

SECTION 2 | # POWERFUL EMPIRES OF INDIA

TEXT SUMMARY

In 321 B.C., the Mauryas conquered most of northern and southern India. They built the first Indian empire. The Maurya dynasty set up a strong government. Officials collected taxes and managed road building. People sought justice in royal courts. Maurya rule was often harsh, and brutal secret police reported problems to the emperor. After almost 150 years, the empire declined.

Fierce rivalries, geography, and distance made it difficult to keep India united. In spite of conflicts, by 100 B.C. India had become a center of world trade. Merchants traded fine cloth, jewels, and spices with faraway civilizations such as China and Egypt.

About 500 years after the Mauryas, the Gupta dynasty again united much of India. This empire also had a strong government. The Gupta period was a golden age, a time of peace and **prosperity,** or wealth. Under the Guptas, advances were made in the arts and sciences. Building, painting, and literature flowered. Mathematicians invented the number system we use today as well as the decimal system. Gupta doctors used herbs to cure sick people. They performed plastic surgery and vaccinated people against smallpox. The Gupta empire lasted for over 200 years, then it too declined.

> ### THE **BIG** IDEA
>
> Two great empires, the Maurya and the Gupta, flourished in ancient India.

GRAPHIC SUMMARY: *Empires of Ancient India*

Empire	MAURYA	GUPTA
Dates	321 B.C.–185 B.C.	A.D. 320–550
Location	Northern and southern India	Northern India
Government	• Harsh rule • Organized government • Officials collected taxes • Government owned factories	• Mild rule • Organized government • Villages and cities had power
Learning	• Schools and libraries in capital • Missionaries spread Buddhism	• Golden age of learning • Number system we use today; decimal system • Plastic surgery; vaccines for smallpox • Carvings of gods and animals

The diverse peoples of India rarely united. Yet the Mauryas and the Guptas were able to unite much of the subcontinent.

REVIEW QUESTIONS

1. List three advances in learning made by the Guptas.

2. Chart Skills How did Maurya rule differ from Gupta rule?

SECTION 3 — PILLARS OF INDIAN LIFE

◼ TEXT SUMMARY

The caste system began in early Aryan times. (See Chapter 3.) By Gupta times, there were many castes. Caste was linked to Hindu beliefs. People in different castes were considered different types of beings. Caste rules developed to prevent mixing among the groups. These rules determined where people lived, what they ate, and what jobs they did. High castes had more status than low castes. People believed that **karma** determined their caste. Karma refers to all of the actions of a person's life that affect his or her next life. Living by caste rules meant that a person would be born into a higher caste in his or her next life. Although the caste system might seem unfair to us, it created a stable society.

In India, the village was the center of everyday life. A village was made up of a group of homes surrounded by fields. Most people farmed and depended on summer monsoons for water. Together, farmers built irrigation systems to control the monsoon rains. A village was left alone as long as it paid taxes to the rulers of the region. A local headman and council made decisions and led the village.

In the village, people lived in **joint families.** Parents, children, and grandchildren lived together. Joint families created unity and security. The oldest male was the head of the household, but property belonged to the whole family. Every family member had certain duties according to caste values. As time passed, the roles of women became more limited.

> ### THE **BIG** IDEA
>
> **The three important parts of Indian life were the caste system, villages, and the family.**

◼ GRAPHIC SUMMARY: *The Caste System*

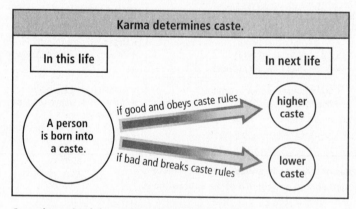

Karma determines caste.

In this life — A person is born into a caste.

if good and obeys caste rules → In next life: higher caste

if bad and breaks caste rules → lower caste

Caste determined the position of a person in Indian society.

◼ REVIEW QUESTIONS

1. How were joint families organized?

2. **Diagram Skills** According to Indian beliefs, what would happen if a person broke caste rules?

PHILOSOPHY AND RELIGION IN CHINA

■ TEXT SUMMARY

The late Zhou dynasty was a troubled time in China. There were many wars, and economic and social changes disrupted everyday life. Thinkers looked for ways to make society better.

China's most important thinker was Confucius. Confucius taught people to accept their place in society. He said that older people were superior to younger people. Husbands were superior to their wives. Respect for parents was the most important duty. Confucius also taught that people were good. Honesty, hard work, and caring promoted harmony. He believed a ruler should set a good example for the people. Rulers should take advice from educated men. Thus, education became the way to advance in Chinese society.

Another thinker, Hanfeizi, believed that people were bad. He taught that a good ruler should use strict laws and harsh punishments. The teachings of Hanfeizi were called **Legalism.** Many rulers used the ideas of Legalism to help them rule.

A third Chinese thinker was Laozi. His teachings were called **Daoism.** Daoists wanted to live in harmony with nature. To Daoists, the best government was the one that governed least.

The ideas of these three thinkers influenced Chinese life. Confucianism taught people how to behave. Legalism punished those who would not do their duty. Daoism affected people's view of nature. Chinese ideas and beliefs also spread to Japan, Korea, and Vietnam.

THE **BIG** IDEA

Three schools of thought— Confucianism, Legalism, and Daoism—influenced the Chinese people.

■ GRAPHIC SUMMARY:

Proper Relationships in Society According to Confucius

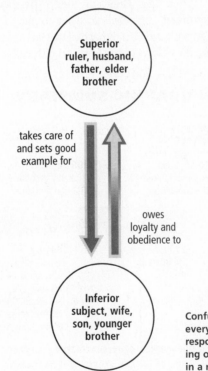

Superior
ruler, husband, father, elder brother

takes care of and sets good example for

owes loyalty and obedience to

Inferior
subject, wife, son, younger brother

Confucius believed that everyone had duties and responsibilities, depending on his or her position in a relationship.

■ REVIEW QUESTIONS

1. According to Confucius, what did a good ruler do?

2. Diagram Skills According to Confucius, what did a subject owe to a ruler?

STRONG RULERS UNITE CHINA

◼ TEXT SUMMARY

By 221 B.C., the ruler of the Qin people had conquered the Zhou. He called himself Shi Huangdi, or "First Emperor." Shi Huangdi used cruel methods to control China. He tortured, jailed, and killed those who did not support him. However, he made measurements standard, created national coins, and repaired canals and roads. The greatest achievement of the Qin was creating the Great Wall to keep out invaders. Thousands of workers labored for years to build the wall.

When Shi Huangdi died, the people **revolted,** or rebelled. They replaced the Qin with the Han dynasty. The Han changed the harsh laws of the Qin and reduced taxes.

The Han developed a civil service system. Exams based on the teachings of Confucius, not family influence, decided who would get government jobs. This system was used for nearly 2,000 years.

Han China was the most advanced civilization of its time. The Han learned to make paper out of wood pulp. They invented the wheelbarrow, the fishing reel, and the **rudder,** a device used to steer ships. In medicine, the Han used **acupuncture,** or treatment with needles, to reduce pain. They built beautiful temples and palaces. Artists carved jade and ivory. The Han opened a trade route called the Silk Road. The Silk Road connected China with lands as far west as Mesopotamia.

> ### THE **BIG** IDEA
>
> **Powerful emperors made China the most advanced civilization of its time.**

◼ GRAPHIC SUMMARY: *Early Civilization in China*

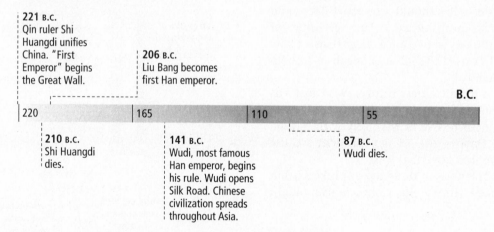

221 B.C.
Qin ruler Shi Huangdi unifies China. "First Emperor" begins the Great Wall.

206 B.C.
Liu Bang becomes first Han emperor.

210 B.C.
Shi Huangdi dies.

141 B.C.
Wudi, most famous Han emperor, begins his rule. Wudi opens Silk Road. Chinese civilization spreads throughout Asia.

87 B.C.
Wudi dies.

B.C.

220   165   110   55

The Qin and Han dynasties created a huge empire that united China.

◼ REVIEW QUESTIONS

1. What was the Silk Road?

2. **Time Line Skills** Who was the first Han emperor? When did he come to power?

CHAPTER 4 *Test*

▪ IDENTIFYING MAIN IDEAS

Write the letter of the correct answer in the blank provided. (10 points each)

____ 1. According to Hinduism, what is the ultimate goal of existence?
   A. to become a priest
   B. to become one with the spiritual force
   C. to be reincarnated
   D. to obey one's dharma

____ 2. Buddha taught that a person could achieve enlightenment through
   A. meditation.
   B. reincarnation.
   C. suffering.
   D. belief in one God.

____ 3. The golden age of India took place during the rule of the
   A. Mauryas.
   B. Romans.
   C. Guptas.
   D. Dravidians.

____ 4. Hindus believed that caste could be changed by
   A. the emperor.
   B. marriage.
   C. the law of karma.
   D. moving.

____ 5. Village decisions were made by
   A. popular vote.
   B. the village headman and council.
   C. outside rulers.
   D. priests and scribes.

____ 6. In an Indian household, the head of the family was the
   A. oldest female.
   B. oldest male.
   C. oldest daughter.
   D. youngest son.

____ 7. Confucius believed the best ruler was
   A. someone who would pass strict laws.
   B. a virtuous man who led by example.
   C. a man with little education.
   D. a great military hero.

____ 8. According to Legalism, the way to achieve order was
   A. to provide a ruler who set a good moral example.
   B. to pass strict laws and enforce them with harsh punishments.
   C. to live by the natural balance of yin and yang.
   D. to appeal to man's natural goodness.

____ 9. Daoists believed that the best government
   A. was one that governed the least.
   B. was one that took control of people's lives.
   C. was one that brought order to human affairs.
   D. was one that forced people to work on government projects.

____ 10. How did Han emperors select officials to run the government?
   A. They appointed people from noble families.
   B. They chose the best-educated priests and scribes.
   C. They set up a system of civil service exams that were open to anyone.
   D. They allowed villages to appoint their own officials.

Ancient Greece (1750 B.C.–133 B.C.)

 SECTION 1

EARLY PEOPLE OF THE AEGEAN

■ TEXT SUMMARY

Around 1750 B.C., the Minoans built the first Greek civilization on the island of Crete in the eastern Mediterranean Sea. The Minoans were sea traders who traveled to Egypt and Mesopotamia. Through trade, they learned new ideas and technology. The Minoans adapted these new ideas to their own culture.

The Mycenaeans conquered Crete around 1400 B.C. and built a new civilization. The Mycenaeans were also sea traders. They traded with Sicily, Italy, Egypt, and Mesopotamia. The Mycenaeans learned many skills, including writing, from the Minoans. They also learned from the Egyptians and Mesopotamians. They passed on these influences to later Greeks.

The Mycenaeans are best remembered for the Trojan War, which took place around 1250 B.C. In this war, the Mycenaeans defeated the trading city of Troy. Much of what we know about this period comes from reading the **epic** poems of Homer. An epic is a long poem that tells the story of a hero or heroes. The *Iliad* and the *Odyssey* give us clues about the lives of the ancient Greeks. The poems have influenced writers and artists for almost 3,000 years.

Around 1200 B.C., sea raiders attacked the Mycenaeans. For the next 300 years, Greek civilization slowly declined.

> ### THE **BIG** IDEA
>
> **The Minoans and Mycenaeans were the first Greek civilizations.**

■ GRAPHIC SUMMARY: *Early Greek Civilizations*

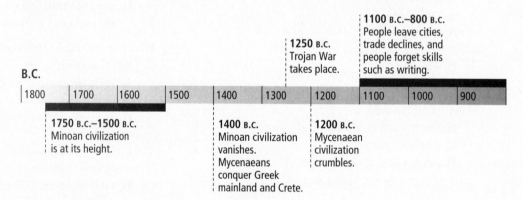

1250 B.C.
Trojan War takes place.

1100 B.C.–800 B.C.
People leave cities, trade declines, and people forget skills such as writing.

B.C.

| 1800 | 1700 | 1600 | 1500 | 1400 | 1300 | 1200 | 1100 | 1000 | 900 |

1750 B.C.–1500 B.C.
Minoan civilization is at its height.

1400 B.C.
Minoan civilization vanishes. Mycenaeans conquer Greek mainland and Crete.

1200 B.C.
Mycenaean civilization crumbles.

Minoan and Mycenaean civilizations learned from Egypt and Mesopotamia.

■ REVIEW QUESTIONS

1. Name two cultures from whom the Mycenaeans borrowed ideas.

2. Time Line Skills When was Minoan civilization at its height?

THE RISE OF GREEK CITY-STATES

◼ TEXT SUMMARY

Greece is made up of many isolated valleys and small islands. This geography prevented the Greeks from building a large empire like that of the Egyptians or Mesopotamians. Instead, the Greeks built small city-states. These city-states frequently fought one another.

Between 750 B.C. and 500 B.C., the Greek city-states tried different types of government. At first, city-states were ruled by kings. This type of government is called a **monarchy.** The landowning nobles won power as time passed. They created an **aristocracy,** or a government ruled by the landholding elite. In some city-states, a middle class of merchants, farmers, and artisans came to power. This form of government is called an **oligarchy.**

The two most powerful city-states were Sparta and Athens. They developed very different ways of life. Sparta was a monarchy, ruled by two kings. The Spartans created a military society. Spartan boys trained to be soldiers. Spartan girls trained to be mothers of soldiers. Athens, on the other hand, developed a limited **democracy,** or government by the people. However, only male citizens could vote in the assembly. Women could not participate. Unlike Sparta, Athens encouraged the arts, trade, and education.

THE BIG IDEA

Two powerful city-states, Athens and Sparta, arose in Greece.

◼ GRAPHIC SUMMARY: Two City-States: Athens and Sparta

ATHENS
- Limited democracy
- Laws made by assembly
- Only male citizens in assembly
- Trade with other city-states
- Education for boys
- Women inferior

(shared)
- Common language
- Shared heroes
- Olympic Games
- Same gods and religious beliefs

SPARTA
- Monarchy with two kings
- Military society
- Trade and travel not allowed
- Military training for all boys
- Girls trained to be mothers of soldiers
- Women obeyed men
- Women owned property

Although Athens and Sparta were similar in some ways, they developed very different styles of life.

◼ REVIEW QUESTIONS

1. How did geography affect early Greek civilization?

2. Diagram Skills Which city-state encouraged trade and education?

SECTION 3 · VICTORY AND DEFEAT IN THE GREEK WORLD

◼ TEXT SUMMARY

In 490 B.C., the Persians attacked the city-state of Athens. Other city-states joined Athens to fight the Persian Wars. After years of fighting, the Greeks defeated Persia. Athens emerged from the fighting as the most powerful city-state in Greece.

> ### THE **BIG** IDEA
>
> Competition among Greek city-states led to conflict.

The years after the Persian Wars were a golden age for Athens. A wise leader named Pericles ruled the city-state. This period is often called the Age of Pericles. Athens had a **direct democracy** under Pericles. This meant that male citizens helped to run the government. Pericles pointed out that citizens had a special responsibility to participate. Athens prospered in the Age of Pericles and became the cultural center of Greece. Many thinkers, writers, and artists came to Athens to take part in the growth of culture.

Sparta and its **allies,** or partners, resented Athenian wealth and power. They formed a league to promote oligarchy. Athens and its allies supported democracy. The Peloponnesian War broke out between the two sides in 431 B.C. After 27 years of fighting, Sparta defeated Athens. Soon after, Sparta fell to Thebes, another Greek city-state. Athenian democracy suffered, and the city declined. Fighting continued among the Greek city-states for almost 50 more years.

◼ GRAPHIC SUMMARY: *Persian Wars, 490 B.C.–479 B.C.*

Great wars and many battles affected the history of Greek city-states.

```
┌─────────────────────────────────────────────┐
│            Athens fights Persia.              │
│  Other Greek city-states fight on Athenian side. │
└─────────────────────────────────────────────┘
                      ▼
┌─────────────────────────────────────────────┐
│            Persians burn city of Athens.      │
└─────────────────────────────────────────────┘
                      ▼
┌─────────────────────────────────────────────┐
│              Greeks defeat Persians.          │
└─────────────────────────────────────────────┘
                      ▼
┌─────────────────────────────────────────────┐
│          Greeks believe gods protect them.    │
│     Athens becomes most powerful city-state.  │
└─────────────────────────────────────────────┘
```

◼ REVIEW QUESTIONS

1. Which city-state became the cultural center of Greece?

2. Diagram Skills What was a result of the Persian Wars?

▣ TEXT SUMMARY

Greek thinkers tried to understand the reasons why things happened. The Greeks called these thinkers **philosophers.** Socrates, Plato, and Aristotle were important Greek philosophers. Socrates taught that people should examine their beliefs and ideas. Plato, a student of Socrates, believed in reason. He taught that people could learn to organize an ideal society through the use of reason. Plato wanted a republic ruled by the best men and women. Aristotle felt that people should try to live balanced lives. These ideas have influenced people since ancient times.

The Greeks believed in beauty, balance, and order in the universe. Greek art and architecture reflected those ideas. Greek paintings and statues were lifelike but also **idealistic,** meaning that they showed individuals in their most perfect form. The most famous Greek building was the Parthenon. Architects today still use ancient Greek ideas in their buildings.

Greek literature began with the epics of Homer. Greek poets wrote about joy and sorrow. Plays had their roots in religious festivals. Actors performed outdoors with few props and little scenery. The characters wore masks that showed that the story was sad or happy. Aeschylus, Sophocles, and Euripides wrote **tragedies,** or plays that told stories of human conflict. Others created comedies. The Greeks also were concerned about accurate history.

THE **BIG** IDEA

Greek thinkers, artists, and writers explored the nature of the universe and the place of people in it.

▣ GRAPHIC SUMMARY: *The Greek Philosophers*

SOCRATES	PLATO	ARISTOTLE
Developed Socratic method: learning about beliefs and ideas by asking questions	Believed government should control lives of people	Believed one strong and good leader should rule
Government puts him to death	Divided society into three classes: workers, philosophers, and soldiers	Believed people should try to live balanced lives

Greek philosophers used reason and observation to discover why things happened.

▣ REVIEW QUESTIONS

1. What was the concern of Greek artists and architects?

2. Chart Skills What three social classes did Plato divide people into?

SECTION 5 ALEXANDER AND THE HELLENISTIC AGE

◪ TEXT SUMMARY

Macedonia was a mountain kingdom in the north of Greece. In 338 B.C., King Philip of Macedonia dominated all of the city-states to the south. His son, Alexander the Great, conquered the Persian empire and parts of India.

> ### THE **BIG** IDEA
>
> **Alexander the Great created a large empire and spread Greek culture throughout the region.**

Alexander spread Greek culture to many parts of the world. The conquered peoples learned Greek ways. The Greeks also learned the ways of the peoples they conquered. A new **Hellenistic** culture arose. It blended parts of Greek, Persian, Egyptian, and Indian life. Women gained rights during the Hellenistic period. Alexander's empire fell apart soon after his death.

However, Greek culture had a lasting impact on the regions he had ruled.

The city of Alexandria, Egypt, was at the heart of Hellenistic civilization. Its location made it the major marketplace of the empire. People from many nations met there. Alexandria was also a center of learning, with a museum, libraries, and a zoo. Its 440-foot-tall lighthouse was one of the wonders of the world.

Hellenistic thinkers made great advances in the sciences and in mathematics. Pythagoras developed a formula used to measure the sides of a right triangle. The astronomer Aristarchus discovered that the Earth moves around the sun. Archimedes explored the physical principles of the lever and pulley.

◪ GRAPHIC SUMMARY: *Hellenistic Civilization*

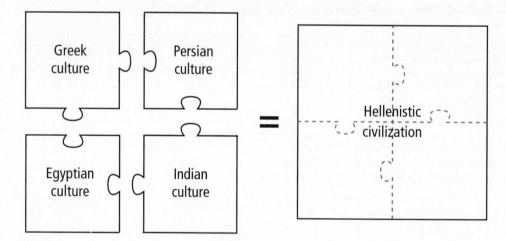

Hellenistic civilization was a blend of many cultures.

◪ REVIEW QUESTIONS

1. Why was Alexandria an important city?

2. **Diagram Skills** Which four cultures contributed to Hellenistic civilization?

CHAPTER 5 *Test*

▣ IDENTIFYING MAIN IDEAS

Write the letter of the correct answer in the blank provided. (10 points each)

____ **1.** Minoan civilization owed its success mainly to
   A. conquering other civilizations.
   B. its isolated location on Crete.
   C. trading with other civilizations.
   D. its strong rulers.

____ **2.** Homer's great epics, the *Iliad* and the *Odyssey,*
   A. reveal much about the lives of ancient Greeks.
   B. were written down and read by all Mycenaeans.
   C. are completely factual.
   D. were lost when the Dorians invaded from the north.

____ **3.** The rocky islands and isolated valleys of Greece contributed to the development of
   A. a large, united Greek empire.
   B. several different Greek languages.
   C. individual city-states.
   D. the Greek alphabet.

____ **4.** From childhood, Spartan boys were trained to be
   A. philosophers.
   B. politicians.
   C. soldiers.
   D. artists.

____ **5.** Athens enjoyed a golden age under the leadership of
   A. Pericles.
   B. Alexander.
   C. Darius.
   D. Themistocles.

____ **6.** The Peloponnesian War resulted from conflict between
   A. Athens and Sparta.
   B. Greece and Persia.
   C. Athens and Macedonia.
   D. Greece and Egypt.

____ **7.** Greek sculptors developed a style that combined realistic, natural poses with
   A. Egyptian influences.
   B. dramatic scenes of human suffering.
   C. images of ordinary people.
   D. an idealistic approach.

____ **8.** According to Plato, rational thought was necessary
   A. to rebuild fallen temples.
   B. to organize an ideal society.
   C. for enforcing ethical values.
   D. for creating realistic sculptures.

____ **9.** Which cultures contributed to the new Hellenistic civilization?
   A. Greek and Indian
   B. Greek, Persian, Indian, and Egyptian
   C. Greek, African, and Italian
   D. Indian and Persian

____ **10.** Alexander's greatest achievement was
   A. the conquest of India.
   B. the spread of Greek culture.
   C. a lasting empire.
   D. an alliance with Persia.

CHAPTER

6

Ancient Rome and the Rise of Christianity

(509 B.C.–A.D. 476)

 **SECTION 1**

THE ROMAN WORLD TAKES SHAPE

TEXT SUMMARY

THE BIG IDEA

Rome's central location helped the Romans unite Italy and all of the Mediterranean world under their control.

Rome began as a small city-state near the coast of central Italy. Italy is a peninsula that sticks out into the Mediterranean Sea. That location helped Rome to expand. The land itself also helped the Romans. Low mountains presented few natural barriers to expansion. People farmed on the fertile plains to support a growing population.

In 509 B.C., the Romans drove out their last king. The Romans did not want a king or a leader with too much power. Thus, they set up a new government called a **republic.** In a republic, officials are chosen by the people. At first, all government officials were **patricians,** or in the landholding upper class. The **plebeians** (farmers, merchants, and traders) had little power. In 450 B.C., the plebeians demanded written laws. Then, they won the right to elect their own officials. Eventually, plebeians served in all government jobs.

By 270 B.C., the Romans had conquered all of Italy. They went on to conquer Carthage, Macedonia, Greece, and parts of Asia Minor. They were able to do so partly because they had a strong, well-disciplined army. The Romans also treated their enemies well. Conquered peoples were allowed to keep their own government and customs. In return, they had to pay taxes to Rome and supply soldiers for the Roman army. Some conquered people even became Roman citizens.

GRAPHIC SUMMARY:

The Early Republic

1. Romans want to prevent one person from gaining too much power.

2. Romans set up republic in 509 B.C.

3. All government officials are patricians. Plebeians have little power.

4. Plebeians demand written laws. Plebeians win right to choose their own officials. Plebeian officials have right to veto laws that harm them. Plebeians can hold any office in the government.

5. More than 2,000 years later, writers of the United States Constitution use Roman ideas about government.

Romans created a republican form of government between 509 B.C. and 133 B.C.

REVIEW QUESTIONS

1. Why did the Romans set up a republic?

2. **Diagram Skills** What are two rights that the plebeians gained?

FROM REPUBLIC TO EMPIRE

■ TEXT SUMMARY

Rome added many conquered lands to the republic and gained control of important trade routes. Some Romans became very rich. However, many people were poor and could not find jobs. Government officials became greedy and **corrupt,** or dishonest. Efforts for reform resulted in civil wars that lasted 100 years.

In 48 B.C., Julius Caesar became dictator. Caesar increased Roman power and made reforms. However, his enemies in the Senate killed him because they feared he wanted to be king.

Civil war began again with the death of Caesar. Then, in 31 B.C., Octavian Augustus was sole ruler. Augustus did not call himself a king. However, he ruled with **absolute,** or complete, power. The Romans did not know it then, but this was the end of the 500-year republic. The age of the Roman empire had begun.

The 200-year period that followed was called the Pax Romana, or Roman Peace. Augustus and later emperors created a strong government. Some reduced taxes and gave people jobs. Ideas and knowledge spread through the empire. Women gained more freedom. However, some emperors were bad. They ignored social and economic problems. They used free food, races, and gladiator fights to control the people.

THE BIG IDEA

When Octavian came to power in 31 B.C., he ended the Roman republic and made Rome an empire.

■ GRAPHIC SUMMARY: *The Roman Empire in 44 B.C.*

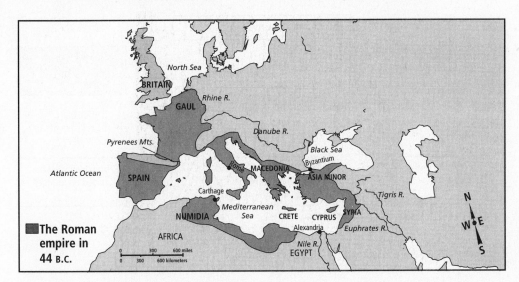

The Roman empire in 44 B.C.

The Romans built an empire that surrounded the Mediterranean Sea. Thousands of miles of roads united the lands.

■ REVIEW QUESTIONS

1. Why did his enemies kill Julius Caesar?

2. Map Skills Name three cities that were part of the Roman empire in 44 B.C.

THE ROMAN ACHIEVEMENT

■ TEXT SUMMARY

Roman civilization spread to faraway lands. Romans also borrowed ideas from other cultures. The blending of Greek, Hellenistic, and Roman cultures is called Greco-Roman civilization.

THE **BIG** IDEA

Romans made great advances in architecture, engineering, literature, and law.

Roman artists, architects, and writers borrowed ideas from these different cultures. The Romans used Greek statues in their homes and public buildings. Romans adapted the realistic Hellenistic style. Statues showed every detail of a subject, even warts and veins. Builders used Greek columns. However, Roman buildings were mighty and grand rather than simple and elegant. Many Romans spoke Greek and used Greek writing styles. Still, the greatest Roman writers such as Virgil, Horace, and Livy used the Roman language of **Latin** for literature.

Romans were practical. They built excellent roads, bridges, harbors, and **aqueducts,** or bridgelike stone structures that brought water from the hills to the cities. The Romans did little scientific investigation. They did, however, put science to practical use. They used geography to make maps and medical knowledge to improve public health. The Romans also developed an important system of law. Under this system, people were innocent until proved guilty. Decisions were based on fairness. Roman law influenced the modern legal systems of the Americas and Europe.

■ GRAPHIC SUMMARY: *The Greatest Achievement of Rome*

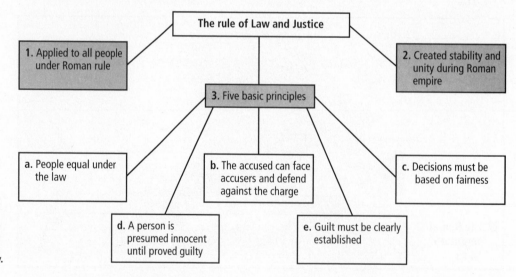

The rule of Law and Justice

1. Applied to all people under Roman rule

2. Created stability and unity during Roman empire

3. Five basic principles

a. People equal under the law

b. The accused can face accusers and defend against the charge

c. Decisions must be based on fairness

d. A person is presumed innocent until proved guilty

e. Guilt must be clearly established

Rome's greatest achievement was its rule of law and justice. Ideas from Roman law are a part of western civilization today.

■ REVIEW QUESTIONS

1. Give an example of how Greco-Roman civilization influenced Roman art.

2. **Diagram Skills** What are three important principles of Roman law?

THE RISE OF CHRISTIANITY

TEXT SUMMARY

Generally, Rome allowed its citizens to worship as they pleased. However, Jewish reformers called Zealots wanted independence. When the Jews revolted, the Romans drove them out of their homeland.

During these difficult times, a new religion emerged. Its founder was a Jew named Jesus. Jesus was born around 4 B.C. He believed in the Jewish idea of one God and accepted the Ten Commandments. Jesus also preached new ideas. He called himself the Son of God and he claimed his mission was to bring spiritual salvation to everyone. Many Jews and Romans worried that Jesus was dangerous. Arrested by the Romans, he was tried and executed Roman-style—nailed to a cross and left to die.

After Jesus died, his followers spread his teachings. They became the first Christians, and they believed Jesus was the Messiah. At first, Rome persecuted the Christians. Still, Christianity continued to spread. Many people found comfort in the belief that Jesus redeemed them from sin and offered them the possibility of a better life after death. Jesus had welcomed all people, including the poor and the troubled. In A.D. 313, the emperor Constantine ended the persecution of Christians. Some eighty years later, Christianity became the official religion of the Roman empire.

THE BIG IDEA

A new religion, Christianity, arose in the Roman empire. By A.D. 392, it was the official religion of the empire.

GRAPHIC SUMMARY:

Growth of Christianity

1. Around 4 B.C. Jesus born

2. Around A.D. 26 Jesus begins preaching new beliefs

3. About A.D. 29 Jesus arrested and crucified

4. Followers spread Jesus' teachings

5. Christians set up organized church

6. Romans persecute Christians

7. A.D. 313–Roman emperor Constantine ends persecution of Christians

8. A.D. 392–Christianity becomes official religion of Roman empire Church preserves and spreads Greco-Roman civilization

Christianity gradually spread throughout the Roman empire. Apostles carried the teachings of Jesus across the region.

REVIEW QUESTIONS

1. What messages did Jesus preach?

2. **Diagram Skills** In which year did Christianity become the official religion of the Roman empire?

THE LONG DECLINE

▨ TEXT SUMMARY

The Pax Romana ended around A.D. 180. The next 100 years were violent times. Many different rulers came to power. Social and economic problems developed. Taxes were high. Poor farmers left their land and sought protection of stronger landowners. Technically, they were free, but they could not leave their landowner's estate.

Two emperors introduced reforms to stop the decay. Diocletian came to power in 284. He divided the empire into two parts to make it easier to rule. Diocletian controlled prices and forced farmers to stay on their land to help the economy. Constantine came to power in 312. He continued the reforms of Diocletian. Constantine became a Christian and ended the persecution of the Christians. He also built a new capital, Constantinople. As a result, the eastern part of the empire became the center of power. However, these improvements did not last.

Historians use the year 476 to mark the fall of Rome. In fact, the empire had been declining for many years. Germanic invasions weakened the empire. Romans forgot the values that made Rome great. The government made people unhappy. Officials became corrupt. Taxes were too high. The army grew weak. Gradually, Germanic customs, ideas, and languages replaced Roman culture.

> **THE BIG IDEA**
>
> Foreign invasions along with political, social, and economic problems led to the fall of the Roman empire.

▨ GRAPHIC SUMMARY: *The Fall of Rome*

Military causes	Economic causes	Political causes	Social causes
• Visigoths and other Germanic peoples invade the empire. • Roman army lacks training and discipline. • Romans forced to hire foreign soldiers to defend borders.	• Heavy taxes necessary to support the government. • Farmers leave land. • Middle class disappears. • Romans use too much slave labor.	• Government becomes too strict. • People stop supporting government. • Many corrupt officials. • Divided empire becomes weak.	• Population declines because of disease and war. • People become selfish and lazy.

Fall of Rome

The fall of Rome was a long, slow process. Historians have identified many causes.

▨ REVIEW QUESTIONS

1. What two changes did Constantine make during his rule?

2. Diagram Skills Give one military cause and one social cause for the decline of the Roman empire.

Test

■ IDENTIFYING MAIN IDEAS

Write the letter of the correct answer in the blank provided. (10 points each)

____ 1. Which of the following geographical aspects *did not* make it easier to unify Italy?
  A. no small, isolated valleys
  B. thousands of rocky islands
  C. broad, fertile plains for settlements
  D. Apennine Mountains were not very rugged.

____ 2. Which statement does not describe how Romans treated the people they conquered?
  A. Some were granted full Roman citizenship.
  B. They were often allowed to keep their own customs and local government.
  C. They were forced to pay taxes and acknowledge Roman leadership.
  D. All conquered people were sold into slavery.

____ 3. As it expanded, Rome was beset by social and economic troubles caused partly by
  A. angry Carthaginians.
  B. a lack of trade.
  C. the widening gap between the rich and poor.
  D. weak leadership.

____ 4. The 200-year period when peace, order, and prosperity flourished is known as the
  A. Pax Romana.
  B. republic.
  C. Circus Maximus.
  D. Punic Wars.

____ 5. What characterized Roman architecture?
  A. Romans emphasized grandeur and built mighty monuments.
  B. Romans aimed for simple elegance in their buildings.
  C. Roman buildings were free of any decorations, such as columns.
  D. Roman architects did not use arches in their buildings.

____ 6. How did Romans supply their cities with water?
  A. Romans built their cities where there were natural springs.
  B. Romans only built cities on the banks of rivers.
  C. Roman engineers built aqueducts that carried water to their cities.
  D. Romans relied exclusively on rainfall to supply water for their cities.

____ 7. What was the Romans' attitude toward Christianity before A.D. 313?
  A. They ignored Christians.
  B. They embraced Christianity.
  C. They tolerated Christianity.
  D. They persecuted Christians.

____ 8. Who ended the persecution of Christians?
  A. Jesus
  B. Constantine
  C. Julius Caesar
  D. Augustus

____ 9. Pax Romana came to an end when Rome was plunged into a time of
  A. economic growth.
  B. peaceful expansion.
  C. political, economic, and social turmoil.
  D. religious fervor.

____ 10. The "fall of Rome" was
  A. a rapid event.
  B. due entirely to military failures.
  C. not a single event, but a long process of change.
  D. the end to Roman civilization.

Civilizations of the Americas

(1400 B.C.–A.D. 1570)

 **SECTION 1** *CIVILIZATIONS OF MIDDLE AMERICA*

■ TEXT SUMMARY

During the last ice age, frozen oceans created a land bridge between North America and Asia. Groups of Paleolithic hunters and food gatherers crossed from Asia into Alaska. They migrated eastward and southward across the Americas. These people were the first Americans.

The Mayas built a civilization in Central America around A.D. 300. Each Mayan city-state had its own ruling chief. Mayan farmers developed complex ways to raise crops. The Mayas built giant pyramids and large palaces. Often, carvings on temple walls recorded historical events. Traders carried valuable goods along hard-packed dirt roads. Mayas developed a system of writing, an accurate calendar, and a number system.

The Aztecs developed another great civilization. In 1325, they founded the city of Tenochtitlán, where Mexico City stands today. The Aztecs were fierce warriors. However, they also made alliances with other peoples. **Tribute,** or payment from conquered peoples, made the Aztecs wealthy. By 1500, the Aztec empire numbered about 30 million people. The Aztecs sacrificed many captured soldiers to their gods. The sacrifices and tributes caused rebellions by the conquered peoples.

> ### THE **BIG** IDEA
>
> The Mayas and the Aztecs both developed advanced civilizations in Middle America.

■ GRAPHIC SUMMARY: *Civilizations of Middle America*

	MAYAS	AZTECS
Time	300—900	1325—1521
Location	southern Mexico through part of Central America	central Mexico
Government	• city-states • ruling chief for each city (sometimes women) • military leaders • public officials	• single ruler • nobles served as officials, judges, governors
Way of Life	• farmers • traders	• farmers • warriors • traders • slaves
Religion	• powerful priests • ceremonies for harvests and war • human sacrifices	• worshiped many gods • sun god most important • priests • human sacrifices

The Mayas and Aztecs were two important civilizations that grew in Middle America.

■ REVIEW QUESTIONS

1. How did the first Americans reach North America?

2. Chart Skills How did Aztec and Mayan governments differ?

THE WORLD OF THE INCAS

◼ TEXT SUMMARY

For more than 2,000 years, Peru was home to many different civilizations. In the 1400s, Incan armies quickly conquered a large empire. By the early 1500s, the Incas ruled an empire that stretched 2,500 miles along the Andes. It reached from Ecuador to Chile and from the mountaintops to the Pacific Ocean.

Efficient centralized government united the empire. The Incan emperor, a god-king, had complete control of everybody and everything in his empire. Nobles ran the provinces. Officials below them collected taxes. The government built an amazing system of roads to unify the empire. (See diagram below.) The Incas strictly controlled the lives of the people within their empire. All people had to speak the Incan language, Quechua. Government officials decided what job each person should do and who each person should marry. Farmers grew food for the emperor. The government stored grain for hard times.

Religion affected all parts of daily life. All people in the empire had to practice the Incan religion. Incas worshiped many gods. The emperor, who was considered the son of the sun, was also the religious leader. Powerful priests conducted ceremonies and monthly festivals of sports and rituals.

> **THE BIG IDEA**
>
> The Incan empire was united by a strong government, a common language, and a complex system of roads.

◼ GRAPHIC SUMMARY: *The Incan System of Roads*

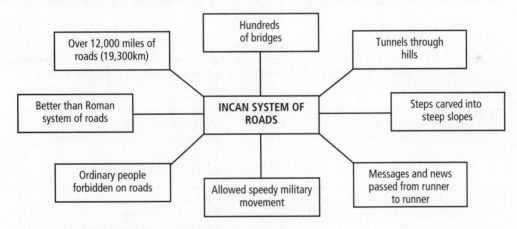

The Incan system of roads was so well built that it was not equaled until modern times.

◼ REVIEW QUESTIONS

1. How did the Incan rulers control the lives of the people?

2. Diagram Skills How did the Incan system of roads help unify the empire?

SECTION 3 PEOPLES OF NORTH AMERICA

■ TEXT SUMMARY

Many different cultures arose in North America. Farming societies developed in the desert in what became the southwestern United States. The Hohokams used irrigation to farm in the desert. They may have learned this from the earlier civilizations of Central America. (See Section 1.) The Anasazi built houses high in the cliffs. Some buildings had more than 500 rooms. These cliff houses protected the Anasazi from invaders.

Other farming societies emerged in the Mississippi and Ohio river valleys around 700 B.C. A group called the Mound Builders built huge mounds made of earth. Mounds were cone-shaped or shaped like animals. Temples probably topped the largest mounds, where priests offered prayers to the sun. Scientists see the mounds as evidence of an organized society and strong leadership.

Many other groups of Native Americans lived in the different regions of North America before 1500. In each region, geography influenced their ways of life. In the Arctic region, the Inuits built igloos to keep warm and used dog sleds to travel across the ice. In the Northwest Coast, people fished for salmon and built large villages with wooden homes. The Iroquois of the Eastern Woodlands cleared land and built villages in the forests.

> **THE BIG IDEA**
>
> **Hundreds of cultural groups arose in North America.**

■ GRAPHIC SUMMARY: *Geography and Three Native American Cultures*

Environment	Culture group	Patterns of life
Arctic/Subarctic—very cold, harsh climate; frozen seas and icy treeless plains; limited supply of food	**Inuits**	• Lived in small groups of nomadic people. • Made igloos, or homes from snow and ice. • Lived by hunting and fishing.
Northwest Coast—mild climate; ocean and rivers; thick forest; large food supply	**Kwakiutls**	• Lived in large permanent villages. • Fished in rivers and ocean and hunted in the forests. • Traded with nearby groups. • Built homes of wood.
Eastern Woodlands—hot summers and cold winters; forests; medium to large food supply	**Iroquois**	• Lived in farming villages. • Hunted in the forests. • Built long houses out of bark. • Five nations formed the Iroquois League.

As Native Americans spread across North America, they developed a great variety of cultures.

■ REVIEW QUESTIONS

1. Give an example of how geography influenced the way of life for Native Americans.

2. **Chart Skills** In what region did the Inuits settle? The Kwakiutls? The Iroquois?

CHAPTER 7 *Test*

IDENTIFYING MAIN IDEAS

Write the letter of the correct answer in the blank provided. (10 points each)

____ **1.** The earliest people who migrated to the Americas came from
  A. Europe.
  B. Asia.
  C. Africa.
  D. Australia.

____ **2.** Which of the following statements describes Mayan government?
  A. Each city had its own ruling chief.
  B. Only men could rule.
  C. A king ruled all Mayan city-states.
  D. The emperor claimed divine power.

____ **3.** How did the Aztecs gain their wealth?
  A. They traded with neighboring empires.
  B. They collected tribute from conquered peoples.
  C. They sold their children into slavery.
  D. They made alliances with other peoples.

____ **4.** Which of the following civilizations ruled an area that included the Andes Mountains?
  A. Mound Builders
  B. Mayas
  C. Aztecs
  D. Incas

____ **5.** The Incan empire was ruled overall by
  A. a tax collector.
  B. a god-king.
  C. nobles.
  D. the army.

____ **6.** The Incan road system was built to allow
  A. people to travel from one village to another.
  B. farmers to carry goods to markets.
  C. armies and news to move rapidly throughout the empire.
  D. traders to come into the empire.

____ **7.** The Incas united their empire by
  A. imposing their language and religion on the peoples they conquered.
  B. forcing the conquered peoples to pay tribute.
  C. encouraging trade throughout the empire.
  D. establishing one common coinage.

____ **8.** What advantage did the Anasazi gain by moving from pueblos to cliff dwellings?
  A. The cliffs offered plenty of water.
  B. The cliffs offered easy access to fields on the canyon floor.
  C. The cliffs offered better hunting.
  D. The cliffs offered protection from raiders.

____ **9.** Scientists believe the mounds built in the Mississippi and Ohio river valleys are evidence of
  A. poor farming skills.
  B. an organized society and strong leadership.
  C. geography influencing lifestyle.
  D. an unorganized society.

____ **10.** What type of housing did the people of the Northwest Coast build?
  A. sod dwellings
  B. pueblos with homes of adobe brick
  C. large villages with homes of wood
  D. igloos

The Rise of Europe (500–1300)

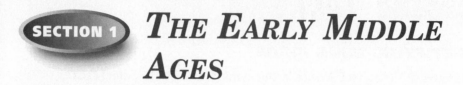

SECTION 1 — THE EARLY MIDDLE AGES

◾ TEXT SUMMARY

The Middle Ages, or **medieval** period, lasted from about 500 to 1500. During this time, Europe was cut off from the world. Population decreased and towns emptied. Trade almost ended. Learning stopped. Still, Europe did have fertile soil and many resources. Seas and rivers provided fish and transportation.

The years between 400 and 700 were frightening. Invaders such as the Huns, the Avars, and the Germanic tribes destroyed communities in Europe. (See Chapter 6, Section 5.) The Germanic people were warriors, farmers, and herders. They had no cities and no written laws. The strongest tribe, the Franks, formed an alliance with the Roman Catholic Church. A new force, Islam, swept out of the Middle East and into the Mediterranean region. Muslims captured Spain and Sicily. Many Christians feared the Muslims. However, Europeans did learn about science and mathematics from the Muslims.

Around 800, a Frankish king, Charlemagne, built a large empire. The pope crowned Charlemagne emperor. (See diagram at right.) Charlemagne wanted his capital to be like Rome. He encouraged Latin learning throughout his empire. He set up schools, even though he himself could not write. He helped the Church spread Christianity. Charlemagne blended Germanic, Roman, and Christian ideas.

> ### THE **BIG** IDEA
>
> The early Middle Ages was a time of conflict in Europe.

◾ GRAPHIC SUMMARY:

Charlemagne's Empire

Charlemagne's conquests nearly doubled Frankish territory.

◾ REVIEW QUESTIONS

1. What are two ways that Charlemagne blended Germanic, Christian, and Roman cultures?

2. Map Skills Name three bodies of water that bordered Charlemagne's empire.

FEUDALISM AND THE MANOR ECONOMY

◼ TEXT SUMMARY

During the Middle Ages, kings were not strong enough to stop invasions by outsiders. People needed protection. A new system, called **feudalism,** developed. In feudal society, powerful lords owned large pieces of land. They divided their land into estates called **fiefs.** Fiefs were given to less powerful lords, called **vassals.** The vassal promised loyalty and service to his lord. The lord promised to protect his vassal.

The noblewoman had an important place in medieval society. She was trained to run a household. Although she probably could not read, she might serve as doctor. When her husband or father was away fighting, the noblewoman took over his duties. Sometimes she even went to war to protect her home. Some noble women got involved in politics. Eleanor of Aquitaine became queen of both France and England.

The medieval economy was based on the **manor,** or lord's estate. Peasants lived and worked on the manor. Most people were peasants or **serfs.** Serfs were not slaves, but they had to stay and work on the land. They farmed for the lord and repaired roads. The lord charged them fees for grinding wheat, inheriting land, or marrying. In exchange, they received a small amount of land to farm. They also received their lord's protection from Viking raids or feudal warfare.

THE **BIG** IDEA

A new political and social system, feudalism, controlled medieval life.

◼ GRAPHIC SUMMARY:

Feudal Society

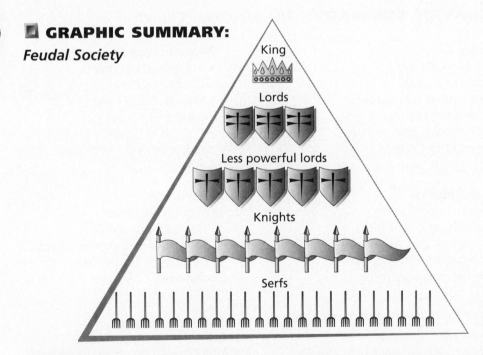

King

Lords

Less powerful lords

Knights

Serfs

Under feudalism, the roles of people were determined by their places in society.

◼ REVIEW QUESTIONS

1. Why was the noblewoman important in medieval society?

2. Diagram Skills Which group was at the bottom of feudal society?

THE MEDIEVAL CHURCH

◼ TEXT SUMMARY

After the fall of Rome, the Christian Church split into eastern and western churches. The western church became the Roman Catholic Church. It was headed by the pope. The pope also claimed to have authority over **secular,** or nonreligious, rulers.

Religion was an important part of medieval life. The Church had absolute power over Christians. A person who did not obey the rules of the Church could be **excommunicated,** or cut off from the Church. People shunned an excommunicated person. Church officials were the only educated people. Rulers often needed them as advisors. The church played an important role in daily life for peasants. Besides providing religious services, it was a social center.

Some Christians became nuns or monks. They spent their lives serving God. Nuns and monks did important work. They cared for sick and poor people. They preserved learning and set up schools for children. These religious people provided food and shelter to travelers. Some were missionaries.

As the Church became rich and powerful, it began to have problems. Some church leaders ignored their vows. Priests paid less attention to religion. Growing corruption caused people such as Abbot Berno and St. Dominic to work to reform the Church.

> ### THE **BIG** IDEA
>
> The Roman Catholic Church played a vital role in medieval life.

◼ GRAPHIC SUMMARY: *The Medieval Church*

Everyday Life
- Christians attend village churches.
- Some priests run schools in village churches.
- All Christians pay taxes to the Church.

Nuns and Monks
- Some set up housing, hospitals, and schools for the sick and poor.
- Some become missionaries.
- Some preserve learning.

Power of Church
- Pope leads Roman Catholic Church.
- Church has its own laws and courts.
- Church excommunicates those who do not obey rules.

Reform
- Church becomes rich and powerful.
- Some clergy become corrupt.
- Reformers try to make changes.

The Church had both spiritual and secular power.

◼ REVIEW QUESTIONS

1. What happened to a person who did not obey Church rules?

2. Diagram Skills What important work did nuns and monks do?

ECONOMIC EXPANSION AND CHANGE

■ TEXT SUMMARY

Around 1000, life began to improve in Europe. The period from 1000 to 1300 is called the High Middle Ages.

By 800, farmers started using new inventions. Among these were the iron plow, the harness, and the windmill. Peasants began to use the three-field system to keep the soil fertile. These changes contributed to an agricultural revolution. Farmers were able to produce more food. With more food available, the population of Europe doubled.

During the High Middle Ages, the economy of Europe grew stronger. As the population grew, people began to trade again. Merchants set up fairs. These meeting places grew into towns and cities. As trade increased, people developed new ways of doing business. They began using money. They developed banks for lending. These and other changes were part of a **commercial,** or business, revolution.

Medieval society also changed. A new middle class emerged. It included traders, merchants, and artisans. Artists formed **guilds,** or associations, to keep the quality of work high. Fewer people were serfs. Instead, peasants rented the land they farmed. As cities grew bigger, they became noisy, crowded, and filthy. Still, cities continued to attract new people.

> ### THE **BIG** IDEA
>
> **During the High Middle Ages, Europe's economy grew. Cities and towns expanded, and a middle class arose.**

■ GRAPHIC SUMMARY: *Changes During the High Middle Ages*

Agricultural Revolution
Increase in food production leads to population growth. A larger population needs more goods so trade increases.

Commercial Revolution
More trade requires new ways of doing business. Middle class of merchants, traders, and craftspeople grows. As centers of trade, towns and cities get bigger.

The growth of towns and the agricultural revolution transformed the way that people lived.

■ REVIEW QUESTIONS

1. What were two ways in which medieval society changed?

2. Chart Skills Which revolution directly caused the growth of the middle class?

CHAPTER 8 *Test*

IDENTIFYING MAIN IDEAS

Write the letter of the correct answer in the blank provided. (10 points each)

_____ 1. Despite the fact that Christians feared Muslims, they
   A. refused to select a Muslim ruler.
   B. learned from Muslim advances in science and mathematics.
   C. treated them with charity and kindness.
   D. lost the battle of Tours in France.

_____ 2. Which of the following is credited to Charlemagne?
   A. the defeat of the Muslims at the battle of Tours
   B. the development of feudalism
   C. the development of banking
   D. the revival of Latin learning

_____ 3. Feudalism evolved in response to a need for
   A. fertile land.
   B. new trading routes.
   C. protection.
   D. organized government.

_____ 4. During the Middle Ages, noblewomen had
   A. little responsibility for the running of the manor.
   B. no rights to their dowry if their husbands died.
   C. an active role in medieval society.
   D. no opportunity to learn how to read and write.

_____ 5. The manor economy was based on
   A. trade among many villages.
   B. farming.
   C. metalworking.
   D. herding and weaving.

_____ 6. Which group made up the largest part of the population in feudal society?
   A. vassals
   B. peasants
   C. knights
   D. lords

_____ 7. How did monks and nuns improve life during the Middle Ages?
   A. They cared for the sick and poor.
   B. They gave land to the peasants.
   C. They opposed the feudal system.
   D. They excommunicated criminals.

_____ 8. Why did some religious people want to reform the Church during medieval times?
   A. It had grown too big.
   B. It had grown corrupt.
   C. It had grown weak.
   D. It had grown too powerful.

_____ 9. What was one result of new farming technologies and methods?
   A. loss of jobs for farmers
   B. population growth
   C. decreased demand for nonfarm goods
   D. a rise in the status of farmers

_____ 10. Who dominated the economic and political life of medieval towns?
   A. apprentices
   B. lords and vassals
   C. merchant guilds
   D. the clergy

The High Middle Ages (1050–1450)

CHAPTER 9

SECTION 1 *GROWTH OF ROYAL POWER IN ENGLAND AND FRANCE*

▇ TEXT SUMMARY

During the Middle Ages, kings, nobles, and the Church struggled for power. Kings slowly began to increase their power. First, they expanded royal lands. Kings then gave rights to townspeople and gained their loyalty.

English and French kings made government stronger. In England, kings created a royal treasury. People paid taxes to the king, not the nobles. King Henry II set up royal courts and a system of common law to broaden royal justice. English kings met with councils made up of nobles and clergy for advice. As time passed, the English council developed into Parliament. It won the right to approve taxes. This provided a balance to royal

power. In France, the ruling family made the throne **hereditary,** passing power from father to son. French kings also formed an alliance with the Church. Rulers collected taxes, organized an army, and created an orderly government. Like English kings, French monarchs met with councils for advice.

Important ideas about government emerged in England. In 1215, English nobles forced King John to sign a document called the Magna Carta. The Magna Carta gave rights to the people. It also stated that the king must obey the law. These ideas are important in governments today.

> ### THE **BIG** IDEA
>
> **Strong monarchs in England and France worked to increase their land holdings and their power over their subjects.**

▇ GRAPHIC SUMMARY: *Kings Increase Their Power*

Kings in England
- Decide who can build castles and where
- Force vassals to obey them
- Establish common law so that all people are treated the same
- Collect records of who owns land

- Add to their lands
- Set up organized government
- Collect taxes
- Create a royal treasury
- Set up royal courts and royal law

Kings in France
- Make throne hereditary
- Become allies with the Church
- Organize army
- Take French lands from English king

During the Middle Ages, European monarchs strengthened their power by centralizing government and developing ties to the middle class.

▇ REVIEW QUESTIONS

1. What was the Magna Carta?

2. Diagram Skills Describe three ways the English kings increased their power.

THE HOLY ROMAN EMPIRE AND THE CHURCH

TEXT SUMMARY

After Charlemagne died in 814, Germany split into many states. Powerful nobles ruled the states. In time, a German king was crowned Holy Roman emperor. Later emperors tried to unify the empire. However, conflicts with powerful German nobles prevented the emperors from succeeding. In addition, emperors and popes clashed over who had the right to pick bishops. The conflict continued because most nobles supported the pope. Finally, in 1122, the pope and emperor reached a settlement about choosing bishops.

During the 1100s and 1200s, Holy Roman emperors tried to gain control of Italy. However, the pope and his Italian allies defeated the emperors. While the emperors focused attention on Italy, German nobles grew more independent. When French and English kings grew stronger, the rulers of Germany lost more control. Thus, Germany stayed divided.

During the 1200s, the Church was very powerful. Pope Gregory VII and Pope Innocent III believed that the pope should have more power than any other ruler. Rulers who objected were excommunicated. After the 1200s, the power of the pope declined.

THE **BIG** IDEA

Conflicts with nobles and the Roman Catholic Church prevented Holy Roman emperors from unifying Germany.

GRAPHIC SUMMARY: *Struggles Between Emperors and Popes*

Conflict

- Emperors and popes both want to choose Church officials.

Resolution

- They reach a compromise.
- Emperor grants land to bishops.
- Pope chooses bishops and gives them spiritual power.

Conflict

- Emperor and pope fight over land in northern Italy.

Resolution

- Pope and his Italian allies defeat Emperor.

The Holy Roman emperors and the pope struggled over important issues from the late 1000s to the 1200s.

REVIEW QUESTIONS

1. What happened to Germany after the death of Charlemagne?

2. Diagram Skills What was the compromise that the pope and the Holy Roman emperor reached about choosing bishops?

EUROPEANS LOOK OUTWARD

■ TEXT SUMMARY

While Europe was still cut off from the world, civilizations in other places were thriving. (See Chapters 3, 4, and 7.) Islamic civilization stretched from the Middle East across Northern Africa to Spain. The Byzantine empire was a rival to Islam.

In the 1050s, the Seljuk Turks invaded the Byzantine empire and conquered Palestine. The pope called for Europeans to rescue the Holy Land from the Turks. For 200 years, thousands of knights fought religious wars called the **Crusades.** In the end, the Crusaders failed to regain the Holy Land.

However, the Crusades had major effects on Europe. People of different religions grew to hate each other. Other effects were more positive. Trade with the East increased, especially from Italian port cities. Kings and popes became more powerful. Since nobles needed more money to pay for armies, they allowed serfs to pay rent in money instead of grain or labor. Europeans realized there was culture and civilization in far-away places. Some Europeans, such as Marco Polo, traveled to far-off lands.

Religious wars also took place in Spain. In 1492, the rulers Ferdinand and Isabella forced out the Muslims and united Spain. The Spanish then persecuted Jews and Muslims who refused to convert to Christianity.

THE **BIG** IDEA

The Crusades brought changes and caused Europeans to learn more about the Middle East and Asia.

■ GRAPHIC SUMMARY: *The Crusades*

Causes

- People want to free the Holy Land from Seljuk control.
- Many people want to get rich and gain new land.
- Some people want to see new places.

The Crusades

Effects

- Trade increases.
- People of different religions grow to hate each other.
- Popes become more powerful.
- Feudal kings become more powerful.
- Renting land helps to free serfs.
- Europeans become interested in traveling.
- People learn about other cultures.

The Crusades helped to speed up changes in Europe and to open it up to new ideas.

■ REVIEW QUESTIONS

1. What happened in Spain after the Spanish defeated the Muslims?

2. Diagram Skills What were three effects of the Crusades?

SECTION 4 LEARNING, LITERATURE, AND THE ARTS

TEXT SUMMARY

By the 1100s, economic, social, and political conditions in Europe had improved. This change created a need for education. The Church wanted a more educated clergy. Rulers needed people who could read and write to help run the government. Wealthy people wanted their sons to have important jobs.

The Church set up schools to train the clergy, but eventually **laymen,** or people who were not in the clergy, could attend. Some of these schools became the first universities. Women were not allowed to attend university. During this period, new learning was reaching Europe. Scholars rediscovered the ideas of ancient Greece, Rome, and the Muslim world.

Important changes took place in medieval European literature. Writers began to use everyday languages that ordinary people could understand. Authors such as Chaucer wrote stories about warrior heroes and ordinary people that showed courage, humor, and morality. Popular works such as these give us an idea of what life was like in the High Middle Ages.

Changes also took place in architecture. Some architects built stone churches that looked like Roman fortresses. This style was called **Romanesque.** Others built huge **Gothic** churches with pointed arches, high ceilings, and supports called **flying buttresses.** Stained glass windows and marble statues showed Bible stories to those who could not read.

> ### THE **BIG** IDEA
>
> **Improved economic and political conditions in Europe led to a revival of learning during the High Middle Ages.**

GRAPHIC SUMMARY: *Life at a Medieval University*

Go to classes in cold rooms with hard benches.	Eat breakfast of soup and oatmeal at 10 A.M.	Take oral exams.

| Wake up at 5 A.M. for prayers. | Memorize arithmetic, geometry, astronomy, music, grammar, rhetoric, and logic. | Go to afternoon classes until 5 P.M. | Have light supper and study. |

Students at medieval universities sat for hours as teachers dictated to them in Latin.

REVIEW QUESTIONS

1. List two changes that took place in Europe during the 1100s.

2. Diagram Skills About how many hours did university students in the Middle Ages spend in class?

A TIME OF CRISIS

◼ TEXT SUMMARY

The late Middle Ages was a hard time for Europeans. During the 1300s, a deadly disease called the **bubonic plague,** or Black Death, spread through Europe. One out of every three people in Europe died from this disease. The economy fell apart because of the loss of workers and rising prices. Landowners converted farmland to sheep pastures to avoid the high wages of farm hands. Peasants who were thrown off their farms rushed to towns, but found no jobs. People everywhere were scared and angry. Revolts all over Europe resulted.

The Roman Catholic Church faced serious problems. Its frightened followers needed comfort. But many priests and monks died from the plague, so the Church was not able to help. In addition, rich popes and bishops who lived in luxury caused great resentment. Angry reformers attacked corruption and elected their own pope. For many years, two or three different popes ruled at the same time.

During this period, England and France fought the Hundred Years' War. The English king wanted French land and wanted to be king of France. A young woman named Joan of Arc led the French to several victories. Then the English captured and killed her. Her execution inspired the French to win the war. Later, the Church made Joan of Arc a saint.

> ### THE **BIG** IDEA
>
> The late Middle Ages was a period of decline in Europe, marked by disease, corruption, and war.

◼ GRAPHIC SUMMARY: *Hard Times During the Late Middle Ages*

FAMINE	BLACK DEATH	PROBLEMS IN THE CHURCH	HUNDRED YEARS' WAR
• Crops fail • People starve	• Bubonic plague spreads from Asia to Europe • One in three people die • Society and economy fall apart	• People resent rich clergy • Church cannot comfort people during plague • Reformers demand change • Reformers choose their own pope	• English king wants to be king of France • Both England and France want French land • They fight for more than 100 years • France defeats England

Although the 1300s and the 1400s were a time of crisis, they marked the end of the Middle Ages and the beginning of modern times.

◼ REVIEW QUESTIONS

1. Why did England and France fight the Hundred Years' War?

2. Chart Skills What were two effects of the Black Death?

CHAPTER 9 *Test*

◻ IDENTIFYING MAIN IDEAS

Write the letter of the correct answer in the blank provided. (10 points each)

____ **1.** What did Henry II do to broaden the system of royal justice?
   A. He established a Supreme Court.
   B. He stiffened the requirements necessary to become a lawyer.
   C. He taxed the rich and used the money to build a court house.
   D. He helped establish English common law.

____ **2.** Why was the Magna Carta important?
   A. It approved money for wars in France.
   B. It asserted that the monarch must obey the law.
   C. It allowed the monarch to abolish Parliament.
   D. It limited the power of the pope.

____ **3.** A major conflict between the Holy Roman emperors and the popes concerned
   A. who would appoint bishops.
   B. the right to succession.
   C. who would control England.
   D. the right to wage war.

____ **4.** What was the chief goal of the Crusades?
   A. to liberate Spain
   B. to conquer England
   C. to conquer the Holy Land
   D. to defeat the Hindus

____ **5.** The Crusades affected the world by
   A. increasing trade between Europe and the Middle East.
   B. strengthening the system of serfdom.
   C. weakening the power of the Church.
   D. causing Europeans to isolate themselves from the world.

____ **6.** A key feature of Gothic architecture is
   A. towers.
   B. tiny windows.
   C. flying buttresses.
   D. low, heavy roofs.

____ **7.** How did medieval cathedrals help to educate people who could not read?
   A. They held religious education classes.
   B. They featured sculptures and stained glass that portrayed biblical stories.
   C. They supported tax-based public education.
   D. They required church members to learn to read the Bible.

____ **8.** What change in education developed in the Middle Ages?
   A. The first universities evolved.
   B. The Church stopped training clergy.
   C. Students with very little training could qualify to be teachers.
   D. Women began to attend universities.

____ **9.** Which of the following was a result of the plague in Europe?
   A. economic decline
   B. political reform
   C. the rebirth of Christianity
   D. the Hundred Years' War

____ **10.** Why is Joan of Arc remembered?
   A. She led a peasant uprising that ended feudalism.
   B. She led the French to victories against the English in the Hundred Years' War.
   C. She led English troops in the Hundred Years' War.
   D. She drove the English from Calais.

The Byzantine Empire and Russia (330–1613)

 **SECTION 1** — *THE BYZANTINE EMPIRE*

■ TEXT SUMMARY

During the early Middle Ages, the cities of the western Roman empire crumbled. At the same time, the eastern part, called the Byzantine empire, became a rich center of world trade. The Eastern (Greek) Orthodox Church, not the Church of Rome, became the religion of the East.

Emperor Justinian ruled the Byzantine empire from 527 to 565. Justinian wanted his empire to be as great as ancient Rome. He started a building program to make the city of Constantinople beautiful. Most important, Justinian collected and organized all the laws of ancient Rome. Justinian's Code influenced legal thinkers for hundreds of years.

The Byzantine empire lasted 1,000 years. Byzantine emperors built a strong government and a strong economy. Byzantine civilization blended Christian beliefs with Greek science, philosophy, arts, and literature. Scholars preserved the classic works of ancient Greece and wrote their own histories. They also expanded Roman engineering and law. However, in 1453, the Ottoman Turks conquered Constantinople. Despite the defeat, Byzantine culture continued to influence western civilizations for centuries.

> **THE BIG IDEA**
>
> The emperor Justinian expanded the Byzantine empire, erected grand buildings, and established a code of laws.

■ GRAPHIC SUMMARY: *The Byzantine Empire*

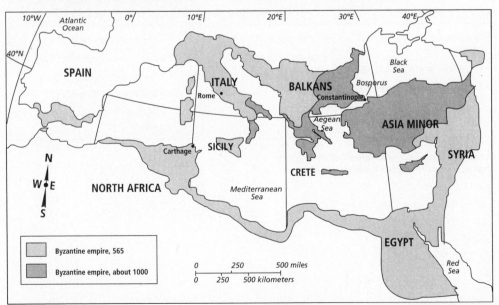

Byzantine empire, 565

Byzantine empire, about 1000

0   250   500 miles
0   250   500 kilometers

The Byzantine empire served as a center of trade and as a buffer between Europe and the Muslim world.

■ REVIEW QUESTIONS

1. What were two accomplishments of the emperor Justinian?

2. Map Skills Name two islands in the Byzantine empire.

THE RISE OF RUSSIA

■ TEXT SUMMARY

THE BIG IDEA

In its early years, Russia was influenced by the Slavs, Vikings, Byzantines, and Mongols.

In the 700s and 800s, the Vikings settled among the native Slavs on the vast Eurasian plain. These two groups mixed and became the early Russians. The city of Kiev was the center of the first Russian state.

Other civilizations influenced the early Russians. Byzantine missionaries brought Christianity to Russia. In time, Byzantine Christians formed the Russian Orthodox Church. The Russians borrowed from Byzantine art, music, and architecture. They built their churches with Byzantine-style domes. In the early 1200s, fierce warriors called Mongols conquered Russia. The absolute power of the Mongols served as a model for later Russian rulers. Most important, Mongol rule cut Russia off from western Europe while Europeans were advancing in science and art.

Little by little, the princes of Moscow grew more powerful. The location of their city on river trade routes helped. When the Russian Orthodox Church moved to Moscow, the city became the spiritual capital of Russia. In 1380, the princes of Moscow defeated the Mongols. Czar Ivan the Great brought most of northern Russia under his control. Ivan the Great and his grandson, Ivan the Terrible, were absolute rulers. They began a tradition of absolute power government in Russia.

■ GRAPHIC SUMMARY: *Absolute Rule in Russia*

1200s–1300s Mongols	1462–1505 Ivan the Great	1547–1584 Ivan the Terrible
• Force Russians to accept their rule • Force Russians to pay tribute • Introduce absolute power	• Limits power of the nobles • Takes title of czar • Claims ruler was like "highest god"	• Centralizes royal power • Takes power from the nobles • Forces serfs to stay on the land • Kills nobles who revolt • Destroys towns that do not support him

The czars of Russia created a centralized system of government that gave them absolute power.

■ REVIEW QUESTIONS

1. What impact did Mongol rule have on Russia?

2. **Chart Skills** What are three ways Russian czars created absolute power for themselves?

SECTION 3 SHAPING EASTERN EUROPE

■ TEXT SUMMARY

During the early Middle Ages, many different groups settled in Eastern Europe. West Slavs settled in Poland. South Slavs and other ethnic groups moved into the Balkans. Jews went to Poland to escape persecution in Western Europe. Waves of Asian peoples, such as the Huns and Magyars, also migrated to this area. As a result, Eastern Europe became a region of many different peoples, languages, and cultures.

Eastern Europe was made up of many small kingdoms. These kingdoms often fought each other. Wars and alliances caused the blending of cultures. Powerful neighboring states also influenced Eastern Europe. Byzantine missionaries brought Eastern Orthodox Christianity and Byzantine culture. German missionaries and knights spread Roman Catholic Christianity to Poland and Hungary.

Eastern European kingdoms faced threats from inside and out. The kingdom of Poland fought against Germans, Russians, and Mongols. In 1386, Poland formed an alliance with another kingdom, Lithuania, that made the combined nation very powerful. However, Polish nobles slowly gained power, which would later cause the decline of Poland. Both Hungary and Serbia had some success enlarging their kingdoms. However, both were eventually conquered by the Ottoman Turks.

THE BIG IDEA

Ethnic diversity contributed to the varied cultural tradiditons of Eastern Europe.

■ GRAPHIC SUMMARY: *People and Cultures of Eastern Europe*

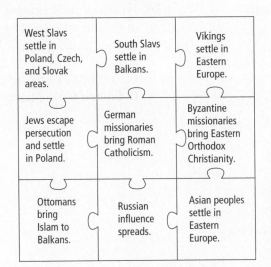

West Slavs settle in Poland, Czech, and Slovak areas.	South Slavs settle in Balkans.	Vikings settle in Eastern Europe.
Jews escape persecution and settle in Poland.	German missionaries bring Roman Catholicism.	Byzantine missionaries bring Eastern Orthodox Christianity.
Ottomans bring Islam to Balkans.	Russian influence spreads.	Asian peoples settle in Eastern Europe.

Many groups of people such as the Slavs, Jews, Huns, and Vikings settled in Eastern Europe and created a very diverse region.

■ REVIEW QUESTIONS

1. Which groups settled in Poland?

2. Diagram Skills Which group brought Roman Catholicism to Eastern Europe?

CHAPTER 10 *Test*

◼ IDENTIFYING MAIN IDEAS

Write the letter of the correct answer in the blank provided. (10 points each)

____ 1. The Byzantine empire reached its greatest size under
   A. Constantine.
   B. Justinian.
   C. Muhammad II.
   D. Vladimir.

____ 2. Of all Justinian's works, he is best remembered for this.
   A. his wife Theodora
   B. his code of laws
   C. his art
   D. war with North Africa, Italy, and Spain

____ 3. Which of the following groups finally conquered the Byzantine empire?
   A. Ottoman Turks
   B. Seljuk Turks
   C. Latin Christians
   D. Arabs

____ 4. Early Russian civilization was strongly influenced by the culture of
   A. Rome.
   B. the Byzantine empire.
   C. the Ottoman Turks.
   D. Persia.

____ 5. How did Mongol rule affect Russia's relations with Western Europe?
   A. It isolated Russia from the West.
   B. It spread Russian learning.
   C. It spread Byzantine Christianity.
   D. It led to war with the West.

____ 6. Which of the following cities became the capital of Russia under the czars?
   A. Kiev
   B. Rome
   C. Constantinople
   D. Moscow

____ 7. What did Ivan the Great believe about czars?
   A. They had absolute power.
   B. They ruined Russia.
   C. They would rule for twenty years.
   D. They should give in to the Mongols.

____ 8. Which of the following groups of people took refuge in Poland during the late Middle Ages?
   A. Slavs
   B. Jews
   C. Serbs
   D. Roman Catholics

____ 9. Eastern Europe is a region of
   A. democratic government.
   B. unpassable mountain ranges.
   C. diverse peoples and cultures.
   D. isolated cities.

____ 10. Which of the following religions took hold in Poland and Hungary?
   A. Hinduism
   B. Islam
   C. Orthodox Christianity
   D. Roman Catholicism

The Muslim World (622–1629)

SECTION 1 · RISE OF ISLAM

TEXT SUMMARY

In 622, a new religion called Islam arose in Arabia. According to Islam, God sent his angel Gabriel with a command to Muhammad to spread the message of Islam. Muhammad spent the rest of his life spreading the word of Islam. Soon thousands of people adopted Islam.

People who practice Islam are called Muslims. Like Jews and Christians, Muslims believe in one God, Allah. Allah is compassionate and all-powerful. Islam teaches that people are responsible for the way they behave. Muslims must pray every day and are expected to **fast,** or go without food, from sunrise to sunset during the holy month of Ramadan. Muslims are supposed to help the poor and visit the holy city of Mecca. If Muslims follow Islamic teachings, they will have eternal happiness after death.

The sacred book of Islam is the Quran. Muslims believe that the Quran contains the word of God, so it is the final authority in all matters. It also provides a complete guide to life. Over time, Muslims developed a system of law, called the Sharia. The laws teach people how to behave in family life, business, and other aspects of the community. In this way, Islam is both a religion and a way of life. The Quran, the Sharia, and the Arabic language helped unite all Muslims.

THE BIG IDEA

Islam arose in Arabia around 622 and became one of the world's major religions.

GRAPHIC SUMMARY: *The Five Duties of Islam*

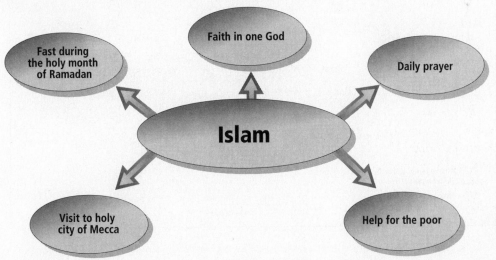

Faith in one God

Fast during the holy month of Ramadan

Daily prayer

Islam

Visit to holy city of Mecca

Help for the poor

All Muslims accept five basic duties called the Five Pillars of Islam.

REVIEW QUESTIONS

1. What do the Quran and the Sharia teach?

2. Diagram Skills Name three duties of Islam.

SECTION 2 ISLAM SPREADS

■ TEXT SUMMARY

Arabs spread Islam across parts of three continents. After Muhammad died, Arab armies built a large empire. They conquered parts of the Byzantine empire, the Persian empire, Egypt, and Spain. The Arabs were strong fighters. Their cavalry, mounted on camels and horses, overwhelmed opponents. The Arabs were successful partly because the Byzantine and Persian empires were weak from fighting wars against each other. Most important, the Arabs were united by their belief in Islam. The Arabs treated conquered people fairly. People in defeated empires welcomed the Arabs after years of living under harsh rulers. Many converted to Islam.

After the death of Muhammad, Muslims disagreed about who should be the leader of Islam. They split into two groups, Sunnis and Shiites. Today, Sunnis and Shiites share most religious beliefs, laws, and ways of life, but they still differ over the issue of who should have succeeded Muhammad as leader of the Islamic community.

Several strong dynasties ruled the Arab empire. However, around 850, the empire began to decline. Independent dynasties arose to rule separate Muslim states. In the 900s, the Seljuk Turks adopted Islam and built their own empire. They took control of the Arab capital, Baghdad. Then, in the 1200s, the Mongols destroyed Baghdad.

> **THE BIG IDEA**
>
> Inspired by Muhammad's teachings, Arab armies spread Islam through parts of three continents.

■ GRAPHIC SUMMARY: *The Spread of Islam*

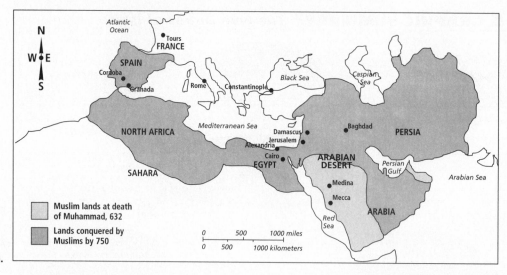

Arab armies made mighty conquests that carried Islam from the Atlantic Ocean to India.

■ REVIEW QUESTIONS

1. Name three reasons that the Arabs were able to build a large empire.

2. **Map Skills** What lands did the Muslims rule at the time of Muhammad's death?

© Prentice-Hall, Inc.

GOLDEN AGE OF MUSLIM CIVILIZATION

◼ TEXT SUMMARY

As the Muslim empire grew, it added Persians, Egyptians, Africans, Europeans, and others to the Arab population. Over time, Muslim culture blended many different traditions.

A strong economy helped to spread Islam. Between 750 and 1350, Muslim merchants built a trade network across the Islamic world and beyond. Muslims invented new ways of doing business that included credit sales and bank checks. Muslim artisans produced fine carpets, glassware, and steel swords. To help farm the deserts, leaders built huge irrigation systems.

The many cultures of the Muslim empire influenced art and literature. For example, Muslim architects adapted Byzantine domes and arches for their buildings. Arabs loved stories, so they collected tales from all over the Islamic world. However, the Quran was the most important piece of Arab literature. Many writers wrote poems and stories based on the Quran.

The Muslims were excellent scientists. They contributed to the development of algebra. Muslim astronomers studied eclipses, and they figured out the **circumference** of, or distance around, the Earth. The government set up hospitals with emergency rooms and wards for women. Doctors had to pass difficult tests to practice. They traveled to jails and to the countryside to care for sick people.

> ### THE **BIG** IDEA
>
> **During the golden age of Muslim civilization, Muslims of many lands made advances in art, literature, and science.**

◼ GRAPHIC SUMMARY: *The Golden Age of Muslim Civilization*

Art	Literature
• Use beautiful writing and patterns to decorate buildings and art • Adapt Byzantine domes and arches • Paint people and animals in nonreligious art	• Consider Quran most important piece of Arabic literature • Chant oral poetry • Collect stories from other people

Muslim Civilization

Learning	Medicine
• Translate writings of Greek philosophers • Develop algebra • Observe Earth turning and measure its circumference	• Require doctors to pass difficult tests • Set up hospitals with emergency rooms • Study diseases and write medical books

Muslim civilization adapted and greatly expanded the learning of other cultures.

◼ REVIEW QUESTIONS

1. How did merchants help to spread Islam?

2. Chart Skills What were three Arab advances in science and medicine?

MUSLIMS IN INDIA

◼ TEXT SUMMARY

In the late 1100s, Turkish Muslims conquered northern India. They set up a dynasty called the Delhi **sultanate.** Muslim rule brought changes to Indian government and society. Muslim sultans introduced Muslim ways of government. Trade between India and the Muslim world increased. Many Muslim scholars went to India. They helped create a brilliant civilization at Delhi.

Muslim rule of India brought together two very different religions and cultures. Hinduism was an ancient religion, with many gods and many sacred texts. Islam was a newer religion with one God and one sacred text. The Delhi sultans allowed Hindus to practice their religion. Over time, Muslim and Hindu cultures blended together. Many Hindus converted to Islam. Indian Muslims adopted Hindu marriage customs and the caste system. A new language, Urdu, mixed Persian, Arabic, and Hindi. Also, a new religion called Sikhism developed. Sikhism blended Muslim and Hindu beliefs.

In 1526, Turkish and Mongol invaders conquered India. They set up the Mughal dynasty. The most important Mughal ruler was Akbar the Great. Akbar built a strong government through his policy of religious tolerance. He married a Hindu princess and allowed Hindu princes to help rule the empire. He modernized the army and encouraged trade.

> ### THE **BIG** IDEA
>
> Muslim invasions resulted in Islamic rule of northern India.

◼ GRAPHIC SUMMARY: *Islam and Hinduism*

Islam	Hinduism
One sacred book	Many sacred books
One God	Many gods and goddesses
Believers do not make statues of God	Believers pray before statues of gods and goddesses
All believers are equal before God	People of different castes are not equal

When the Muslims conquered India, two very different religions came into contact.

◼ REVIEW QUESTIONS

1. Describe two ways in which Muslim rule changed India.

2. Chart Skills Name two differences between Hinduism and Islam.

 **SECTION 5**

THE OTTOMAN AND SAFAVID EMPIRES

■ TEXT SUMMARY

Starting in the 1400s while the Mughals ruled India, two other Muslim dynasties arose. Both used new weapons and military strategies to win territory. One group, the Ottomans, built a huge empire in the Middle East, Eastern Europe, and northern Africa. The other group, the Safavid dynasty, built a powerful empire in Persia.

Muslim traditions influenced both empires. Ottoman Sultan Suleiman the Magnificent strengthened the government and improved the system of justice. Ottoman law was based on the Sharia. (See Section 1.) Government officials worked with religious leaders who interpreted the law. The Safavids created a strong government, strengthened the army, and formed alliances with European states. Wise lead-ers of both empires accepted people of other religions. However, the Ottomans and Safavids were bitter enemies because of their opposing views of Islam.

Both the Ottomans and the Safavids enjoyed a golden age under great leaders. During the reign of Suleiman, Ottoman painters used Persian styles to create beautiful manuscripts. Architects built many palaces and places of worship called **mosques.** Safavid leader Shah Abbas the Great restored the culture of Persia. He welcomed artists, poets, and scholars to his capital city. His palace workshops produced beautiful porcelains, clothes, and rugs.

> ### THE **BIG** IDEA
>
> **New military technology helped both the Ottomans and Safavids to create powerful empires.**

■ GRAPHIC SUMMARY: *Powerful Muslim Empires*

Ottoman Empire

- Empire extends from Hungary to Arabia and across North Africa
- Suleiman the Magnificent rules from 1520 to 1566
- Sunni Muslims
- Capital city is Istanbul, previously Constantinople
- Sultan improves the legal system

(shared)

- Armies use new weapons such as muskets and cannons
- Other religious beliefs tolerated in the empire
- Use Persian and Arab ideas in literature
- Empires fight each other in religious wars

Safavid Empire

- Empire controls the area of Iran
- Shah Abbas the Great rules from 1588 to 1629
- Shiite Muslims
- Isfahan, the capital, is center of arts and learning
- Alliances with European states

The period from about 1450 to 1650 is sometimes called "the age of gunpowder empires" because the Ottomans and the Safavids used new military technology.

■ REVIEW QUESTIONS

1. What helped both the Ottomans and Safavids to win new territory?

2. Diagram Skills Name a great Ottoman ruler. Name a great Safavid ruler.

CHAPTER 11 *Test*

▪ IDENTIFYING MAIN IDEAS

Write the letter of the correct answer in the blank provided. (10 points each)

____ 1. Which of the following beliefs is held by Muslims, Jews, and Christians?
   A. belief in reincarnation
   B. belief in Jesus as the messiah
   C. belief in one God
   D. belief in Muhammad

____ 2. To Muslims, the Quran is
   A. a theoretical work with little application to daily life.
   B. only a guide written by a group of Muslim scholars.
   C. superseded by the Sharia.
   D. the final authority on all matters.

____ 3. According to the Five Pillars of Islam, every Muslim must
   A. read the Bible.
   B. give alms.
   C. believe in many gods.
   D. obey official priests.

____ 4. The key reason for Muslim success in conquest was
   A. the weakness of the Persians.
   B. the Arab camel cavalry.
   C. their common faith.
   D. their bravery.

____ 5. The split between Sunni and Shiite Muslims began with disagreement over
   A. the choice of a leader.
   B. a belief in one God.
   C. acceptance of the Quran.
   D. the required pilgrimage to Mecca.

____ 6. Extensive trade led Muslims to invent new
   A. products.
   B. ways of doing business.
   C. highways.
   D. religious beliefs.

____ 7. Which of the following events created a Muslim empire in India?
   A. the fall of the Gupta empire
   B. the establishment of the Delhi sultanate
   C. the invasion by Tamerlane
   D. the conquest by Mahmud

____ 8. Sikhism blended the beliefs of Islam with those of
   A. Christianity.
   B. Judaism.
   C. Buddhism.
   D. Hinduism.

____ 9. Which of the following statements describes the Ottoman and Safavid empires?
   A. Both were ruled by a caliph.
   B. Both persecuted non-Muslims.
   C. Both preserved peace.
   D. Both based their government on Muslim traditions.

____ 10. How did the arts fare under Suleiman?
   A. They declined.
   B. They remained the same.
   C. They flourished.
   D. They were outlawed.

Kingdoms and Trading States of Africa (750 B.C.–A.D. 1586)

CHAPTER 12

SECTION 1 EARLY CIVILIZATIONS OF AFRICA

■ TEXT SUMMARY

Geography has always influenced how Africans live. Most Africans live in the **savanna.** These grassy plains are good for farming and cattle herding. Many people also settled in the fertile Nile River valley. Several large deserts made it difficult to travel in parts of Africa. Steep waterfalls on several of Africa's major rivers limited contact between the coast and the interior of the continent. However, people did migrate and trade.

The kingdom of Nubia emerged in North Africa at the same time Egyptian civilization developed. Nubia and Egypt had contact through trade and war. As a result, the Nubians adopted many Egyptian ways. They built palaces and pyramids in the Egyptian style. At the same time, the Nubians developed their own civilization. By controlling trade routes, Nubia grew wealthy. The Nubian system of writing used an alphabet, not hieroglyphics.

Several early civilizations influenced North Africa. Trade linked Egypt with Greece and Mesopotamia. Later, Roman conquerors built roads and cities across North Africa. Under Roman rule, Christianity spread. Merchants used camels brought from Asia to create new trading networks across the Sahara. In the 600s, Arab armies spread Islam throughout North Africa. Over time, Islam replaced Christianity and the Arabic language replaced Latin.

> ### THE **BIG** IDEA
>
> **The varied climates, physical features, and natural resources of Africa helped create diverse ways of life.**

■ GRAPHIC SUMMARY: *Early Civilizations and North Africa*

GREEKS
- Trade with Egypt
- Rule Egypt

ROMANS
- Conquer and rule North Africa
- Build roads, aqueducts, dams, and cities
- Spread Christianity

NORTH AFRICA

ARABS
- Conquer cities in North Africa
- Spread Islam
- Bring Arabic language
- Spread Muslim ideas and learning

ASIANS
- Introduce camels

Early African civilizations had strong ties to other cultures, especially those that developed in the Mediterranean region.

■ REVIEW QUESTIONS

1. Why was the use of camels important in Africa?

2. Diagram Skills What were two ways in which early Roman civilization influenced North Africa?

KINGDOMS OF WEST AFRICA

▇ TEXT SUMMARY

By A.D. 100, farming villages in West Africa were growing into towns. Over time, these towns became part of an important trade network. Gold and salt were the most important products traded. People needed salt in their diet to prevent **dehydration,** or the loss of water. There was plenty of salt in the Sahara, but there was little in the savanna. There, a block of salt was worth its weight in gold.

Strong West African rulers created powerful kingdoms. These kingdoms gained control of the trade routes. By 800, the kingdom of Ghana controlled trade in gold and salt across West Africa. Around 1250, the kingdom of Mali crushed Ghana and won control of the gold trade routes. Mali built the great trading city of Timbuktu. Timbuktu became a center of learning. Around 1450, a new kingdom called Songhai emerged. The ruler of Songhai built the largest state that had ever existed in West Africa.

Muslim merchants brought their religion when they settled throughout West Africa. In time, however, Islam became an important influence. The emperor of Mali, Mansa Musa, converted to Islam. He based his system of justice on the Quran. West African kingdoms also used Muslim military technology. They adopted Muslim ideas, including the written language, coins, and business methods.

> **THE BIG IDEA**
>
> **West African rulers built powerful kingdoms by gaining control of trade routes and defeating their enemies.**

▇ GRAPHIC SUMMARY: *Kingdoms of West Africa*

Ghana (800–1000)	Mali (1200–1450)	Songhai (1450–1600)
• Controls trade in gold and salt across West Africa	• Mali conquers kingdom of Ghana	• Songhai grows into largest West African state
• Women work in business and government	• Mansa Musa becomes great emperor	• Controls important trade routes
• King has Muslim advisers	• Mali controls gold trade routes	• Emperor sets up Muslim dynasty
	• Timbuktu becomes a great trading city and center of learning	

West Africa was the home of three important civilizations.

▇ REVIEW QUESTIONS

1. What were the two most important products traded in West Africa?

2. Chart Skills Which kingdom conquered Ghana?

 **SECTION 3**

TRADE ROUTES OF EAST AFRICA

■ TEXT SUMMARY

The kingdom of Axum was located on the coast of East Africa. In A.D. 350, Axum conquered and absorbed Nubia. Axum controlled a trade network that linked Africa, India, and the Mediterranean world. In the cities of Axum, Africans mixed with people from other lands.

In the 300s, the king of Axum converted to Christianity. Over time, Christianity spread throughout the kingdom. Civil war and the spread of Islam in Northern Africa led to the decline of Axum. However, people living in the mountains continued to practice Christianity. These people became the ancestors of the Ethiopians. Ethiopian Christians borrowed many different traditions from other cultures. They adapted East African music and dance. They observed Jewish holidays and rules about diet.

While Axum declined, other trading cities arose along the East African coast. In the 600s, Arab and Persian merchants set up Muslim communities there. By 1000, merchant ships from port cities such as Mogadishu sailed to India to trade. Trade led to a mixing of cultures in East Africa.

Starting in the 600s, trading cities grew along the East African coast.

Over time, this blending of cultures resulted in a new language called **Swahili.** Swahili mixed Arabic words with Bantu, an African language.

THE BIG IDEA

Trade routes across the Indian Ocean linked East Africa with other regions.

■ GRAPHIC SUMMARY:
The Rise of East African Trading Cities

- Early trade with Phoenician, Greek, Roman, Arab, Chinese, and Indian merchants
- Trading communities set up on the eastern coast

East African trading cities develop

SHORT-TERM EFFECTS
- Growth of cities on coast into strong city-states
- Rise of slave trade

LONG-TERM EFFECTS
- Rich mix of cultures
- Development of Swahili language

■ REVIEW QUESTIONS

1. How did the Swahili language develop?

2. Chart Skills Name two results of the rise of East African trading cities.

MANY PEOPLES, MANY TRADITIONS

■ TEXT SUMMARY

Across Africa, people lived in different ways. In the deserts, people gathered roots and herbs and hunted small animals. They lived in small groups. In some parts of the savanna, nomadic people raised cattle. Along the coasts, people fished. They traded extra fish for grains and animal skins. Farming communities grew many crops, such as grains, yams, and bananas.

The village, the family, and religion were important in Africa. Most farming people lived in villages. Villagers helped each other with planting and harvesting. Each African family belonged to a **lineage,** or group of households who claimed a common ancestor. Several lineages formed a clan. Belonging to a family, lineage, or clan helped each person to feel part of a community. Africans had many different religious beliefs. Villagers worshiped many gods and goddesses. Many Africans believed that the spirits of their ancestors could help them. They tried to influence the spirits of nature with rituals and ceremonies.

Art and literature strengthened African society. African artists used ivory, wood, and bronze. Some art was only for decoration. Statues and masks were often used in religious ceremonies. Many African societies used stories to teach history and values. In West Africa, storytellers called **griots** passed stories from generation to generation.

> ### THE BIG IDEA
>
> Village governments, family bonds, and religious beliefs gave people a sense of community.

■ GRAPHIC SUMMARY: *Diverse African Traditions*

Village Life	Family Patterns	Religious Beliefs
• Elders share government power	• Each family belongs to a lineage	• Worship many gods and goddesses
• Villagers help each other with planting and harvesting	• Several lineages form a clan	• Elders ask spirits for rain and good harvests
• Some villages ruled by larger kingdoms, such as Songhai	• Elders teach children the clan's history and religious beliefs	• Ask spirits of ancestors for help

Each family belonged to a lineage. Several lineages formed a clan.

■ REVIEW QUESTIONS

1. How did Africans live in the savanna? In the deserts?

2. Chart Skills What is a clan?

CHAPTER 12 *Test*

◼ IDENTIFYING MAIN IDEAS

Write the letter of the correct answer in the blank provided. (10 points each)

_____ 1. What geographic features created a barrier to the movement of people and goods in Africa?
   A. oceans
   B. harbors
   C. mountains
   D. deserts

_____ 2. Trade across the Sahara was revolutionized by this.
   A. camel caravans
   B. desertification
   C. horse-drawn chariots
   D. new roadways

_____ 3. The Sahara trade was dominated by what two products?
   A. copper and gold
   B. salt and pepper
   C. gold and salt
   D. diamonds and iron ore

_____ 4. How did Islam influence Mali emperor Mansa Musa?
   A. He adapted Islamic education techniques.
   B. He rejected Muslim military techniques.
   C. He based his system of justice on the Quran.
   D. He revised the Arabic language based on Islamic traditions.

_____ 5. Axum prospered partly because it had a port on the
   A. Mediterranean Sea.
   B. Indian Ocean.
   C. Atlantic Ocean.
   D. Red Sea.

_____ 6. What religious tradition did the Axumites pass on to the Ethiopians?
   A. Christianity
   B. Islam
   C. Hinduism
   D. Buddhism

_____ 7. Over the centuries, Ethiopian Christians
   A. remained isolated.
   B. borrowed many traditions from other cultures.
   C. converted to Islam.
   D. sent missionaries to other states.

_____ 8. In dry desert areas, people adapted by practicing
   A. slash-and-burn agriculture.
   B. herding and fishing.
   C. hunting and gathering.
   D. ancestor worship.

_____ 9. African art masks were tied to
   A. literature.
   B. lineages.
   C. economics.
   D. religion.

_____ 10. The griots of West Africa preserved
   A. oral traditions.
   B. written records.
   C. woven cloth.
   D. religious statues.

Spread of Civilizations in East Asia (500–1650)

SECTION 1 — TWO GOLDEN AGES OF CHINA

TEXT SUMMARY

After the Han dynasty declined, China remained divided for nearly 400 years. Then, in 618, the Tang dynasty reunited the Chinese empire. The Tang conquered parts of Central Asia and forced Vietnam, Korea, and Tibet to become **tributary states.** That is, the states remained independent, but their rulers had to recognize China's power and send tribute to the emperor. In 960, the Song dynasty came to power. The Song period was a golden age. The Chinese economy grew. Chinese culture dominated East Asia. Merchants traded with Persia, India, and the Middle East.

The two main classes of Chinese society were the **gentry,** or rich landowners, and the peasants. Many members of the gentry studied Confucian thought. Some became government officials. Most Chinese were peasants who worked the land. Some Chinese became merchants. According to Confucian tradition, merchants had an even lower social status than peasants. This was because their riches came from the work of other people.

The arts were important during the Tang and Song periods. In literature, Chinese writers wrote short stories and poetry. Li Bo was probably the greatest Tang poet. Chinese landscape painting became popular during the Song period. Chinese architects created the **pagoda,** a temple with a roof that curved up at the corners. The Chinese became experts at making **porcelain,** a kind of pottery. Chinese porcelain was the finest in the world.

> ### THE **BIG** IDEA
>
> The Tang and the Song dynasties restored culture and prosperity to China.

GRAPHIC SUMMARY:

Chinese Society

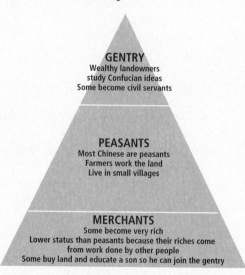

GENTRY
Wealthy landowners
study Confucian ideas
Some become civil servants

PEASANTS
Most Chinese are peasants
Farmers work the land
Live in small villages

MERCHANTS
Some become very rich
Lower status than peasants because their riches come from work done by other people
Some buy land and educate a son so he can join the gentry

Under the Tang and the Song dynasties, there were three social classes in China.

REVIEW QUESTIONS

1. Which lands became tributary states of China under the Tang dynasty?

2. **Diagram Skills** Which group had time to study Confucian ideas?

THE MONGOL AND MING EMPIRES

■ TEXT SUMMARY

Under their leader Genghiz Khan, the Mongols built the largest empire in the world. The Mongols were fierce conquerors from the deserts north of China. Despite their violent reputation, they were fair rulers. During the 1200s and 1300s, the heirs of Genghiz Khan established peace and order within the Mongol empire. They gained control of the Silk Road. Trade allowed people from different cultures to mix within the empire.

In 1279, Kublai Khan, the grandson of Genghiz Khan, conquered the Song dynasty in China. He set up the Yuan dynasty. The Mongols ruled China for 150 years. The Yuan improved transportation, encouraged trade, and created an efficient mail system. However, Kublai Khan did not want the Mongols to be absorbed into Chinese civilization. He gave the best government jobs to Mongol workers. Only Mongols were allowed to serve in the army. Many Chinese disliked Mongol domination.

In 1368, the Chinese drove the Mongols out of China. They set up the Ming dynasty. The Ming brought back the civil service system. Confucian learning became important again. Ming rulers improved the government and the economy. Chinese cities developed industries. The Ming also made advances in the arts and literature. In 1433, the Ming emperor forbade the Chinese from having contact with the rest of the world.

> **THE BIG IDEA**
>
> Powerful Mongol armies conquered China, much of Asia, and part of Europe. The Ming dynasty ended Mongol control of China.

■ GRAPHIC SUMMARY: *The Mongol Empire*

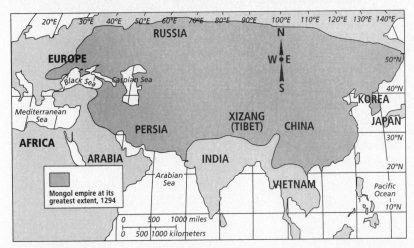

At its height, the Mongol empire was the largest in the world.

■ REVIEW QUESTIONS

1. What did the Ming do when they came to power?

2. Map Skills Why do you think that contact between China and Europe increased while the Mongols controlled China?

SECTION 3 · KOREA AND ITS TRADITIONS

◼ TEXT SUMMARY

Korea is located on a peninsula in the east of Asia. Steep mountains and the Yalu River separate Korea from China. The southern tip of Korea points toward Japan. Since Korea is near both China and Japan, it has served as a link between China and Japan. Throughout its history, Koreans have adapted Chinese ideas and passed them on to the Japanese.

Chinese civilization has always influenced Korea. Chinese missionaries brought Buddhism to Korea. Korean monks traveled to China and brought home Chinese arts and learning. Koreans adopted Confucian ideas, including the belief that the family was the basis of the state. In fact, Koreans saw the relationship of their kingdom to China as the younger brother who owes loyalty to the older brother. Koreans adapted the Chinese civil service system. Scholars used Chinese models for their histories and poems. Art and architecture also had strong Chinese influences.

Despite strong ties to China, Koreans also developed their own ways. For example, their language is not related to Chinese. Koreans invented their own system of writing that was easier to use than the Chinese system. They perfected a type of blue-green porcelain glaze called celadon. People all over Asia admired celadon vases and jars made in Korea.

> **THE BIG IDEA**
>
> Due to Korea's location, its history and culture were linked closely to China and Japan.

◼ GRAPHIC SUMMARY: *China Influences Korea*

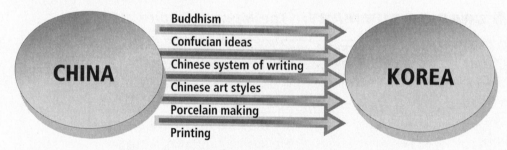

CHINA → KOREA
- Buddhism
- Confucian ideas
- Chinese system of writing
- Chinese art styles
- Porcelain making
- Printing

Korea borrowed many ideas from Chinese culture. Later, these ideas were adapted to fit Korean culture.

◼ REVIEW QUESTIONS

1. How has Korea served as a link between China and Japan?

2. Diagram Skills Name three ideas that Korea borrowed from China.

THE EMERGENCE OF JAPAN

■ TEXT SUMMARY

Japan is located on an **archipelago,** or chain of islands, near the Asian mainland close to China and Korea. Japan is part of the Ring of Fire, which has many earthquakes, volcanoes, and tidal waves called **tsunamis.** Because the land is very mountainous, people settled along the coast and in the narrow river valleys. In early times, the mountains prevented unity.

Around A.D. 500, the Yamato clan gained control of Japan and set up its first and only dynasty. The current emperor still traces his roots to the Yamato clan. Through the Koreans, the Japanese learned about Chinese culture. Then, in the early 600s, a Yamato ruler sent Japanese nobles to China to study. They brought back Chinese ideas and technology. The Japanese adopted many Chinese ways. (See chart below.) By the 800s, the Tang dynasty in China began to decline and the Japanese became less interested in China. The Japanese began to blend the Chinese ideas with their own to create a unique civilization.

The blending of Japanese and Chinese cultures in Japan took place between 794 and 1185. This time is called the Heian Period. During the Heian Period, the emperor lost power to one clan, the Fujiwara, who ran the country. Rich nobles lived in beautiful homes with gardens and pools. They developed elegant manners and new ways to dress. Noblewomen wrote important works of Japanese literature. One Heian woman wrote the world's first novel.

THE **BIG** IDEA

Japan borrowed elements of Chinese civilization but remained free of Chinese control.

■ GRAPHIC SUMMARY: *Japan Adapts Chinese Ideas*

600s–700s	800s	900s–1200s
• Japanese study Chinese civilization. • Emperor builds capital city modeled on Chinese capital. • Japanese nobles adopt Chinese language, food, and style of dress. • Japanese nobles adopt Chinese tea ceremony, music and dance, and gardens.	• Japanese stop traveling to China.	• Japanese keep some Chinese ways but build their own civilization. • Japanese artists develop their own styles. • Japanese change the Chinese system of writing.

The Japanese borrowed many ideas from the Chinese but developed their own unique civilization.

■ REVIEW QUESTIONS

1. How did the location of Japan near China and Korea affect its early development?

2. Diagram Skills What were three ideas the Japanese borrowed from China?

JAPAN'S FEUDAL AGE

▨ TEXT SUMMARY

In Japan during the 1100s, local warlords fought one another. While armies battled for power, feudalism developed. The emperor had no real power. Military rulers called **shoguns** set up dynasties called shogunates. The shoguns gave land to vassal lords called **daimyo.** The daimyo, in turn, gave land to lesser warriors called **samurai.** (See diagram at right.)

THE **BIG** IDEA

Military rulers called shoguns dominated Japanese society during feudal times.

In 1603, the Tokugawa shogunate came to power. The Tokugawa ended wars between feudal lords. However, they continued the feudal system. They imposed restrictions on society by taking control of the daimyo and forcing the peasants to remain on the land. Only the samurai could serve in the army or hold government jobs. Under the Tokugawa shogunate, agriculture improved. Farmers used new seeds and tools to grow more food. The population of Japan grew. Towns were linked by roads and trade increased.

During this time, a form of Buddhism called Zen spread through Japan. Zen Buddhists valued peace, simple living, nature, and beauty. Many Japanese learned Zen practices, such as the tea ceremony and landscape gardening. At the same time, the Japanese made advances in the arts and theater. In **kabuki** theater, actors wore colorful costumes and acted out stories about families or events in history. In literature, Japanese poets created a form of poetry called **haiku.**

▨ GRAPHIC SUMMARY:

Feudal Society in Japan

EMPEROR
Held highest rank in society but had no political power

SHOGUN
Actual ruler

Daimyo
Large landowners

Samurai
Warriors loyal to daimyo

Peasants
Three fourths of population

Artisans

Merchants
Low status but gradually gained influence

The Japanese developed a feudal society very similar to the feudal system in medieval Europe.

▨ REVIEW QUESTIONS

1. What are two changes that occurred during the Tokugawa shogunate?

2. Diagram Skills Who had the most power in Japanese feudal society? What three groups had the least power?

CHAPTER 13 *Test*

■ IDENTIFYING MAIN IDEAS

Write the letter of the correct answer in the blank provided. (10 points each)

_____ 1. Under the Tang, the Chinese empire
   A. expanded.
   B. shrank.
   C. stayed the same.
   D. conquered all of Asia

_____ 2. In Chinese society under the Tang and Song, peasants ranked
   A. higher than gentry.
   B. lower than merchants.
   C. higher than merchants.
   D. the same as merchants.

_____ 3. Mongol rule in China was a time of
   A. peace and order.
   B. violence and oppression.
   C. restricted trade.
   D. widespread poverty.

_____ 4. The Ming dynasty came about when
   A. Kublai Khan invaded China.
   B. the Chinese economy revived.
   C. the Song dynasty collapsed.
   D. the Mongols were pushed out of China.

_____ 5. Korea's role between China and Japan has been that of a
   A. trading partner.
   B. cultural bridge.
   C. defensive fortress.
   D. highway to the outside world.

_____ 6. Which of the following cultures had the greatest influence on Korea?
   A. Chinese
   B. Japanese
   C. European
   D. African

_____ 7. Because most of Japan is mountainous, its people lived mostly
   A. in the mountains.
   B. on the smallest islands.
   C. in river valleys and coastal plains.
   D. on boats.

_____ 8. Heian nobles influenced Japanese culture by
   A. studying the Chinese language.
   B. producing important works of literature.
   C. supervising family estates.
   D. training in the military arts.

_____ 9. Who held the real power in Japan's feudal society?
   A. the emperor
   B. women
   C. samurai
   D. the shogun

_____ 10. The Tokugawa shoguns created an orderly society by
   A. ending feudalism.
   B. forbidding trade.
   C. giving peasants greater freedom.
   D. imposing restrictions on social classes.

The Renaissance and Reformation (1300–1650)

SECTION 1 — THE RENAISSANCE IN ITALY

▪ TEXT SUMMARY

The period from the 1300s to the 1500s was a time of creativity and change in Europe. This period is called the **Renaissance,** which means "rebirth." It was a golden age in the arts, literature, and sciences. Europeans developed new ideas about the world. During the Middle Ages, thinkers had wondered about life after death. Renaissance thinkers, on the other hand, were curious about life in the present.

The Renaissance began in Italy in the mid-1300s and then spread north. Renaissance thinkers were interested in ancient Rome. Visible reminders of Roman culture were everywhere in Italy. In addition, Italian cities such as Florence and Venice had become centers of trade and manufacturing. Rich merchants in these cities spent large sums of money on art and education.

The ideas of the intellectual movement known as **humanism** influenced the Renaissance. Instead of religious issues, humanists studied worldly subjects that the ancient Greeks and Romans had studied. They hoped to use ancient learning to increase knowledge about their own times. Renaissance artists studied ancient Greek and Roman art. They copied the ancient realistic style. Painters developed new ways to make their paintings realistic. For example, they studied the human body and used live models when they painted.

▪ GRAPHIC SUMMARY:

Artists of the Italian Renaissance

Leonardo da Vinci
- Painter, sculptor, inventor, architect, musician, engineer
- Painting of *Mona Lisa*
- Sketches and plans for flying machines and submarines

Michelangelo
- Sculptor, engineer, poet, painter, architect
- Statue of *David*
- Dome of St. Peter's Church in Rome

Raphael
- Painter
- Student of Michelangelo and Leonardo da Vinci
- Paintings of the madonna, mother of Jesus

Sofonisba Anguissola
- Woman artist
- Painter for King Philip II of Spain

The Renaissance was a time of glorious painting, sculpture, and architecture.

> ### THE **BIG** IDEA
>
> The Renaissance was characterized by an interest in learning and the arts, and a desire to explore the human experience.

▪ REVIEW QUESTIONS

1. Give two reasons why the Renaissance began in Italy.

2. Chart Skills The ideal Renaissance person had many talents. Which of these artists do you think was closest to this ideal?

THE RENAISSANCE MOVES NORTH

◼ TEXT SUMMARY

Northern Europe took a long time to recover from the Black Death. (See Chapter 9.) As a result, the Renaissance did not begin there until the 1400s. It slowly spread to Spain, France, Germany, and England. A German artist named Albrecht Dürer traveled to Italy to study Italian art. When he returned home, he helped spread the ideas of the Italian Renaissance throughout Germany.

Like Italian humanists, northern humanists believed that education was important and studied ancient Greeks and Romans. However, they also explored religious ideas and believed that learning should change society. Erasmus, for example, wanted to reform the Church. Sir Thomas More wanted to build a perfect society of peace and harmony.

The northern Renaissance produced many talented artists and writers. Pieter Bruegel used bright colors to paint scenes from peasants' lives. William Shakespeare wrote 37 plays that are still performed all over the world. Cervantes wrote *Don Quixote*, a story about the adventures of a foolish knight. After the invention of the printing press, more people were able to read these and other works. (See diagram below.)

> ### THE **BIG** IDEA
>
> The Renaissance slowly spread to northern Europe, where artists and writers experimented with new methods and ideas.

◼ GRAPHIC SUMMARY: *The Printing Press*

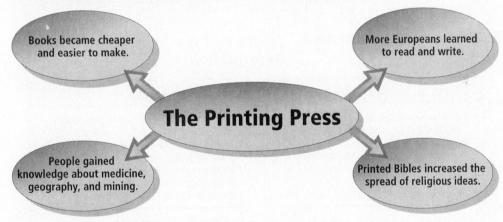

Books became cheaper and easier to make.

More Europeans learned to read and write.

The Printing Press

People gained knowledge about medicine, geography, and mining.

Printed Bibles increased the spread of religious ideas.

Johann Gutenberg and his successors developed the printing press and movable metal type. The invention of the printing press caused great changes in Europe.

◼ REVIEW QUESTIONS

1. What did northern humanists believe about learning?

2. Diagram Skills What were two effects of the invention of the printing press?

THE PROTESTANT REFORMATION

TEXT SUMMARY

During the Renaissance, the Roman Catholic Church faced serious problems. Popes fought wars for power and land. They lived a rich lifestyle and acted like kings instead of God's representatives on Earth. The Church increased its fees for religious services such as marriage and baptism. It also sold **indulgences.** An indulgence forgave a person for his or her sins and allowed entrance into heaven.

By the 1500s, many Christians wanted to reform the Church. A German monk named Martin Luther wrote 95 arguments against indulgences. He believed that Christians reach heaven only through faith in God.

Because of his radical views and outspoken ideas, Luther was excommunicated and declared an outlaw. However, the ideas of Martin Luther spread through Europe. To many, Luther was a hero. His actions began what became the Protestant Reformation. His followers set up the Lutheran Church. They were called Protestants.

John Calvin was another important reformer. Like Luther, Calvin believed that Christians could reach heaven only through faith in God. Calvin also believed that people were born sinners. He preached **predestination,** the idea that God decided long ago who would go to heaven. His followers lived strict, disciplined lives. Calvinism spread to Germany, France, Scotland, and England.

> ### THE **BIG** IDEA
>
> The ideas of Martin Luther and John Calvin led people to separate from the Roman Catholic Church and form new Protestant churches.

GRAPHIC SUMMARY: *Leaders of the Protestant Reformation*

Martin Luther	John Calvin
• Did not believe in sale of indulgences. • Believed Christians reached heaven only through faith in God. • Did not believe that priests had special powers. • Ideas spread to northern Germany and Scandinavia. • Followers later called themselves Protestants.	• Believed Christians reached heaven only through faith in God. • Believed people are born sinners. • Preached predestination. • Ideas spread to Germany, France, Holland, England, and Scotland. • Led a community in Switzerland.

Martin Luther and John Calvin were two very important reformers during the Reformation.

REVIEW QUESTIONS

1. What were two problems the Roman Catholic Church faced during the Renaissance?

2. Chart Skills What did Martin Luther believe about priests?

REFORMATION IDEAS SPREAD

◪ TEXT SUMMARY

Throughout Europe, Catholic rulers and the Catholic Church fought back against Protestantism. In England, King Henry VIII originally supported the Church. However, when he asked the pope to **annul,** or cancel, his marriage, the pope refused. Henry was very angry. With the help of Parliament, he took control of the English Church. Henry then set up the Church of England, called the Anglican Church.

As the Protestant Reformation continued, Catholics began to work for reform from within the Church. This change was called the Catholic Reformation. Catholics wanted to strengthen the Church and stop other Catholics from converting to Protestantism. They took steps to end corruption and set up schools to train the clergy. A group of priests called Jesuits spread Catholicism throughout the world. Teresa of Avila reorganized and reformed monasteries and convents in Spain.

The Protestant and Catholic Reformations divided Europe into a Catholic south and a Protestant north. Terrible religious wars broke out throughout Europe. Both sides tortured and killed people who did not agree with their teachings. The strong religious feeling contributed to a wave of witch hunting. Both Protestants and Catholics persecuted and **expelled,** or drove out, Jews.

THE **BIG** IDEA

Both the Protestant and Catholic Reformations brought sweeping changes to Europe.

◪ GRAPHIC SUMMARY: *The Protestant Reformation*

Long-Term Causes
- Roman Catholic Church becomes more worldly
- Humanists urge return to simple religion
- Strong kings emerge and resent power of Church

Long-Term Effects
- Religious wars break out in Europe for more than 100 years
- Catholic Reformation takes place
- Inquisition becomes stronger
- Many Jews forced into Eastern Europe

The Protestant Reformation

Short-Term Causes
- Indulgences are sold in Germany
- Martin Luther writes 95 Theses
- Luther translates Bible into German
- Printing press helps spread ideas
- Reformers call for change

Short-Term Effects
- Peasants revolt
- Lutheran, Calvinist, Anglican, and other Protestant churches founded
- Holy Roman emperor weakened

The Protestant Reformation brought great changes to Western Europe.

◪ REVIEW QUESTIONS

1. Why did Henry VIII set up the Church of England?

2. Diagram Skills Name one long-term cause and one short-term cause of the Protestant Reformation.

SECTION 5 · THE SCIENTIFIC REVOLUTION

■ TEXT SUMMARY

Beginning in the 1500s, new ideas about science changed the way Europeans thought about the world. This period of change was called the Scientific Revolution. Since ancient times, people had believed that the Earth was at the center of the universe. However, in the 1500s and 1600s, scientists such as Copernicus and Galileo showed that the planets revolved around the sun.

At first, the discoveries of Copernicus and Galileo upset many Europeans. Over time, however, a new way of thinking about science emerged. Scientists began to observe the world around them and to develop ideas about why things happened. They did experiments to test these ideas. This new way of thinking was called the **scientific method.**

With the scientific method, scientists made important advances in many areas. Isaac Newton discovered a force that kept the planets in their orbits around the sun. He called that force **gravity.** In chemistry, Robert Boyle made important discoveries about gases. In medicine, a French doctor named Paré developed an ointment for preventing infection and began using stitches to close wounds.

The scientific method changed the way people thought. Two important thinkers were Francis Bacon and René Descartes. Bacon stressed experimentation and observation as the best way to learn the truth. Descartes argued that human reasoning was the best way to gain understanding.

> **THE BIG IDEA**
>
> A new way of thinking, based on experimentation and observation, changed the way Europeans looked at the world.

■ GRAPHIC SUMMARY: *The Scientific Method*

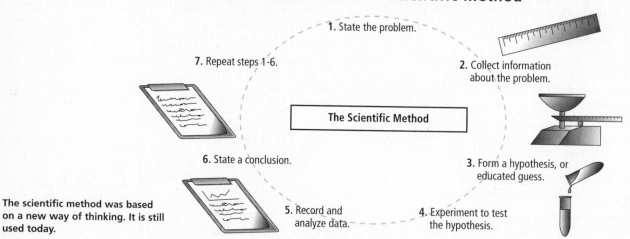

1. State the problem.
2. Collect information about the problem.
3. Form a hypothesis, or educated guess.
4. Experiment to test the hypothesis.
5. Record and analyze data.
6. State a conclusion.
7. Repeat steps 1-6.

The Scientific Method

The scientific method was based on a new way of thinking. It is still used today.

■ REVIEW QUESTIONS

1. How did scientists such as Copernicus and Galileo change the way people viewed the universe in the 1500s and 1600s?

2. Diagram Skills Why do you think scientists need to repeat their work, as shown in Step 7?

SURVEY CHAPTER 14
MODERN ERA CHAPTER 1   *Test*

■ IDENTIFYING MAIN IDEAS

Write the letter of the correct answer in the blank provided. (10 points each)

____ 1. The artists of the Renaissance focused on
   A. humans and their experiences.
   B. the spiritual world.
   C. the universe.
   D. the Catholic Church.

____ 2. Which of the following best explains why the Renaissance occurred in northern Europe later than it did in Italy?
   A. There was little interest in the arts in northern Europe.
   B. The Black Death delayed economic growth in northern Europe.
   C. Few people were educated in northern Europe.
   D. Northern Europe was a region of peasants.

____ 3. How did the printing press affect Europe?
   A. The price of books rose to pay for the new technology.
   B. More people learned to read and write.
   C. Books were available to only a limited few.
   D. Trade declined with the increase in the number of books.

____ 4. The Roman Catholic Church reacted to Luther's ideas by
   A. spreading them to non-Christians.
   B. sentencing him to death.
   C. excommunicating him.
   D. adapting Church doctrine.

____ 5. Luther believed that Christians could reach heaven only through
   A. the Church.
   B. faith.
   C. buying indulgences.
   D. participating in a crusade.

____ 6. Calvin taught that humans were born
   A. saints.
   B. sinners.
   C. believers in God.
   D. Catholics.

____ 7. Why did Henry VIII break from the Catholic Church?
   A. to please his subjects
   B. to keep wealth in England
   C. to annul his marriage
   D. to become an Anabaptist

____ 8. Which of the following was a result of the Catholic Reformation?
   A. new schools to train the clergy
   B. increased tolerance for religious minorities
   C. the end of the Protestant religion
   D. the spread of Calvinism

____ 9. The new scientific method was based on
   A. religion.
   B. ancient teachings.
   C. observation and experimentation.
   D. reasoning.

____ 10. Descartes believed people could discover basic truths through
   A. observation.
   B. experimentation.
   C. reason.
   D. religion.

The First Global Age: Europe and Asia (1415–1796)

SECTION 1 THE SEARCH FOR SPICES

TEXT SUMMARY

When the Black Death ended, the population of Europe increased again. The growing population wanted Asian goods, particularly spices. They used spices to keep foods from spoiling and to make medicines and perfumes. During the 1400s, Muslim and Italian merchants controlled the trade routes between Asia and Europe. Europeans knew direct trade with Asia would make them rich. They began to look for new routes to Asia.

Advances in technology helped Europeans explore the oceans. Map makers created better maps and charts of the seas. European sailors learned to use the **astrolabe,** an instrument for determining latitude when at sea, and the magnetic compass to navigate. Europeans also built bigger and better ships.

Portugal was the first European nation to search for a new sea route to Asia. In 1497, Vasco da Gama sailed around the southern tip of Africa to India. In 1492, the Spanish king and queen sent Christopher Columbus on a voyage to India. Although he did not know it, Columbus landed in the West Indies. Later explorers realized that Columbus had found a route to a continent they had never seen before. The region became known as the Americas. In 1520, Ferdinand Magellan sailed around South America to the Pacific Ocean. His crew was the first to sail around the world.

> **THE BIG IDEA**
>
> A desire to share in the rich spice trade of the East spurred Europeans to explore the oceans.

GRAPHIC SUMMARY: *The Early Explorers*

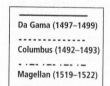

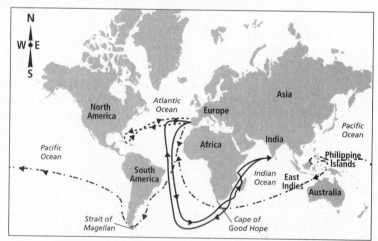

Da Gama (1497–1499)

Columbus (1492–1493)

Magellan (1519–1522)

Beginning in the 1400s, European nations sent explorers to look for new routes to Asia.

REVIEW QUESTIONS

1. Why did European merchants want to find a new route to Asia?

2. Map Skills Describe the route taken by Ferdinand Magellan.

 **SECTION 2**

DIVERSE TRADITIONS OF SOUTHEAST ASIA

■ TEXT SUMMARY

Southeast Asia is composed of a mainland and scattered islands. It is located between China and India. Modern countries there include Myanmar (Burma), Thailand, Cambodia, Laos, Vietnam, Indonesia, the Philippines, Singapore, Brunei, and Malaysia. Ships traveling between China and India had to pass through Southeast Asian waters. Between monsoon seasons, ships waited in Southeast Asian ports. These ports became centers of trade and culture.

India and China influenced the culture of Southeast Asia. Indians traveling to Southeast Asia brought ideas about government, law, art, and architecture. They introduced Buddhism, Hinduism, and Islam to the region. In 111 B.C., China

conquered northern Vietnam. The Chinese ruled Vietnam for 1,000 years. During that time, the Vietnamese adopted many Chinese ideas.

Kingdoms emerged in Southeast Asia that blended Indian and Southeast Asian ways. (See chart below.) The ruler of the kingdom of Pagan united the region in A.D. 1044 and introduced Buddhism. The Khmer empire thrived between 800 and 1350. Khmer rulers became Hindus. The Srivijaya nation prospered between the 600s and 1200s. As in other nations, its people added Hindu and Buddhist ideas to their own religious practices.

> ### THE **BIG** IDEA
>
> **Because of its location, Southeast Asia was affected by the cultures of China and India.**

■ GRAPHIC SUMMARY: *Kingdoms and Empires in Southeast Asia*

Kingdom of Pagan	Khmer Empire	Srivijaya
• Located where Myanmar is today • King Anawrata united region in 1044 • Anawrata brought Buddhism • Pagan an important Buddhist center • Conquered by Mongols in 1287	• Controlled much of present-day Cambodia, Thailand, and Malaysia • Powerful between 800 and 1350 • Adapted Indian writing, mathematics, art, and architecture • Rulers were Hindu • Most people were Buddhist • Great temple at Angkor Wat	• Located where Indonesia is today • Powerful from the 600s to the 1200s • Combined Hinduism and Buddhism with traditional nature beliefs • Trading empire • Controlled Malacca Strait

Indian and Chinese culture influenced the kingdoms and empires in Southeast Asia.

■ REVIEW QUESTIONS

1. How did Southeast Asian ports become centers of trade and culture?

2. Chart Skills How did India influence the Khmer empire?

EUROPEAN FOOTHOLDS IN SOUTHEAST ASIA AND INDIA

◼ TEXT SUMMARY

In 1510, the Portuguese took control of the Indian Ocean trade network from the Muslims. The Portuguese seized the port of Malacca, the most important Arab trading city. They also conquered cities on the east coast of Africa and destroyed Arab ships at sea. In a short time, Portugal controlled the spice trade between Europe and Asia.

By the late 1500s, Portuguese power in the Indian Ocean was declining. Meanwhile, the Dutch were setting up trading colonies around the world. In 1641, the Dutch captured Malacca from the Portuguese and began trading with China. Before long, the Dutch controlled the Asian spice trade.

Before the 1700s, the Mughal empire in India was richer and more powerful than any European empire. The Mughals did not want to trade with the Europeans. Still, Mughal emperors allowed European trading companies to build forts and warehouses along the coast of India. In the early 1700s, Mughal leaders ended their policy of religious toleration and conflicts began to arise. Civil war led to a decline in Mughal power. Then, the British East India Company forced the Mughal emperor to allow it to collect taxes in northeast India. Before long, the company was the real ruler of the region. Slowly the company spread its influence to other parts of India.

THE BIG IDEA

Europeans used military power to build trading empires in Southeast Asia.

◼ GRAPHIC SUMMARY: *European Trade in the East, 1700*

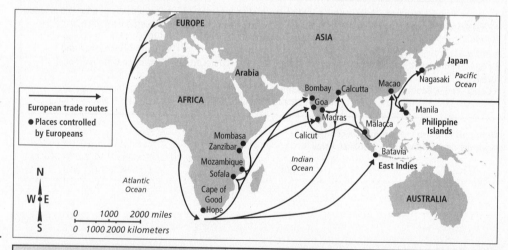

European trade routes
● Places controlled by Europeans

EUROPE
ASIA
Arabia
AFRICA
Bombay
Calcutta
Macao
Nagasaki
Japan
Pacific Ocean
Goa
Madras
Manila
Philippine Islands
Mombasa
Calicut
Malacca
Zanzibar
Indian Ocean
Mozambique
Batavia
Sofala
East Indies
Atlantic Ocean
Cape of Good Hope
AUSTRALIA

N W·E S

0   1000   2000 miles
0 1000 2000 kilometers

Europeans gained control of key trading cities in Africa and Asia.

◼ REVIEW QUESTIONS

1. What did the British East India Company do when Mughal power began to decline?

2. **Map Skills** Where was the trading city of Malacca located?

ENCOUNTERS IN EAST ASIA

TEXT SUMMARY

European traders reached China in 1514. The Ming rulers of China were not interested in European goods because they thought the goods were not well made. They allowed the Europeans to trade only at Canton and forced them to leave after each trading season ended. When the Ming dynasty declined, Manchu conquerors from the west set up the Qing dynasty. The Qing continued to limit European traders, reject foreign goods, and refuse treaties. Later, this policy would prove disastrous.

Before 1500, Korean traders traveled all over East Asia. Then, in the 1590s, Japan conquered Korea. Less than fifty years later, the Manchus forced Korea to become a tributary state of China. In response, the Koreans decided to isolate themselves. They did not allow foreigners to come to Korea. When European sailors landed on Korean shores, the Koreans put them in prison. Korea became known as the "Hermit Kingdom."

At first, the Japanese welcomed European traders and ideas. The Japanese bought European weapons and learned how to build castles in the European style. Many Japanese converted to Christianity. However, Japanese rulers did not trust the Europeans. In time, they forced all Europeans to leave Japan and persecuted Japanese Christians. By 1638, they ended western trade and banned travel outside the country. Japan remained isolated for the next 200 years.

THE BIG IDEA

China, Korea, and Japan limited contact with western nations.

GRAPHIC SUMMARY: Asia and the European Powers

1400s	1500s	1600s
China Ming dynasty ends overseas exploration by the Chinese	**China** Ming allow Europeans to trade only at Canton and force them to leave after each trading season	**China** British pressure Qing dynasty to open up more cities but Qing continue policy of limiting European trade
Korea Korean traders travel all over East Asia	**Korea** Japan conquers Korea	**Korea** Koreans decide to isolate themselves and forbid foreigners from coming to Korea
Japan No contact with Europeans	**Japan** Japanese welcome European traders	**Japan** Shoguns end European trade and foreign travel and Japan remains isolated for next 200 years

China, Korea, and then Japan restricted contact with the outside world during the 1500s and 1600s.

REVIEW QUESTIONS

1. How did the Ming limit European traders in China?

2. **Chart Skills** What was the Korean policy toward foreigners during the 1600s?

Name _____ Class _____ Date _____

Test

◼ IDENTIFYING MAIN IDEAS

Write the letter of the correct answer in the blank provided. (10 points each)

_____ 1. Why was the astrolabe helpful to sailors?
   A. It showed the location of the Pacific Ocean.
   B. It helped them determine their latitude.
   C. It showed the curved surface of the Earth on a flat chart.
   D. It projected wind currents.

_____ 2. Who was the first explorer to reach India by sailing around Africa?
   A. Prince Henry
   B. Christopher Columbus
   C. Vasco da Gama
   D. Bartholomeu Dias

_____ 3. Which of the following best describes Southeast Asia?
   A. a region completely dominated by China
   B. a completely isolated region
   C. a region composed of a mainland and scattered islands
   D. a region located between China and Japan

_____ 4. Why did Chinese influences have a greater effect on Vietnam than Indian influences?
   A. Chinese influences were more acceptable to the Vietnamese.
   B. India was weaker than China.
   C. Indian influences were spread through trade, while Chinese influences were spread through conquest.
   D. People in Vietnam were originally from China.

_____ 5. How did the Portuguese gain control of trade in Southeast Asia?
   A. They used military force.
   B. They established ties with local rulers.
   C. They paid money for trading rights.
   D. They agreed to share their navigational know-how with rulers of the region.

_____ 6. In the 1600s, the Portuguese lost control of trade in the Indian Ocean to the
   A. French.
   B. Spanish.
   C. Dutch.
   D. English.

_____ 7. What began the decline of the Mughal empire in India?
   A. war
   B. lack of religious toleration
   C. invasion
   D. increased trade with China

_____ 8. Why were the Chinese uninterested in trading with Europeans?
   A. They thought trade might lead to war.
   B. European goods were inferior to Chinese goods.
   C. The Chinese were already trading with too many nations.
   D. Chinese goods were in short supply.

_____ 9. The Ming and Qing dynasties followed which of the following policies regarding foreign trade?
   A. They restricted foreign trade.
   B. They encouraged foreign trade.
   C. They allowed foreign trade in all of China's coastal cities.
   D. They forbade foreign trade entirely.

_____ 10. What event(s) led Korea to adopt a policy of isolationism?
   A. war with Europe
   B. drought and famine
   C. war with Japan and the Manchus
   D. signing of the Treaty of Tordesillas

The First Global Age: Europe, the Americas, and Africa (1492–1750)

SECTION 1 · CONQUEST IN THE AMERICAS

■ TEXT SUMMARY

In 1492, Christopher Columbus landed in the West Indies. At first, the Native Americans were friendly and generous toward the Spanish. However, these friendly feelings did not last. The Spanish soon forced the Indians to work for them. Many Indians died from cruel treatment.

Many Spanish **conquistadors,** or conquerors, followed Columbus to the Americas. They came to find riches. Some also wanted to convert Native Americans to Christianity. Within a few years, the Spanish had conquered several Indian civilizations. Hernan Cortés defeated the powerful Aztec empire in Mexico. Francisco Pizarro destroyed the Incan empire in Peru. (See timeline below.)

The Spanish were able to conquer these empires so quickly for several reasons. The Spanish used horses and powerful weapons that the Indians had never seen before. They also had Native American allies who fought on the Spanish side. Diseases brought by the Europeans also killed millions of Indians. Their deaths made others feel that their gods had deserted them.

> ### THE **BIG** IDEA
>
> Desire for riches, as well as religious zeal, encouraged Spanish explorers to travel to the Americas.

■ GRAPHIC SUMMARY: *Early Spanish Conquests in the Americas*

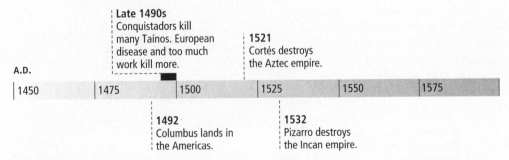

Late 1490s
Conquistadors kill many Taínos. European disease and too much work kill more.

1521
Cortés destroys the Aztec empire.

A.D.

| 1450 | 1475 | 1500 | 1525 | 1550 | 1575 |

1492
Columbus lands in the Americas.

1532
Pizarro destroys the Incan empire.

The Spanish conquered the Aztec and Incan empires.

■ REVIEW QUESTIONS

1. Give two reasons that the Spanish were able to conquer the Native American empires.

2. **Time Line Skills** Name two Native American civilizations that were destroyed by the Spanish conquistadors.

SPANISH AND PORTUGUESE COLONIES IN THE AMERICAS

◢ TEXT SUMMARY

The Spanish introduced new forms of government, religion, economy, and culture to the Americas. During the 1500s, the Spanish empire stretched from California through South America. Even though the colonies were far away, Spain kept strict control over them. The king decided who ran the colonial government. He allowed the colonies to trade only with Spain.

> ### THE **BIG** IDEA
> Native American, African, and European traditions blended to form the distinct cultures of the Americas.

The Catholic Church was very important in the colonies. Church leaders often helped to run the government. They also worked to convert Native Americans to Christianity.

Growing sugar cane became a large business. At first, Native Americans were forced to work on sugar **plantations,** large estates run by an owner or overseer. They were treated cruelly, and many died. The Spanish then brought slaves from Africa to do the work.

A new social structure developed. People born in Spain made up the highest social class. Those of European descent born in the colonies were next. People of mixed European and Indian or African descent were in the middle. Native Americans and people of

African descent were in the lowest classes.

Over time, the people in the colonies developed a new culture. They combined European, Native American, and African traditions. Their art, buildings, and daily life were influenced by all three cultures.

◢ GRAPHIC SUMMARY:
Social Structure of the Spanish Colonies

Most Power   **Fewest People**

Peninsulares
People born in Spain

Creoles
People of European descent born in the colonies

Mestizos
People of mixed Native American and European descent

Mulattoes
People of mixed African and European descent

Native Americans and People of African descent

Least Power   **Most People**

In Spanish America, the mix of peoples led to a new social structure.

◢ REVIEW QUESTIONS

1. What were two ways in which Spain controlled its colonies?

2. **Diagram Skills** What group had the most power in the Spanish colonies? What group had the least power?

 **SECTION 3** # STRUGGLE FOR NORTH AMERICA

◻ TEXT SUMMARY

During the late 1600s, the French settled Canada. They called their colony New France. Settlers there were traders and fur trappers. They worked and lived with Native Americans. The French king chose the officials who ran the colonial government.

England also set up colonies in North America. Large numbers of settlers came to these colonies. Some came to make a profit. Others hoped to own land. Still others, like the Pilgrims, wanted religious freedom. The English kings also wanted to control their colonies. However, they allowed the colonists more self-government than the French or Spanish did. (See chart below.) Each colony had an **assembly,** or legislature. Its members were elected by men who owned property in the colony. An assembly advised the governor and made laws.

During the 1700s, France and Britain fought for power and territory all over the world. In the Americas, they fought each other in the French and Indian War. The British finally won in 1763. In the Treaty of Paris, France was forced to give up Canada. Thus, England gained control of much of North America.

> **THE BIG IDEA**
>
> **During the 1600s and 1700s, England and France claimed territory in North America.**

◻ GRAPHIC SUMMARY: *British and French Settlements in North America*

	BRITISH	FRENCH
Settlement	• First permanent settlement: Jamestown, Virginia, in 1607	• First permanent settlement: Quebec, Canada, in 1608
Economy	• Profits made growing sugar and tobacco on large plantations • Most settlers live on small farms	• Profits made by hunting and trading for furs • A few settlers support themselves by fishing
Religion	• Protestants, Catholics, and Jews settle in colonies	• Colony allows settlers to practice only Catholicism
Government	• British king chooses some colonial officials • Colonies allowed some self-government	• French king chooses all colonial officials • Colony strictly controlled by France

The French and British settlements in North America were very different.

◻ REVIEW QUESTIONS

1. How was government in the French colonies similar to government in the British colonies? How was it different?

2. Chart Skills Where in North America did the French first settle?

TURBULENT CENTURIES IN AFRICA

▣ TEXT SUMMARY

In the 1400s, Europeans began to trade directly with Africa. This contact led to troubled times. The Atlantic slave trade began in the 1500s when Europeans started buying slaves to ship to the Americas. The voyage on the slave ships was called the Middle Passage. Conditions were terrible and many Africans died along the way. Those who survived were forced to work on tobacco and sugar plantations in the American colonies.

> **THE BIG IDEA**
>
> **The Atlantic slave trade sent millions of Africans to the Americas.**

The Atlantic slave trade did not end until the 1800s. By then, an estimated 11 million Africans had been sent to the Americas. West Africa lost many young women and men. As a result, some societies and small states disappeared forever. During the 1600s and 1700s, new African states formed. These new states depended on the slave trade. (See time line below.)

During the 1700s and 1800s, conflicts arose in southern Africa. The Zulus were a powerful African group. The Boers were Dutch farmers who had settled in southern Africa. When the two groups came into contact in the early 1800s, fighting broke out. The struggle between the Boers and the Zulus lasted until the end of the century.

▣ GRAPHIC SUMMARY: *Africa and the Atlantic Slave Trade*

1500s
Atlantic slave trade begins. Africans are shipped to the Americas as slaves.

1700s
Slave trade peaks. Tens of thousands of Africans are shipped each year.

A.D.

| 1400 | 1500 | 1600 | 1700 | 1800 |

1400s
Europeans trade directly with West Africans.

1600s
New states form in West Africa based on slave trade.

1833
Britain outlaws slavery in its empire.

The Atlantic slave trade had terrible effects on Africans.

▣ REVIEW QUESTIONS

1. What were two effects of the slave trade?

2. Time Line Skills When did the slave trade officially end in the British empire?

CHANGES IN EUROPE

◼ TEXT SUMMARY

European exploration between 1500 and 1700 led to many changes in the world. A global exchange of people, plants, animals, ideas, and technology began. (See map below.) Since this exchange started with Columbus, it is called the Columbian exchange.

The building of European empires in the Americas led to major economic changes in Europe. The huge amounts of gold and silver coming from the Americas caused prices to rise. This caused **inflation.** Inflation is an economic cycle that involves a rise in prices linked to an increase in the amount of money available. The increase in trade with the colonies encouraged European **capitalism**—the investment of money to make a profit. (See Chapter 20.) European nations adopted a new policy, called **mercantilism.** Under this policy, nations tried to build up their supply of gold and silver. They did this by exporting more goods than they imported. Colonies were supposed to benefit the parent nation. A parent nation used colonies to supply it with raw materials and to buy its goods.

These economic changes affected the lives of some Europeans. The nobility became less powerful. Many merchants became rich and a middle class developed. However, the lives of peasants did not change much during the 1500s and 1600s.

THE **BIG** IDEA

European explorations resulted in a global exchange of people, animals, food, plants, technology, and disease.

◼ GRAPHIC SUMMARY:

The Columbian Exchange

From the Americas to Europe, Africa, and Asia

maize (corn)
potato
sweet potato
beans
peanut
squashes
pumpkin

tomato
chili pepper
avocado
pineapple
cocoa
tobacco
quinine (a medicine)

wheat
sugar
banana
rice
grape (wine)
dandelion
horse
pig

cattle
goat
sheep
chicken
smallpox
measels
typhus

From Europe, Africa, and Asia to the Americas

The arrival of Columbus started a global exchange between the Americas and the rest of the world.

◼ REVIEW QUESTIONS

1. What was one change caused by European exploration?

2. Diagram Skills Imagine that you live in Europe in the 1600s. What is one way that the Columbian exchange might affect you?

SURVEY CHAPTER 16
MODERN ERA CHAPTER 3
Test

◼ IDENTIFYING MAIN IDEAS

Write the letter of the correct answer in the blank provided. (10 points each)

_____ **1.** Conquistadors were attracted to the Americas by
  A. rumors of the Indians' advanced technology.
  B. stories of riches and Spanish religious zeal.
  C. warm weather.
  D. an opportunity for peasants to move up in a new society.

_____ **2.** Which of the following resulted from encounters between the Spanish and Native Americans?
  A. Spanish treasures flowed into the Americas.
  B. The Native American population declined.
  C. Native Americans defeated Spanish conquerors.
  D. Spanish explorers treated Native Americans with respect.

_____ **3.** Why did the Spanish bring enslaved Africans to the Americas?
  A. to learn from them new agricultural techniques
  B. to convert them to Christianity
  C. to provide labor for working Spanish plantations
  D. to allow them to earn enough money to buy their freedom

_____ **4.** Which of the following groups was at the bottom of the new social structure?
  A. Native Americans
  B. creoles
  C. mulattoes
  D. viceroys

_____ **5.** In North America, power struggles between France and Britain resulted in the
  A. French and Indian War.
  B. loss of New England to the French.
  C. end of trade with Native Americans.
  D. beginning of a French empire in Canada.

_____ **6.** As part of the terms of the Treaty of Paris, France was forced to give up
  A. the Caribbean islands.
  B. Canada.
  C. New England.
  D. Paris.

_____ **7.** By the 1500s, the most important elements of African trade with Europeans was
  A. ivory.
  B. gold.
  C. hides.
  D. enslaved Africans.

_____ **8.** The Middle Passage was a horror due to
  A. hunger and seasickness.
  B. disease and mistreatment.
  C. evil spirits.
  D. unfavorable weather conditions.

_____ **9.** What was one cause of European inflation?
  A. mercantilism
  B. the joint stock company
  C. increased supplies of gold and silver
  D. the population explosion

_____ **10.** How were European peasants affected by Europe's growing involvement with the world?
  A. They moved up in society.
  B. Their lives did not change very much.
  C. They prospered as a result of the new food crops.
  D. Many died as a result of diseases brought from the Americas.

The Age of Absolutism (1550–1800)

SECTION 1 — EXTENDING SPANISH POWER

■ TEXT SUMMARY

In the 1500s, riches from the Americas were flowing into Spain. As a result, Spain became the most powerful nation in Europe. King Philip II ruled Spain from 1556 until 1598. Philip, an absolute monarch, believed that God had given him the right to rule. Philip thought of himself as **guardian,** or protector, of the Catholic Church. He persecuted people who were not Catholic and fought against the spread of Protestantism. He also fought with the Muslim empire of the Ottomans.

Philip II helped to make the period from 1550 until 1650 a golden age in Spain. He set up schools of science and mathematics and supported the arts. The artist Diego Velázquez painted portraits of the royal family. El Greco used bright colors to paint religious pictures and portraits of Spanish nobles. In literature, Lope de Vega wrote more than 1,500 plays, including comedies and romances. Cervantes wrote *Don Quixote,* the first novel in Europe.

In the 1600s, Spanish power slowly declined because rulers spent too much money on wars overseas. The Spanish relied on gold and silver from their American colonies. As a result, they neglected business at home. At the same time, the middle class felt they were being taxed too much so they stopped supporting the government. By the late 1600s, France had replaced Spain as the most powerful European nation.

THE **BIG** IDEA

Philip II extended Spain's power and helped establish a golden age.

■ GRAPHIC SUMMARY: *Spain's Golden Age*

GOVERNMENT	WARS	ARTS	RELIGION
• Philip II makes himself absolute ruler	• Builds strong navy	• Supports arts and learning	• Supports Catholic Reformation
• Controls all parts of government	• Defeats Ottoman navy in 1571	• Sets up schools of science and mathematics	• Stops Catholics from converting to Protestantism
• Believes God had given him right to rule	• English navy defeats Spanish navy in 1588	• Encourages painters and writers	• Persecutes Protestants in Spain
			• Fights against Dutch Protestants for many years

Philip II did much to create a golden age in Spain.

■ REVIEW QUESTIONS

1. Give three reasons why Spanish power declined in the 1600s.

2. Chart Skills How did Philip II help create a golden age in Spain?

FRANCE UNDER LOUIS XIV

TEXT SUMMARY

The period from the 1560s to the 1590s was a turbulent time in France. Catholics fought bloody religious wars against French Protestants, called **Huguenots.** Then, in 1589, Henry IV became king. He granted religious toleration to the Huguenots. France then had peace.

French kings, like the Spanish, were absolute rulers. Henry IV and later kings increased royal power by making the government stronger and controlling the nobles. Louis XIII destroyed the walled cities of the Huguenots yet allowed them to practice their religion. The king defeated the private armies of the nobles, but gave them high posts in court to keep them loyal. Louis XIV continued to strengthen the monarchy. He sent officials to collect taxes and rule the provinces. Louis made his army the strongest in Europe.

During the 72-year reign of Louis XIV, French culture spread throughout Europe. However, many of his foreign and domestic policies failed. Louis fought many wars for power and land. Other European nations thought France was too powerful, so they formed alliances with one another. These alliances created a balance of power that prevented any one nation from dominating Europe. At home, Louis persecuted the hard-working Huguenots, so more than 100,000 of them fled. The French economy suffered as a result.

> ### THE **BIG** IDEA
>
> **Under the absolute rule of Louis XIV, France became the leading power of Europe.**

GRAPHIC SUMMARY: *Louis XIV Rules France*

GOVERNMENT	WARS	ARTS	RELIGION
• Louis XIV rules for 72 years	• Makes French army the strongest in Europe	• Supports music, ballet, and theater	• Persecutes the Huguenots
• Becomes absolute ruler	• Fights many wars to gain territory	• Increases popularity of French styles all over Europe	
• Called the "Sun King"	• Causes European nations to join together to stop France	• Sets high standards for the arts	
• Sends officials to collect taxes and rule the provinces			

Louis XIV ruled France longer than any other king.

REVIEW QUESTIONS

1. Why did other European nations join together against France?

2. Chart Skills How long did Louis XIV rule France?

SECTION 3 — TRIUMPH OF PARLIAMENT IN ENGLAND

TEXT SUMMARY

From 1485 until 1603, Tudor kings and queens ruled England and worked well with Parliament. When the Tudors wanted to make changes, they consulted Parliament first. Then, in 1603, the Stuarts came to power. They angered Parliament by acting like absolute rulers.

One Stuart king, Charles I, got into trouble with Parliament. He put his enemies in prison without trials, collected very high taxes, and angered the Puritans. When Parliament tried to stop him, Charles **dissolved**, or broke up, Parliament. In 1642, civil war broke out between Charles I and Parliament. Seven years later, Parliament put Charles on trial and beheaded him. Charles was the first European king to be executed. For a time, England did not have a king. It was a republic, known as the Commonwealth.

Then, in 1660, Parliament invited Charles II to become king.

In 1688, another Stuart king, James II, angered Parliament. This time, Parliament invited Mary, the daughter of James, and her husband William to replace the king. James fled to France. This was called the Glorious Revolution because it took place without any fighting. Before William and Mary took power, they accepted the English Bill of Rights. It stated that the king must work with Parliament and gave Parliament control of money. Now Parliament had a great deal of power. In this way, England became a **limited monarchy,** a government in which a legislative body limits the monarch's powers.

THE BIG IDEA

Clashes between Parliament and the kings of England led to limited power for the monarchy.

GRAPHIC SUMMARY: *Revolution in England*

A.D.

| 1600 | 1610 | 1620 | 1630 | 1640 | 1650 | 1660 | 1670 | 1680 | 1690 |

1649 English execute Charles I

1688 In Glorious Revolution, William and Mary become king and queen

1603 Stuart dynasty takes power in England

1625 Charles I becomes king

1642-9 English Civil War takes place

1660 England restores the monarchy

1685 James II becomes king

In the age of absolute monarchy, England developed a limited monarchy.

REVIEW QUESTIONS

1. Why did the Stuarts have trouble with Parliament?

2. Time Line Skills In what year did the English execute Charles I?

RISE OF AUSTRIA AND PRUSSIA

▣ TEXT SUMMARY

Between 1618 and 1648, the nations of Europe fought each other in the Thirty Years' War. What started as a fight between Catholics and Protestants soon became a political battle. Armies burned villages and destroyed cities. One third of the population of the German states died. When the Thirty Years' War finally ended, France had won territory from both Germany and Spain. The Netherlands and Switzerland became independent states. The war left Germany divided into more than 360 states, and the Hapsburgs, rulers of the Holy Roman Empire, lost land.

After the Thirty Years' War, two new powers emerged. Although the war weakened the Hapsburgs of Austria, they still wanted a strong empire. They conquered Bohemia, Hungary, and parts of Poland and Italy. However, the Hapsburgs were unable to completely control their empire. Around the same time, the Hohenzollern family united a number of German states. The Hohenzollerns built a powerful Protestant nation called Prussia.

By 1750, Austria, Prussia, France, England, and Russia were the strongest nations in Europe. These nations tried to maintain the balance of power. Two or more nations formed alliances to keep another nation from becoming too strong. To maintain the balance of power, nations sometimes went to war.

> ### THE **BIG** IDEA
>
> Two great empires, Austria and Prussia, rose out of the ashes of the Thirty Years' War.

▣ GRAPHIC SUMMARY: *Austria and Prussia Become Great Powers*

AUSTRIA under the Hapsburgs	PRUSSIA under the Hohenzollerns

• Works to build unified state
• Adds Bohemia, Hungary, and parts of Poland and Italy
• Maria Theresa is a powerful ruler
    Wins support of the people
    Organizes the government
    Improves tax collection
    Taxes the nobles and the clergy
    Defends empire against Prussian invaders
	• Unites territory across Germany
	• Establishes strong government
	• Takes power away from the nobles
	• Hohenzollerns rule absolutely
	• Creates one of the strongest armies in Europe
	• Frederick II is a powerful ruler
	    Attacks Austria and seizes Silesia
	    Fights wars and wins territory for Prussia

While Austria was building a strong Catholic empire, Prussia grew to be a new Protestant power.

▣ REVIEW QUESTIONS

1. What were three results of the Thirty Years' War?

2. Chart Skills What ruling family began to unite the German states?

ABSOLUTE MONARCHY IN RUSSIA

TEXT SUMMARY

In 1682, Peter the Great became czar and absolute ruler of Russia. Peter wanted to make Russia modern and powerful. He introduced western technology, improved education, developed new industries, and encouraged trade. He strengthened the Russian government and reduced the power of the nobles. However, Peter forced the Russian people to become more western, using terror to carry out his plans. His policies maintained serfdom in Russia, long after it had died in Western Europe.

In foreign policy, Peter built the strongest army in Europe, expanded Russian territory, and gained ports on the Baltic. Peter wanted a port city where the water did not freeze during the winter. This way, Russia could trade with the West all year long. However, Peter was not successful in gaining a warm-water port. Still, Russian pioneers crossed to Siberia and explored the Bering Strait between Siberia and Alaska. Some Russians even settled in California.

In 1762, Catherine the Great, another absolute monarch, came to power. She reorganized the government and the laws, set up state schools for boys and girls, and encouraged western ways. Under Catherine, Russia finally won a warm-water port on the Black Sea. In the 1770s, Catherine and the rulers of Prussia and Austria agreed to divide up Poland. By 1795, the kingdom of Poland had disappeared.

> ## THE **BIG** IDEA
>
> Czar Peter the Great and his successor Catherine the Great strengthened Russia and expanded Russian territory.

GRAPHIC SUMMARY: *Important Russian Rulers*

	PETER THE GREAT (1689–1725)	CATHERINE THE GREAT (1762–1796)
Government	• Absolute ruler • Strengthens government • Takes power from the nobles • Spreads serfdom	• Absolute ruler • Organizes the government • Gives more rights to the nobles • Allows peasants to suffer
Reforms	• Improves education • Develops new industries • Encourages trade	• Organizes the system of laws • Sets up state schools for children
Wars	• Creates largest army in Europe • Conquers land along Baltic	• Conquers port where water did not freeze in winter • Seizes territory from Poland
Ideas from Western Europe	• Builds capital city, St. Petersburg, in western style • Forces Russians to dress like western Europeans	• Encourages Western European ways • Introduces French language and ways of life

Both Peter the Great and Catherine the Great were absolute rulers who wanted to westernize Russia.

REVIEW QUESTIONS

1. Why was it important for Russia to conquer a port city where the water did not freeze?

2. **Chart Skills** Describe two ways in which Peter the Great introduced western ways to Russia.

SURVEY CHAPTER 17
MODERN ERA CHAPTER 4
Test

◼ IDENTIFYING MAIN IDEAS

Write the letter of the correct answer in the blank provided. (10 points each)

____ **1.** What role did Philip II of Spain play in regard to the Catholic Church?
   A. He was an opponent to the Church.
   B. He was a protector of the Church.
   C. He was a disinterested party.
   D. He was a supporter of Protestantism.

____ **2.** What was one reason that the arts and literature were able to flourish during the golden century in Spain?
   A. Philip II supported them
   B. wars stimulated creativity
   C. the Church supported artists
   D. more women than men were artists

____ **3.** What was the effect on the French army of Louis XIV's reign?
   A. It became the strongest in Europe.
   B. It became the weakest in Europe.
   C. It lost many wars.
   D. It ceased to exist.

____ **4.** What was the result of Louis XIV's persecution of Huguenots?
   A. They rose against him in war.
   B. They left France, causing a blow to the French economy.
   C. The entire group was killed off.
   D. They formed a new French state.

____ **5.** The Stuart kings' claims to absolute power in England were challenged by
   A. the Tudors.
   B. the Parliament.
   C. the Cavaliers.
   D. the Church of England.

____ **6.** What were William and Mary required to accept before taking the throne of England?
   A. Levellers
   B. English Bill of Rights
   C. Glorious Revolution
   D. Long Parliament

____ **7.** Which of the following was divided into many small states as a result of the Thirty Years' War?
   A. France
   B. Spain
   C. Germany
   D. the Netherlands

____ **8.** By 1750, the great powers of Europe had formed alliances to maintain the
   A. balance of power.
   B. democratic system of government.
   C. Parliament.
   D. right to trade with other continents.

____ **9.** Peter the Great forced Russians to accept social reforms that would make their culture more like that of
   A. Native Americans.
   B. Chinese.
   C. Western Europeans.
   D. Ottoman Turks.

____ **10.** What Russian dream did Catherine the Great achieve?
   A. a modern economy
   B. the end of serfdom
   C. modernizing the Russian alphabet
   D. a warm-water port

The Enlightenment and the American Revolution (1707–1800)

SECTION 1 — *PHILOSOPHY IN THE AGE OF REASON*

◼ TEXT SUMMARY

During the Scientific Revolution, scientists used reason to explain why things happened in the universe. By the early 1700s, Europeans also used reason to discover the **natural laws** of human behavior that explained why people act the way they do. With these laws, they hoped to solve the problems of society. This was the Age of Reason, or the Enlightenment.

Some Enlightenment thinkers wanted to reform government. John Locke believed that the government must protect the **natural rights** of the people. Natural rights are rights that belong to all humans from birth. If the government did not protect these rights, the people had the right to overthrow it. The Baron de Montesquieu wanted to divide the government into three branches to create a separation of powers. Each branch would make sure the other two branches did not become too powerful. This system is called checks and balances. In France, thinkers said that Enlightenment ideas could improve society. Jean-Jacques Rousseau argued that in a perfect society, people made and obeyed the laws. Voltaire argued for freedom of thought and of speech.

Other thinkers used reason to reform the economy of Europe. They believed that government should let business run itself. This belief is called **laissez faire.** The economist Adam Smith argued that a free market works through supply and demand.

> **THE BIG IDEA**
>
> Enlightenment thinkers tried to apply the laws of nature to human society.

◼ GRAPHIC SUMMARY: *Thinkers of the Enlightenment*

Thomas Hobbes	**John Locke**
People are greedy and selfish. Only a powerful government can create a peaceful, orderly society.	People have natural rights. It is the job of government to protect these natural rights. If government does not protect these rights, the people have the right to overthrow it.
Baron de Montesquieu	**Jean-Jacques Rousseau**
The powers of government should be separated into three branches. Each branch will keep the other branches from becoming too powerful.	In a perfect society, people both make and obey the laws. What is good for everyone is more important than what is good for one person.

The ideas of the philosophers of the Enlightenment continue to influence us today.

◼ REVIEW QUESTIONS

1. What ideas did Montesquieu have about government?

2. **Chart Skills** What did John Locke believe to be the role of government?

ENLIGHTENMENT IDEAS SPREAD

◨ TEXT SUMMARY

As Enlightenment ideas spread across Europe, people began to question the old ways and demand reform. A fair society, they thought, should provide material well-being, justice, and happiness. However, government and the Church believed that God had set up society as it was. To stop the new ideas, they burned Enlightenment books and put the writers in prison.

Philosophers asked rulers to adopt reforms. **Enlightened despots** were absolute rulers who used their power to reform society. Frederick II of Prussia improved the government and tolerated different religions. He gave tools and seeds to peasants.

Catherine the Great of Russia reformed Russian law and government. Joseph II of Austria made the most reforms.

During the 1600s and 1700s, the arts also changed to reflect Enlightenment ideas. **Baroque** paintings were huge and full of excitement. **Rococo** art tended to be personal and charming. Ballet and opera became popular. Brilliant musicians such as Mozart and Handel wrote beautiful symphonies and operas.

During this period, most Europeans were peasants living in small villages. They knew little of the Enlightenment. (See chart below.) In Western Europe, serfdom had almost disappeared. In central and Eastern Europe, however, most peasants were still tied to the land.

> ### THE **BIG** IDEA
>
> Enlightenment ideas spread across Europe and prompted some rulers to make reforms.

◨ GRAPHIC SUMMARY: *The Lives of the Majority*

Peasants During the Enlightenment
- Untouched by middle-class culture
- Lived in small, rural villages

In West
1. No longer serfs
2. Rented or owned land
3. Hired as day laborers
4. By late 1700s, some sought reform and justice

In East
1. Still serfs
2. Could be sold with land
3. Owed labor to lords
4. Some forced to serve as soldiers

Most Europeans were peasants. Conditions for peasants in Western and Eastern Europe were very different.

◨ REVIEW QUESTIONS

1. Give two ways enlightened despots made reforms based on Enlightenment ideas.

2. **Diagram Skills** In which part of Europe had serfdom died out by the 1700s?

BRITAIN AT MID-CENTURY

TEXT SUMMARY

During the 1600s and 1700s, Britain built an empire that reached around the world. Its island location allowed Britain to control trade during the Renaissance. Unrestricted trade helped merchants build settlements in the West Indies, North America, and India. In addition, the British gained control of the slave trade in Spanish America, which brought riches to Britain. Finally, Britain built a powerful navy and was on the winning side in most conflicts during the period.

During the 1700s, the British built a **constitutional government** where governmental power was defined and limited by law. The new government included three important new institutions. These were political parties, the **cabinet,** and the office of **prime minister.** The first political parties were made up of rich, powerful men who shared beliefs. The Tories were conservative. The Whigs were liberal. The cabinet was a group of members of Parliament who advised the King and helped make policy. The prime minister was the leader of the cabinet.

Even with these changes, British government remained an **oligarchy**—a government where a few powerful nobles and rich landowners controlled Parliament. Only male property owners could vote. A small middle class controlled the towns and cities. Most people were poor farmers who struggled to survive. They had no power in the British government.

THE BIG IDEA

Britain's island location, colonial possessions, and powerful navy contributed to its rise to world power.

GRAPHIC SUMMARY:

Britain Builds an Empire

1. Britain controls trade during the Renaissance.
2. In the 1700s, Britain wins territory in several wars.
3. British merchants build settlements in the West Indies, North America, and India.
4. Britain gains control of the slave trade in Spanish America.
5. Britain builds a powerful navy.
6. The British government supports business and trade.

Britain Builds an Empire

Britain was a small island kingdom on the edge of Europe that became very powerful in the 1700s.

REVIEW QUESTIONS

1. What three ideas did the British use to create a constitutional government?

2. Diagram Skills Give two reasons Britain was able to build a world empire.

BIRTH OF THE AMERICAN REPUBLIC

■ TEXT SUMMARY

By 1750, the British empire included 13 colonies along the eastern coast of North America. People from many religions and backgrounds made their home there. The colonies were part of a trade network linking North America, the West Indies, Africa, and Europe.

After 1763, serious problems developed between Britain and the colonies. The British wanted to control colonial trade and manufacturing as well as raise taxes. This made the colonists angry. The colonists felt that the king was taking away their rights as British citizens.

In 1775, war broke out between the colonists and the British government. The following year, the colonists declared independence from Britain. Using Enlightenment ideas, the writers of the Declaration of Independence stated that the colonists had the right to revolt against an unfair government. They called their new nation the United States of America.

In 1781, the colonists defeated the British. The leaders of the United States of America set up a federal republic and adopted a Constitution in 1787. The Constitution included many Enlightenment ideas. Among these were separation of powers and checks and balances. The Constitution also stated that the duty of the government was to protect the rights of the people.

> ### THE **BIG** IDEA
>
> Colonial opposition to British trade and tax policies led to independence and the founding of the United States of America.

■ GRAPHIC SUMMARY:

Enlightenment Ideas and the Declaration of Independence

DECLARATION OF INDEPENDENCE

• Approved, July 4, 1776.

• People have the right to overthrow government that does not protect their rights.

• The British government has not protected the rights of the colonists.

• The colonists declare independence from Britain and create the United States of America.

The Declaration of Independence included ideas of the Enlightenment.

■ REVIEW QUESTIONS

1. Why did problems develop between Britain and the North American colonists?

2. **Diagram Skills** When was the American Declaration of Independence signed?

SURVEY CHAPTER 18
MODERN ERA CHAPTER 5
Test

■ IDENTIFYING MAIN IDEAS

Write the letter of the correct answer in the blank provided. (10 points each)

_____ **1.** The principles of checks and balances and separation of powers were put forward by
  A. Mary Wollstonecraft.
  B. Diderot.
  C. Montesquieu.
  D. Rousseau.

_____ **2.** Adam Smith believed that the free market should regulate business. As such, he was a supporter of
  A. natural laws.
  B. the Enlightenment.
  C. government regulation of business.
  D. laissez faire.

_____ **3.** Government and church officials fought against Enlightenment ideas by
  A. teaching old ideas.
  B. setting up a new social order.
  C. burning books.
  D. making reform illegal.

_____ **4.** Catherine II's contribution to Russia was
  A. a system of education.
  B. reformed law and government.
  C. a smaller empire.
  D. expanded rights for women.

_____ **5.** Which of the following is a true statement about European peasants during the Enlightenment?
  A. Their life changed greatly.
  B. Most moved to the cities.
  C. The Enlightenment had little effect on their life.
  D. They acquired material wealth.

_____ **6.** Which of the following helped Britain become a global power in the 1700s?
  A. its rich resources
  B. its strong navy
  C. its favorable climate
  D. its declining population

_____ **7.** What work did the majority of people in Britain do during the 1700s?
  A. ran small businesses
  B. held public office
  C. farmed
  D. manufactured goods

_____ **8.** What was the main role of the 13 colonies in the British empire?
  A. They supplied laborers for British factories.
  B. They served as trade links between Britain and North America, the West Indies, and Africa.
  C. They supplied slave labor to Britain.
  D. They supplied Britain with food.

_____ **9.** Why were colonists angry about the British taxes they were required to pay?
  A. The taxes were extremely high.
  B. They had never paid them before.
  C. They wanted their independence.
  D. They felt the king was taking away their rights as British citizens.

_____ **10.** Where did the ideas for the Constitution originate?
  A. the French monarchy
  B. the British Parliament
  C. the common people
  D. Europe's Enlightenment thinkers

The French Revolution and Napoleon (1789–1815)

 **SECTION 1** ## ON THE EVE OF REVOLUTION

TEXT SUMMARY

Since the Middle Ages, everyone in France had belonged to one of three social classes called **estates.** The clergy and the nobles belonged to the First and Second Estates. These two groups were rich and powerful. They had many special privileges. For example, they did not have to pay taxes. Most French people belonged to the Third Estate. Nine out of ten people in the Third Estate were peasants. Their tax burden was huge.

In 1789, France faced several crises. For many years, the government had spent more money than it earned. In addition, bad harvests caused food prices to rise. Many peasants did not have enough to eat. In towns and in the countryside, starving people rioted.

To deal with these problems, King Louis XVI met with the leaders of the three estates. Most common people wanted financial relief, but the elected members of the Third Estate wanted government reform. After weeks of meetings, its leaders took a daring step. They created a new government called the National Assembly. Some reform-minded nobles and clergy joined them. The National Assembly promised to write a new constitution for France. However, dangerous rumors, increasing food shortages, and an attack on the Bastille (a Parisian political prison) kept the problems from being solved. A violent revolution was starting.

> ### THE **BIG** IDEA
>
> Social unrest, government debt, and food shortages contributed to the outbreak of the French Revolution in 1789.

GRAPHIC SUMMARY: *Population and Landownership in France, 1789*

First Estate

Second Estate

Third Estate

Great discontent was caused by the unequal treatment of members of the three estates.

PERCENTAGE OF POPULATION, BY ESTATE

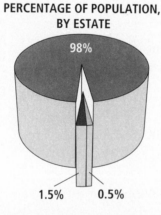

98%

1.5%   0.5%

PERCENTAGE OF LAND-OWNERSHIP, BY ESTATE

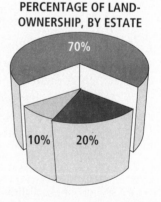

70%

10%   20%

REVIEW QUESTIONS

1. What crises did France face in 1789?

2. Diagram Skills Which estate had the greatest number of people?

CREATING A NEW FRANCE

▦ TEXT SUMMARY

In 1789, a terrible famine occurred in France. Starving peasants attacked the homes of nobles. Revolutionary groups took over Paris and demanded an end to the monarchy. Finally, the nobles agreed to give up their special privileges.

The National Assembly began making reforms. They agreed to abolish feudalism. In 1791, the Assembly finished writing a new constitution that used Enlightenment ideas. Under this constitution, people had natural rights and the government had to protect those rights.

▦ GRAPHIC SUMMARY:

The French Declaration of Rights

DECLARATION OF THE RIGHTS OF MAN AND THE CITIZEN

- Written in 1789
- Uses American Declaration of Independence as model
- States that all men have natural rights
- Declares the job of government is to protect the natural rights of the people
- Guarantees all male citizens equality under the law
- States that people are free to practice any religion they choose
- Promises to tax people according to how much they can afford

The constitution created a limited monarchy. The Assembly also reformed French laws and supported trade. When it took control of the French Catholic Church and sold its lands to pay back the government debt, the pope, clergy, and many peasants rejected the revolution. Other groups, however, wanted more changes. Violent disagreements soon caused the downfall of the Assembly.

News about the French Revolution spread across Europe. While many Europeans supported the revolution, rulers and nobles were afraid that revolutionary ideas would spread to their own countries. After the French king and his family made an unsuccessful attempt to flee, the king of Prussia promised that he would fight to save the French monarchy. In 1792, France declared war on Austria, Prussia, Britain, and several other European states. The fighting lasted for over 20 years.

THE BIG IDEA

The National Assembly instituted political and social reforms in the early stages of the revolution.

The French Declaration of Rights, like the American Declaration of Independence and Constitution, used ideas of the Enlightenment.

▦ REVIEW QUESTIONS

1. How did European rulers feel about the French Revolution?

2. Chart Skills According to the French Declaration of Rights, how must the government tax the people?

RADICAL DAYS

◼ TEXT SUMMARY

The war with other European nations went badly for the French forces. People thought the king was helping the enemy.

Mobs attacked the king's guards and killed nobles. Radical revolutionaries, supported by Paris crowds, took control of the Assembly in 1792. These radicals ended the monarchy, made France a republic, and wrote another new constitution. In 1793, they **executed,** or put to death, the king and queen for treason.

By 1793, France was at war with most of Europe. Within France, peasants rioted for food, and revolutionary groups fought against each other. To restore order, the new government set up the Committee of Public Safety, which had absolute power. Using a new invention called the guillotine, the committee, led by Maximilien Robespierre, beheaded thousands of people for treason, even supporters of the revolution. They put thousands more in prison. This period is called the Reign of Terror.

By 1799, life in France had changed. The monarchy and the old class system were gone. The government controlled the Church. French people began to feel proud of France. This feeling of pride is called **nationalism.** The new government continued to make important reforms. It set up schools for children and organized a system to care for the poor. Slavery in the French colonies ended. Religious tolerance was the law.

> ### THE **BIG** IDEA
>
> The French Revolution, driven by leaders determined to preserve and extend the revolution, entered a radical phase.

◼ GRAPHIC SUMMARY: *Radical Days of the French Revolution*

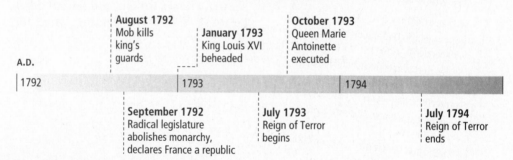

August 1792
Mob kills king's guards

January 1793
King Louis XVI beheaded

October 1793
Queen Marie Antoinette executed

A.D.

1792 | 1793 | 1794

September 1792
Radical legislature abolishes monarchy, declares France a republic

July 1793
Reign of Terror begins

July 1794
Reign of Terror ends

During the Reign of Terror, the Committee of Public Safety used the guillotine to execute thousands of people.

◼ REVIEW QUESTIONS

1. What changes did radical revolutionaries make when they took over the French government?

2. **Time Line Skills** About how long did the Reign of Terror last?

THE AGE OF NAPOLEON BEGINS

SECTION 4

◼ TEXT SUMMARY

When the French Revolution started, Lieutenant Napoleon Bonaparte began to earn rapid promotions. He led the French army in victories against Britain and Austria. A general by 1799, Napoleon helped overthrow the French government. He organized a new government and put himself in charge. Five years later, Napoleon took the title Emperor of the French. At each step of his rise to power, the French voted their support.

The policies that Napoleon set up show why he was so popular. Napoleon strengthened the French government and restored order. He improved the economy and encouraged new industry. Napoleon built roads and canals and supported public schools. Some of his reforms continued the spirit of the revolution. Peasants could legally keep the Church land they bought. Careers were opened to anyone with ability. One of his most important reforms was a new set of laws called the Napoleonic Code. These laws included many Enlightenment ideas but undid some reforms of the Revolution.

From 1804 to 1814, Napoleon defeated the greatest nations of Europe and built an empire. He conquered the Netherlands, Belgium, and parts of Italy and Germany. He ended the Holy Roman Empire and divided Prussia. Napoleon replaced the monarchs of the defeated nations with friends and family. Only Britain remained outside Napoleon's empire.

> ### THE BIG IDEA
>
> Napoleon built a large empire by annexing lands, making alliances, and placing family members on the thrones of Europe.

◼ GRAPHIC SUMMARY: *Napoleon in Europe, 1812*

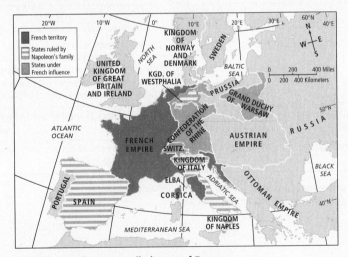

By 1812, Napoleon controlled most of Europe.

◼ REVIEW QUESTIONS

1. What were three reforms Napoleon made in France?

2. **Map Skills** Name two kingdoms or empires ruled by family or friends of Napoleon in 1812.

THE END OF AN ERA

TEXT SUMMARY

Under Napoleon, French armies spread the ideas of the French Revolution across Europe. The French overthrew European monarchs and set up their own governments. They reduced the power of the Church and ended serfdom. Many Europeans welcomed the ideas of the French Revolution. However, they did not welcome the French rulers. Nationalism caused conquered people to reject French control. From Italy to Spain to the Netherlands, people rebelled against the French.

The end of the empire began in 1812 when Napoleon invaded Russia. The invasion was a disaster. Many French soldiers died during the long Russian winter. The following year, an alliance of Russia, Britain, Austria, and Prussia defeated Napoleon at the town of Leipzig and forced him to live on an island in the Mediterranean.

After the defeat of Napoleon, European leaders met at the Congress of Vienna. They hoped to create peace after 25 years of war. One of their goals was to return Europe to the way it was in 1792, before Napoleon. To accomplish this goal, they gave power back to the monarchs of Europe. The leaders of Europe also took steps to create a balance of power. To prevent France from going to war again, they strengthened the countries around it. To protect the new order, European states formed a peacekeeping organization. Peace lasted 100 years.

> ### THE BIG IDEA
>
> After suffering defeat, Napoleon was removed from power. European leaders restored peace and redrew the map of Europe.

GRAPHIC SUMMARY: *The Congress of Vienna*

GOAL	ACTION
To prevent France from going to war again	Strengthen countries around France • Add Belgium and Luxembourg to Holland to create the kingdom of the Netherlands • Give Prussia lands along the Rhine River • Allow Austria to take control of Italy again
To return Europe to the way it was in 1792, before Napoleon	Give power back to the monarchs of Europe
To protect the new system and maintain peace	Create the Concert of Europe, an organization to maintain peace in Europe

At the Congress of Vienna, European leaders tried to prevent France from going to war again and to keep the peace.

REVIEW QUESTIONS

1. What were the results of Napoleon's invasion of Russia?

2. **Chart Skills** What did European leaders do to prevent France from going to war again?

SURVEY CHAPTER 19
MODERN ERA CHAPTER 6   *Test*

■ IDENTIFYING MAIN IDEAS

Write the letter of the correct answer in the blank provided. (10 points each)

_____ 1. Which group made up the vast majority of French society?
A. the clergy
B. the First Estate
C. the *ancien regime*
D. the Third Estate

_____ 2. Which of the following contributed to France's financial crisis?
A. a drop in the gold supply
B. an extended period of peace
C. peasant uprisings
D. bad harvests

_____ 3. Peasant uprisings and the storming of the Bastille forced the National Assembly to do this.
A. attack Versailles
B. abolish feudalism
C. jail thousands of peasants
D. behead the king

_____ 4. European rulers denounced the French Revolution because
A. it promoted the French monarchy.
B. they were afraid it would spread.
C. it took away the power of the Church.
D. it took too long.

_____ 5. In 1792, the National Convention voted to abolish the monarchy and declare France
A. dissolved.
B. bankrupt.
C. a republic.
D. a nation.

_____ 6. In 1793, King Louis XVI and Queen Marie Antoinette were
A. returned to the throne.
B. deported to England.
C. saved from the mob by Lafayette.
D. beheaded.

_____ 7. Which European country was Napoleon unable to conquer?
A. Britain
B. France
C. Italy
D. Belgium

_____ 8. What was the result of Napoleon's invasion of Russia?
A. defeat of the Russians
B. defeat of the French
C. a stalemate
D. French annexation of Russia

_____ 9. Which of the following was the chief goal of the Congress of Vienna?
A. to punish France
B. to create a united Europe
C. to create a lasting peace
D. to strengthen Germany

_____ 10. Why did the Congress of Vienna redraw the boundaries of some European countries?
A. to encircle France with strong countries
B. to create more countries
C. to distribute land more fairly
D. to prevent the growth of nationalism

The Industrial Revolution Begins (1750–1850)

SECTION 1 *DAWN OF THE INDUSTRIAL AGE*

■ TEXT SUMMARY

Since the beginning of civilization, most people have lived in small villages and used simple handmade tools. Beginning in the 1750s, important changes took place in the way people lived and worked. This turning point is known as the Industrial Revolution.

The Industrial Revolution began with an agricultural revolution in Western Europe. In the 1600s, the Dutch built **dikes,** or dams, to protect drained farmland from the sea, and used animal fertilizer to improve the soil. Then, in the 1700s, British farmers discovered ways to produce more food. A British man invented the seed drill that planted seeds in rows. Another pioneer bred stronger horses for work and fatter sheep and cattle for meat. Rich landowners forced many peasants off the land. With no work in the country, peasants moved to cities. There, they became the laborers who would soon operate the new machines.

The agricultural revolution helped to create a population explosion. Since women ate better, they had healthier and stronger babies. At the same time, medical care improved. People lived longer lives.

In the 1700s, an energy revolution occurred. People began to use giant water wheels to power new machines. English inventors used coal to power the steam engine. Steam engines became the power source of the early Industrial Revolution.

> **THE BIG IDEA**
>
> The Industrial Revolution was driven by a growing labor force and by new sources of power.

■ GRAPHIC SUMMARY:

Causes of the Industrial Revolution

> **AGRICULTURAL REVOLUTION**
> • Dutch build dikes to protect farmland from the sea and use animal fertilizer to improve soil
> • British discover ways to produce more food and invent seed drill
> **BETTER FOOD PRODUCTION**

> **POPULATION EXPLOSION**
> • People eat better
> • Women give birth to healthier babies
> • Better medical care slows death rate
> **MORE DEMAND FOR GOODS**

> **ENERGY REVOLUTION**
> • Water wheels power new machines
> • Coal used to fuel steam engine
> **FASTER PRODUCTION OF GOODS**

> **INDUSTRIAL REVOLUTION**

The Industrial Revolution was a long, slow process in which production shifted from hand tools to complicated machines.

■ REVIEW QUESTIONS

1. Describe three changes that were part of the agricultural revolution.

2. Diagram Skills Give two reasons for the population explosion.

BRITAIN LEADS THE WAY

■ TEXT SUMMARY

The Industrial Revolution began in Britain. Britain had plenty of natural resources and many workers for the new mines and factories. The British overseas empire made the economy strong. As a result, the middle class had money to invest in mines, railroads, and factories.

During the early Industrial Revolution, iron and coal were very important. Iron was needed to produce machines and steam engines. In 1709, the British began using coal, instead of wood, for fuel in the production of iron. Experiments led to the production of iron that was cheaper and stronger.

The textile industry was the first to use inventions of the Industrial Revolution. In the 1600s, families spun raw cotton into thread and then wove the thread into cloth at home. By the 1700s, new machines allowed people to make cloth much faster. However, the machines were too large and expensive to be operated at home. Instead, spinners and weavers worked in long sheds that became the first factories.

As production increased, people needed a faster and cheaper means of transportation to move goods from place to place. In the 1700s, people built **turnpikes** (privately built roads that charged a fee to travelers who used them), canals, and stronger bridges. James Watt improved the steam engine that powered boats along canals. Most important, the invention of the steam locomotive made the growth of railroads possible.

> ### THE **BIG** IDEA
>
> The Industrial Revolution began in Britain where there were favorable economic, political, and social conditions, as well as sufficient resources.

■ GRAPHIC SUMMARY: *Travel Time to London*

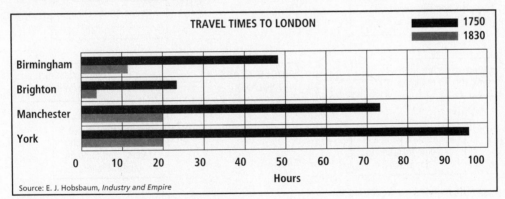

Advances in transportation during the Industrial Revolution made travel between cities much faster.

■ REVIEW QUESTIONS

1. Give two reasons why the Industrial Revolution began in Britain.

2. **Graph Skills** How long did it take to travel from York to London in 1750? In 1830?

HARDSHIPS OF EARLY INDUSTRIAL LIFE

TEXT SUMMARY

The Industrial Revolution brought great riches but also great misery. Many people moved from small villages to towns and cities. The movement of large numbers of people to cities is called **urbanization.** In the cities, most people were poor, living in crowded buildings. There were no sewers. Garbage rotted in the streets and diseases spread quickly.

The heart of the new industrial city was the factory. Men, women, and children worked hard in the factories 12 to 16 hours a day for only a few cents an hour. The work was boring, and the machines were dangerous. If workers were sick or injured, they lost their jobs. Children worked as hard as adults, for even lower wages. Parents let their children work because the money children earned was needed to support their families. Eventually, however, Parliament passed laws to improve working conditions.

Historians have debated whether the Industrial Revolution was a blessing or a curse. The Industrial Revolution created hardships for many people. Low pay, unemployment, and horrible living conditions caused social problems. Still, the Industrial Revolution had many positive effects. Factories created new jobs. More goods became available. Railroads made it possible to visit family members in other towns. The middle class, especially merchants and inventors, benefited financially. Most important, opportunities for all classes of people increased.

THE **BIG** IDEA

Factory work meant long hours, hard jobs, unsafe conditions, and low pay.

GRAPHIC SUMMARY: *The New Middle Class*

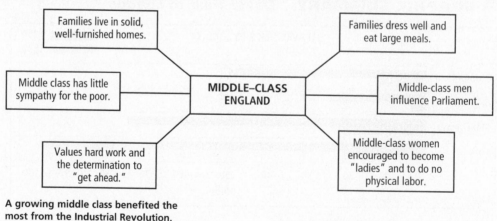

Families live in solid, well-furnished homes.

Families dress well and eat large meals.

Middle class has little sympathy for the poor.

MIDDLE–CLASS ENGLAND

Middle-class men influence Parliament.

Values hard work and the determination to "get ahead."

Middle-class women encouraged to become "ladies" and to do no physical labor.

A growing middle class benefited the most from the Industrial Revolution.

REVIEW QUESTIONS

1. What was work like in a factory during the Industrial Revolution?

2. **Diagram Skills** What new role was assigned to middle-class women?

NEW WAYS OF THINKING

■ TEXT SUMMARY

During the Enlightenment, thinkers developed the policy of laissez faire. They believed that the free market would help everyone, not just the rich. In the early 1800s, thinkers tried to understand the changes created by the Industrial Revolution. Two economists, Thomas Malthus and David Ricardo, believed that as long as the population kept increasing, the poor would suffer. They believed that poor people could improve their lives only by working hard and having fewer children. They did not believe that government should help the poor.

By the 1800s, some thinkers began to argue that government should help the poor. They worked to reform society without making radical changes. Jeremy Bentham taught **utilitarianism,** the idea that the goal of a society should be the happiness of its people. Another utilitarian, John Stuart Mill, wanted government to improve the lives of the poor. Mill and other utilitarians worked for many reforms, including child labor and public health.

Other thinkers condemned industrialism. They believed it was unfair that some people were rich while others were poor. To end poverty, they introduced **socialism.** Under socialism, farms and businesses belonged to all the people, not to individuals. The goal of socialists was a society that worked for the good of all the people. Karl Marx called for an international struggle to end capitalism.

> ## THE **BIG** IDEA
>
> **The Industrial Age gave rise to new ways to think about the economy.**

■ GRAPHIC SUMMARY: *Thinkers of the Industrial Revolution*

THINKER	IDEA
Thomas Malthus	As long as the population increases, the poor suffer. Poor people should have fewer childern.
David Ricardo	When wages are high, families have more children, but more children lead to lower wages.
Jeremy Bentham	**Utilitarianism** The goal of society should be the happiness of its people.
John Stuart Mill	Government should help to improve the lives of the poor.
Karl Marx	**Scientific Socialism** History is a class struggle between the people who have wealth and those who do not. The working class will defeat the people who own the industries and end capitalism.

Many thinkers tried to understand the great changes that the Industrial Revolution caused.

■ REVIEW QUESTIONS

1. What did Malthus and Ricardo say that poor people could do to improve their lives?

2. Chart Skills What did John Stuart Mill believe to be a duty of government?

SURVEY CHAPTER 20
MODERN ERA CHAPTER 7 *Test*

■ IDENTIFYING MAIN IDEAS

Write the letter of the correct answer in the blank provided. (10 points each)

_____ **1.** Which of the following was an agricultural improvement of the 1600s?
   A. fertilizer from livestock
   B. animal domestication
   C. chemical pesticides
   D. warmer weather for growing crops

_____ **2.** What was one way that the agricultural revolution contributed to the Industrial Revolution?
   A. It triggered a population explosion.
   B. It tied peasants even more closely to the land.
   C. It ended feudalism.
   D. It replaced strip farms.

_____ **3.** Which of the following was the most important source of power for the early Industrial Revolution?
   A. the steam engine
   B. animals
   C. the windmill
   D. the dynamo

_____ **4.** What natural resources gave Britain an advantage in the Industrial Revolution?
   A. water and forests
   B. wildlife and precious gems
   C. coal and iron
   D. good harbors

_____ **5.** In what industry did the Industrial Revolution first take hold in Britain?
   A. textiles
   B. iron production
   C. agriculture
   D. transportation

_____ **6.** What invention made possible the growth of railroads?
   A. the spinning jenny
   B. the factory
   C. the turnpike
   D. the steam locomotive

_____ **7.** What was one reason that parents accepted child labor?
   A. They didn't care for their children.
   B. The law gave them no choice.
   C. The children were fed at work.
   D. They needed the additional money.

_____ **8.** Which group benefited the most from the Industrial Revolution?
   A. the working class
   B. farmers
   C. the middle class
   D. the nobility

_____ **9.** Why did Malthus urge families to have fewer children?
   A. He disliked children.
   B. Children were a burden for the state.
   C. He believed that population growth would outpace the food supply.
   D. He knew that as population grew, the economy would decline.

_____ **10.** Which groups worked to reform many aspects of society without altering it radically?
   A. the Socialists
   B. the Communists
   C. the Utilitarians
   D. the Utopians

Revolutions in Europe and Latin America (1790–1848)

SECTION 1 AN AGE OF IDEOLOGIES

■ TEXT SUMMARY

At the Congress of Vienna in 1815, European leaders tried to return Europe to the way it had been before the French Revolution. (See Chapter 19.) These leaders were part of a group known as **conservatives.** Conservatives included monarchs, noble landowners, and church leaders. Conservatives wanted to return the kings of Europe to power and restore historic social classes. Conservative ideas also appealed to peasants who wanted to preserve traditional ways.

Liberals disagreed with the ideas of the conservatives. Liberals included members of the middle class. Many of their ideas came from the Enlightenment. Liberals wanted governments to be based on written constitutions. They believed that

people had natural rights. Disagreements between conservatives and liberals led to 30 years of turmoil in Europe.

Another challenge to the conservatives came from the **nationalists.** They believed that each national group should have its own country. For centuries, European rulers had won and lost territory in war. They passed lands back and forth, from one country to another. By 1815, several European empires included people of many different nationalities. Nationalists wanted to create their own homelands. During the 1800s, nationalist groups across Europe revolted against the empires.

> ## THE **BIG** IDEA
>
> Conflicts arose in Europe between people with opposing systems of thought and belief.

■ GRAPHIC SUMMARY: *Liberal and Conservative Ideas in the 1800s*

	LIBERALS	CONSERVATIVES
Who they were	Lawyers, business owners, writers, and other members of the middle class	Kings, noble landowners, and church leaders
Who should rule	Male property owners	King and nobles
Goals of government	Protect natural rights	Keep peace and order
What kind of government	Republic with constitution and separation of powers	Monarchy
Business	Laissez faire	Government regulated business

Liberals challenged conservatives at every turn.

■ REVIEW QUESTIONS

1. Which groups made up the conservatives?

2. Chart Skills According to liberals, what were the goals of government? According to conservatives?

REVOLUTIONS OF 1830 AND 1848

TEXT SUMMARY

In 1815, the Congress of Vienna put a king back in power in France. In 1830, King Charles X began to act like an absolute ruler, and liberals and radicals revolted. Charles fled. Liberals then set up a constitutional monarchy. By the 1840s, France faced an economic and political crisis. Workers lost their jobs and bread prices rose. The people accused the government of corruption. Once again, the French revolted. In 1848, they set up a republic.

As in 1789, people throughout Europe heard of the French revolutions of 1830 and 1848. The French success inspired other groups to act. Liberals wanted protection for their rights. They also demanded more power. Workers wanted relief from the suffering caused by the Industrial Revolution. Nationalists hoped for independence from foreign rulers.

Across Europe, uprisings occurred in 1848. In the Austrian empire, Hungarian, Italian, and Czech nationalist groups demanded independence. In the German states, peasants burned the homes of wealthy landowners while students demanded reforms. For the most part, the revolts were short-lived. Revolutionaries failed to achieve their goals because powerful government forces crushed them.

However, even when they failed, the revolutionaries frightened the rulers. Later on, many of these frightened rulers began to agree to reforms.

> ### THE BIG IDEA
>
> Social and political discontent sparked revolutions in France in 1830 and 1848, which in turn inspired revolts in other parts of Europe.

GRAPHIC SUMMARY:

Revolutions in Europe, 1830 and 1848

In 1830 and 1848, French revolutions inspired other rebellions.

REVIEW QUESTIONS

1. Why did the French revolt in 1830?

2. **Map Skills** Name three places where revolutions took place in 1848.

LATIN AMERICAN WARS OF INDEPENDENCE

◾ TEXT SUMMARY

By the late 1700s, revolutionary ideas spread from Europe to Latin America. The French colony of Haiti was the first to revolt. Nearly half a million enslaved Africans worked there on French sugar plantations. In 1791, Toussaint L'Ouverture led the slaves in revolt. After a long, difficult struggle, the slaves won freedom, and soon Haiti declared its independence.

In the Spanish colonies, many groups were unhappy that social and political life was dominated by peninsulares. Creoles wanted power for themselves. Mestizos and mulattoes were angry about how the Spanish treated them. Enslaved Africans wanted freedom. In the 1700s, educated Creoles read about Enlightenment ideas. They watched the colonists in North America win their independence. Then, in 1808, Napoleon overthrew the Spanish king. Latin American leaders knew it was time to act.

In Mexico, peasants revolted in 1810. Eleven years later, they overthrew their Spanish rulers. In South America, a Creole named Simón Bolívar led wars of independence in Venezuela, Colombia, and Ecuador. Central America declared independence from Spain in the early 1820s. Local leaders united the region in a republic, although the republic later split into separate, independent states. Most of the new nations faced many problems, including civil war and poverty.

> ### THE BIG IDEA
>
> Enlightenment ideas, revolutions in other lands, and dissatisfaction with European rule caused revolutions in Latin America.

◾ GRAPHIC SUMMARY: *Latin America Fights for Independence*

1798 Haitian slaves win their freedom from French owners

1810 Mexican peasants revolt

1821 Mexicans overthrow Spanish rulers and win independence

1822 Portuguese king makes Brazil independent; accepts constitution

A.D.

| 1790 | 1800 | 1810 | 1820 | 1830 |

1791 Toussaint L'Ouverture leads African slaves in a revolt in Haiti

1804 Haiti declares independence from France

1820 Haiti becomes a republic

Revolutions flamed across Latin America in the 1800s.

◾ REVIEW QUESTIONS

1. Where did the first revolution in Latin America take place?

2. Time Line Skills When did Brazil become independent?

SURVEY CHAPTER 21
MODERN ERA CHAPTER 8
Test

■ IDENTIFYING MAIN IDEAS

Write the letter of the correct answer in the blank provided. (10 points each)

_____ 1. Which of the following goals represents conservative ideology in Europe in the early 1800s?
   A. restoration of power to royal families
   B. establishment of a homeland for each national group
   C. support for freedom of the press
   D. tolerance for religious differences

_____ 2. A liberal was likely to be a
   A. monarch.
   B. middle-class merchant.
   C. church leader.
   D. noble landowner.

_____ 3. Liberals wanted governments to be based on
   A. divine right.
   B. nationalism.
   C. the economy.
   D. written constitutions.

_____ 4. The goal of nationalists was to unify
   A. Italy.
   B. people with a common national heritage.
   C. Europe's monarchies.
   D. all European nations.

_____ 5. How did Charles X incite the July 1830 revolution in Paris?
   A. by ignoring peasants' pleas for bread
   B. by acting like an absolute monarch
   C. by executing radicals in the government
   D. by allowing too much liberty

_____ 6. How did people in other countries react to the French revolutions of 1830 and 1848?
   A. They ignored them.
   B. They joined the French revolutionaries.
   C. They spoke out against them.
   D. They were inspired by them to act.

_____ 7. Which word best describes the results of the 1848 revolts in Europe?
   A. permanent
   B. short-lived
   C. peaceful
   D. laughable

_____ 8. Which of the following places won independence from France and became the first nonslave nation in the Western Hemisphere?
   A. Haiti
   B. Mexico
   C. Venezuela
   D. Brazil

_____ 9. Which group dominated Latin American social and political life in the early 1800s?
   A. creoles
   B. peninsulares
   C. mestizos
   D. mulattoes

_____ 10. Educated creoles in the 1700s were influenced by
   A. Spanish cruelty toward the mestizos.
   B. the peninsulares.
   C. Bolívar's vow to free his country.
   D. Enlightenment ideas and revolutions in other lands.

Life in the Industrial Age (1800–1914)

 SECTION 1

THE INDUSTRIAL REVOLUTION SPREADS

■ TEXT SUMMARY

Britain, with its steam-powered factories, once stood alone as the leader of industry. However, by the mid-1800s, the Industrial Revolution had spread to other nations. Germany and the United States had more coal and iron than Britain. Both nations made use of British technology. By the late 1800s, they led the world in production.

Political and social problems slowed the growth of industry in the South and East of Europe. In East Asia, Japan industrialized rapidly after 1868. This was remarkable since it had few natural resources. By 1900, nations of the West had a great amount of economic power.

Factories used new ways to produce goods. **Interchangeable parts** (parts that could be used in place of one another) and assembly lines made work faster and less costly.

In the mid-1800s, companies hired scientists to improve technology. A new form of power, electricity, changed industry. New ways to send messages and move goods linked cities and nations. (See chart below.)

New equipment was costly. To get enough capital, owners began selling stock in their companies. The late 1800s brought the rise of big business. Huge **corporations,** or businesses that are owned by many investors who own stock, soon ruled industry.

> ### THE **BIG** IDEA
>
> During the 1800s, the United States and several European countries joined Britain in the Industrial Revolution.

■ GRAPHIC SUMMARY: *Technology of the Industrial Age*

INVENTOR OR DEVELOPER	NATION	INVENTION OR DEVELOPMENT	YEAR
Henry Bessemer	Britain	Process to turn iron ore into steel	1856
Alexander Graham Bell	United States	Telephone	1876
Thomas Edison	United States	Electric light bulb	1879
Gottlieb Daimler	Germany	Automobile	1887
Henry Ford	United States	Mass-produced automobile	1903
Orville & Wilbur Wright	United States	Airplane	1903

New technology of the Industrial Age brought economic growth.

■ REVIEW QUESTIONS

1. Which countries led the world in industry by the late 1800s?

2. Chart Skills Choose one invention and tell how you think it changed everyday life.

THE WORLD OF CITIES

◻ TEXT SUMMARY

The spread of the Industrial Revolution brought change, especially to the cities of the world. Populations grew rapidly in the 1800s. (See diagram below.) The boom came because people were living longer. New farming methods meant better diets. Medical discoveries slowed death rates. French scientist Louis Pasteur showed that germs cause disease. In England, Joseph Lister found that antiseptics kill germs. Better health habits and cleaner hospitals brought a drop in disease, infections, and death.

As workers moved from farms to factories, cities took on a new look. Department stores and offices lined streets and public squares. In the late 1800s, American builders put up very tall steel-framed buildings called **skyscrapers.** New sewers made cities healthier places. First gas and then electric street lights made them safer. Trolley lines meant people could live miles from their jobs. The rich moved to fine homes on the edge of town. The poor crowded into slums near the city center. There they lived in run-down tenement buildings near the factories. In spite of crowds and high crime rates, people kept moving to cities. They came for the music halls, parks, libraries, and most of all for the jobs.

Many city factories were unsafe and unhealthy. Men, women, and children worked long hours for low pay. By the late 1800s, labor unions were legal in most western nations. They called for new laws to improve conditions, limit work hours, and end child labor.

> ### THE **BIG** IDEA
>
> **The population of cities grew as people moved to urban centers for jobs.**

◻ GRAPHIC SUMMARY: *Western Populations in the Late 1800s*

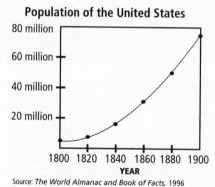

Population of the United States

Source: *The World Almanac and Book of Facts, 1996*
Chronology of the Modern World, 1763-1992

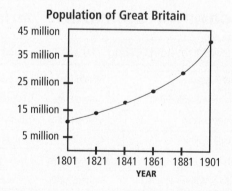

Population of Great Britain

The Industrial Revolution brought rapid population growth.

◻ REVIEW QUESTIONS

1. What was one way the industrial revolution improved city life? What was one way it made city life worse?

2. Diagram Skills What happened to the populations of the United States and Great Britain in the late 1800s?

SECTION 3 CHANGING ATTITUDES AND VALUES

◼ TEXT SUMMARY

In the late 1800s, people of the industrial world developed new ways of thinking and living. Class systems had always divided western society. The spread of industry changed these systems. Wealthy industrial and business families joined nobles and rich landowners as members of a small upper class. (See diagram below.)

The values and practices of a growing middle class shaped western life. The ideal family was made up of two parents and their children. They lived together in a house. The middle-class husband worked in an office or a shop. The wife raised children and directed servants. This ideal rarely applied to the lower classes. Most working-class women labored for low pay in factories or as servants.

Some women called for new rights. They entered schools and professions that had banned them. By the late 1800s, some countries let married women control their own property. At the same time, women began asking for voting rights. In New Zealand, Australia, and some United States territories, women won the vote before 1900. In Europe and most of the United States, **suffrage,** or the right to vote, came decades later.

Scientific theories of the 1800s challenged beliefs. In 1859, British naturalist Charles Darwin caused an uproar. He said that humans had developed to their present state over millions of years. This **theory of evolution,** as it was called, stirred conflicts between religion and science.

> ### THE BIG IDEA
>
> The Industrial Revolution slowly changed the old social order in the western world.

◼ GRAPHIC SUMMARY: *Social Classes in the Industrialized West*

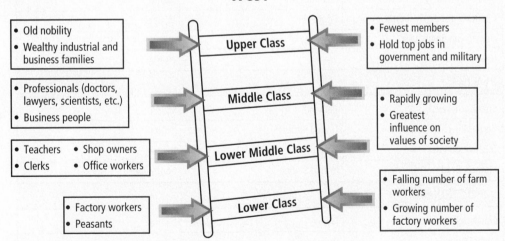

- Old nobility
- Wealthy industrial and business families

Upper Class

- Fewest members
- Hold top jobs in government and military

- Professionals (doctors, lawyers, scientists, etc.)
- Business people

Middle Class

- Rapidly growing
- Greatest influence on values of society

- Teachers   • Shop owners
- Clerks   • Office workers

Lower Middle Class

- Factory workers
- Peasants

Lower Class

- Falling number of farm workers
- Growing number of factory workers

The growth of industry brought the rise of a large middle class.

◼ REVIEW QUESTIONS

1. What were three rights women worked to gain in the late 1800s?

2. Diagram Skills Who made up the lower class?

A NEW CULTURE

▦ TEXT SUMMARY

Artists, musicians, and writers took new directions during the Industrial Age. From about 1750 to 1850, a movement called **romanticism** thrived. The romantics appealed to emotion rather than reason. They aimed to capture the beauty and force of nature. Composers used swelling notes to stir feelings. Writers created a new kind of hero. He was a sad figure, often with a deep secret. Artists found romance in days gone by. Architects copied old buildings. Writers set novels in past times.

The mid-1800s brought a movement known as **realism** to the West. Realists tried to show the world as it was. They often looked at the harsh sides of life. They showed working-class life. They told of women without rights. Many realists hoped to improve the society they described.

In the 1840s, a new art form, photography, emerged. At first, most photos were stiff portraits. In time, realists took the camera into factories and slums. Photos captured real life better than paintings could. So, in the 1870s, some artists took painting in a new direction. A movement called **impressionism** began in Paris. While earlier artists had worked to hide brush strokes, impressionists brushed colors without blending. They created a fresh view of scenes and objects.

> ### THE **BIG** IDEA
>
> **In the 1800s, two very different movements, called realism and romanticism, dominated the arts.**

▦ GRAPHIC SUMMARY: *The Arts in the Industrial Age*

ROMANTICISM		
Lord Byron	England	Writer
Johann Wolfgang von Goethe	Germany	Writer
Charlotte and Emily Brontë	England	Writers
Ludwig van Beethoven	Germany	Composer
Eugène Delacroix	France	Painter
REALISM		
Charles Dickens	England	Writer
Harriet Beecher Stowe	United States	Writer
Gustave Courbet	France	Painter
Mathew Brady	United States	Photographer
IMPRESSIONISM		
Claude Monet	France	Painter
Edgar Degas	France	Painter

While the romantics looked to days gone by, the realists took a hard look at life in their own times.

▦ REVIEW QUESTIONS

1. How was realism different from romanticism?

2. **Chart Skills** Name two English sisters who became well known for their romantic novels.

SURVEY CHAPTER 22
MODERN ERA CHAPTER 9
Test

■ IDENTIFYING MAIN IDEAS

Write the letter of the correct answer in the blank provided. (10 points each)

____ 1. The two countries that came to lead the world in industrial production were
  A. Russia and Canada.
  B. Germany and the United States.
  C. the United States and Russia.
  D. Spain and New Zealand.

____ 2. The assembly line was one new development that made
  A. production faster and cheaper.
  B. only cars.
  C. production slower.
  D. the Bessesmer process possible.

____ 3. One example of a new invention that changed communications is
  A. the electric light bulb.
  B. dynamite.
  C. the telephone.
  D. the Bessemer process.

____ 4. Why did populations soar between 1800 and 1900?
  A. People had larger families.
  B. People did not eat very well.
  C. Food production decreased.
  D. The death rate fell.

____ 5. In nineteenth-century cities, the poor lived
  A. in planned residential neighborhoods.
  B. on the outskirts of the city.
  C. in skyscrapers.
  D. in tenements near the factories.

____ 6. The saying "a woman's place is in the home" reflected the values of which of the following groups in 1850?
  A. the working class
  B. the middle class
  C. the upper class
  D. farmworkers

____ 7. The women's suffrage movement made faster strides in
  A. Europe.
  B. rural areas.
  C. the eastern United States.
  D. New Zealand, Australia, and the western United States.

____ 8. Darwin challenged traditional beliefs by asserting that
  A. Earth was older than formerly thought.
  B. women were equal to men.
  C. humans evolved over millions of years.
  D. the sun was the center of the universe.

____ 9. What new art form captured real life better than paintings?
  A. impressionism
  B. photography
  C. collage
  D. sculpture

____ 10. How did impressionist paintings differ from previous works of art?
  A. The colors were washed out.
  B. The brush strokes were not blended.
  C. Impressionist artists never painted the same subject twice.
  D. They portrayed the subject in a clear, realistic manner.

Nationalism Triumphs in Europe (1800–1914)

SECTION 1 — BUILDING A GERMAN NATION

■ TEXT SUMMARY

In the early 1800s, most German-speaking people were loyal to their own states. From 1807 to 1812, Napoleon of France raided German lands. Feelings of nationalism stirred in those who fought French rule. Some called for a unified Germany.

In the 1830s, Prussia set up a trade agreement among German states. Each state still governed itself, but Prussia had become a clear leader under King William I.

Otto von Bismarck, appointed chancellor in 1862, guided policies. Bismarck aimed to unite the German states under Prussian rule. He was not, however, driven by nationalism. His goal was to make the ruling class of Prussia masters of a German empire.

Bismarck followed a tough policy he called "blood and iron." He led Prussia into three wars. Each moved the German states closer to unity. In 1864, Prussia teamed up with Austria to take lands from Denmark. In 1866, the great Prussian army turned against Austria. Bismarck let Austria keep self-rule but took some northern states. In 1870, he encouraged war between Prussia and France. His triumph in the Franco-Prussian War stirred German pride. In 1871, the German states united under William I. **Kaiser** (emperor)

William I and Chancellor Otto von Bismarck became two of the most powerful people in Europe.

■ GRAPHIC SUMMARY:

The Franco-Prussian War

CAUSES
• Rivalry between Prussia and France
• Struggle over the throne of Spain
• The Ems Dispatch (Bismarck angers France by releasing false reports of insults towards French ambassador.

Franco-Prussian War, 1870

RESULTS
• Quick victory for Prussia
• Downfall of Second Empire of France
• German states unite under William I of Prussia
• German empire takes leading role in Europe
• Control of German empire rests with Kaiser William I and Chancellor Otto von Bismarck

The Prussian victory sparked the spirit of nationalism needed to unite the German states.

THE **BIG** IDEA

Otto von Bismarck, the chancellor of Prussia, led the drive for German unity.

■ REVIEW QUESTIONS

1. What was the goal of Chancellor Otto von Bismarck? What policy did he follow to meet that goal?

2. Diagram Skills What was one result of the Franco-Prussian War?

SECTION 2 STRENGTHENING GERMANY

TEXT SUMMARY

After Germany unified in 1871, it became the leader of industry in Europe. Before unification, many states had big factories and fine railroads. The new nation built upon this progress. Germany had plenty of coal and iron, both needed by industries of the late 1800s. A population boom provided Germans to work and to buy products.

Chancellor Otto von Bismarck had great plans for Germany. Foreign goals included keeping France weak and isolated and building ties with Austria and Russia. At home, he set out to crush all threats to the empire. He feared that Catholics put their church before their state and launched an anti-Catholic campaign. The moves against the Church were met with outrage, and Bismarck ended his attack. The Chancellor also feared that the growing power of socialists could lead to revolt. He banned their meetings. When workers ignored the bans, Bismarck set up new programs to meet their needs. He felt that happy workers would not turn to socialism.

In 1888, William II took the place of his grandfather as Kaiser. The new ruler wanted total power and, in 1890, he shocked Europe by asking Bismarck to step down. William II stopped all moves towards democracy. He made sure his people had good services, including schools that taught students to obey their kaiser. He funded the largest army in Europe and built up the navy. Then he set out to gain colonies in other lands.

THE BIG IDEA

Germany increased its power by building up its industry and military.

GRAPHIC SUMMARY:

The German Industrial Giant

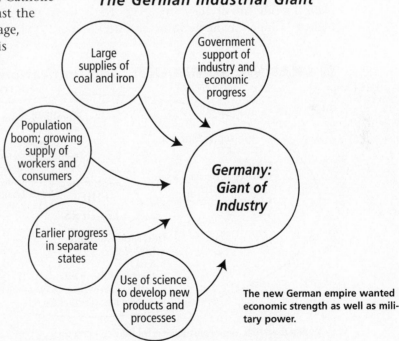

Large supplies of coal and iron

Government support of industry and economic progress

Population boom; growing supply of workers and consumers

Germany: Giant of Industry

Earlier progress in separate states

Use of science to develop new products and processes

The new German empire wanted economic strength as well as military power.

REVIEW QUESTIONS

1. What two groups did Bismarck see as a threat to the German empire? Why did he fear each group?

2. **Diagram Skills** How did a population boom help the growth of German industry?

UNIFYING ITALY

▧ TEXT SUMMARY

When the Roman empire fell in the 400s, Italy split into many kingdoms. In the 1800s, Napoleon of France combined some of the kingdoms. Italians began to dream of one free land.

After the reign of Napoleon, Italy was still divided. Nationalists wanted unity, but regional differences worked against them. Mighty Austria ruled in northern Italy. The Roman Catholic Church controlled central Italy.

Skilled leaders fought for unification. (See diagram below.) In the 1830s, Giuseppe Mazzini founded a rebel group called Young Italy. In the kingdom of Sardinia, King Victor Emmanuel II made plans to rule all of Italy. In 1852, he named Camillo Cavour as prime minister.

Sardinia became the center of the fight for unity. Cavour joined with France in a war against Austria. As he gained lands and respect, more northern states united with Sardinia.

Giuseppe Garibaldi led a force that won Sicily and then moved north. Meanwhile, Cavour sent troops south. The two armies overran all Italian states but Venetia and Rome. As of 1861, Victor Emmanuel ruled the united lands. By 1871, all foreign control had ended. The pope could not fight off Italian troops. Rome became the capital of the unified nation.

The new Italy faced conflicts. The urban North quarreled with the rural South. The Catholic Church resisted new leaders. Unrest grew as groups called for social change and the right to vote for all men.

THE **BIG** IDEA

In the 1800s, influential leaders helped to create a united Italy.

▧ GRAPHIC SUMMARY: *The Unification Movement in Italy*

Giuseppe Mazzini
- 1805–1872
- A rebel
- Founds Young Italy, a secret nationalist society
- Spends many years in exile

Camillo Cavour
- 1810–1861
- A statesman
- Prime minister of Sardinia
  - Strengthens Sardinian economy, forms foreign alliances
  - Launches wars to gain lands and build power

THE LEADERS

Giuseppe Garibaldi
- 1807–1882
- A soldier
- Member of Young Italy
- Leads volunteer army known as the Red Shirts
- Spends many years in exile

During the 1800s, nationalist leaders worked to unite Italy.

▧ REVIEW QUESTIONS

1. What two powerful forces stood in the way of Italian unity?

2. **Diagram Skills** Name three men who helped unify Italy.

NATIONALISM THREATENS OLD EMPIRES

▣ TEXT SUMMARY

The spirit of nationalism helped unite Germany and Italy. It also helped break up two empires. (See diagram below.)

In 1800, the Hapsburgs of Austria were the oldest ruling family in Europe. They controlled Bohemia and Hungary. They also ruled parts of Romania, Poland, Ukraine, and Italy. However, loyalties to regions and ethnic groups were growing. Nationalist minority groups wanted to be free from the Austrian empire. They wanted self-rule.

In 1867, the leaders of Hungary worked out a deal with Austria. They set up the Dual Monarchy of Austria-Hungary. The emperor of Austria still ruled as King of Hungary, but Austria and Hungary were separate states. Each made its own laws.

By 1900, nationalists in other lands were pressing for liberty.

Like the Hapsburgs, the Ottomans ruled a huge empire. It was home to many groups. Among them were Serbs, Greeks, Bulgarians, and Romanians. During the 1800s, groups in the Balkans rebelled. Serbia won freedom in 1817. The south of Greece freed itself in the 1830s. The powers of Europe saw a chance to gain Ottoman lands. Russia, Austria-Hungary, Britain, and France all took part in wars and changing alliances. At the same time, groups within the empire launched revolts and fought among themselves.

> ### THE **BIG** IDEA
>
> Desires for national independence threatened to break up the Austrian and Ottoman empires.

▣ GRAPHIC SUMMARY: *Nationalism Changes the Map of Europe*

NATIONALISM

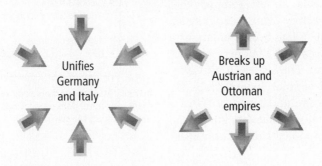

Unifies Germany and Italy

Breaks up Austrian and Ottoman empires

Nationalism could be a uniting or dividing force.

▣ REVIEW QUESTIONS

1. What was the Dual Monarchy and why was it formed?

2. **Diagram Skills** How did nationalism change each of the following: (a) Italy (b) Germany (c) Austrian empire (d) Ottoman empire?

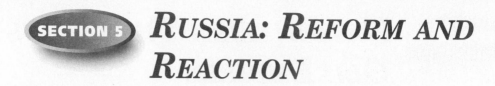

RUSSIA: REFORM AND REACTION

■ TEXT SUMMARY

By 1800, Western Europe had entered the industrial age. Russia, on the other hand, saw little economic growth. The czars feared change might weaken their control. Also, a rigid system of social classes blocked progress. Wealthy nobles owned all farmlands. They cared little about industry. The middle class was too small to have much power. Most Russians were serfs who toiled for the landowners. As long as people served masters, Russia could not move forward.

> ### THE **BIG** IDEA
>
> **Industrialization and reform came more slowly to Russia than to Western Europe.**

Alexander II freed the serfs in 1861. His few **reforms,** or changes, did not satisfy many Russians. He was killed in 1881. His son, Alexander III, persecuted all non-Russians. He insisted on one language, Russian, and one church, Russian Orthodox. Jews were beaten and killed in attacks known as **pogroms.** Many fled to other lands.

Under Alexander III and his son, Nicholas II, Russia at last entered the industrial age. Factory owners could be as unfair as the nobles had been. On January 22, 1905, a priest led marchers to the palace of the czar. They called for an end to poverty and a voice in government. Soldiers opened fire and killed hundreds of the demonstrators. That day, known as Bloody Sunday, sparked a revolution. (See diagram at right.)

In 1905, Nicholas II agreed to set up an elected **Duma,** or body of lawmakers. However, its powers were limited. Unrest among peasants and workers did not end.

■ GRAPHIC SUMMARY:

The Russian Revolution of 1905

> **CAUSES**
> - Low spirits after defeat in 1904 war with Japan
> - Poverty and bad working conditions
> - Corrupt government
> - Persecution of minority groups
> - "Bloody Sunday" killings

Russian Revolution of 1905

> **RESULTS**
> - The "October Manifesto"– Czar Nicholas II announces reforms and new freedoms
> - Nicholas II sets up the Duma which must approve all laws
> - Nicholas II dissolves the first Duma when its leaders criticize the government
> - Pogroms continue
> - New voting laws limit powers of later Dumas

In 1905, Russian workers took over local government, peasants demanded land, and minority groups called for self-rule.

■ REVIEW QUESTIONS

1. What were two reasons why Russia was slow to industrialize?

2. Diagram Skills Do you think the Revolution of 1905 brought the results that the people wanted? Give reasons for your answer.

SURVEY CHAPTER 23
MODERN ERA CHAPTER 10   *Test*

▣ IDENTIFYING MAIN IDEAS

Write the letter of the correct answer in the blank provided. (10 points each)

____ 1. Napoleon's advances in the early 1800s had the effect of
   A. disintegrating German unity.
   B. sparking German nationalism.
   C. tightening laws against Jews.
   D. making trade more difficult.

____ 2. Which of the following was a result of the Franco-Prussian War?
   A. Prussia defeated France.
   B. France defeated Prussia.
   C. Austria defeated Prussia.
   D. France defeated Austria.

____ 3. What was Bismarck's foreign policy goal toward France?
   A. to aid their industrial growth
   B. to compete against their navy
   C. to keep them isolated
   D. to forge strong links with them

____ 4. How did William II shock Europe?
   A. by invading Britain
   B. by asking Bismarck to resign
   C. by abdicating the throne
   D. by closing public schools

____ 5. Which of the following made Italy hard to unite into a single country?
   A. lack of a common language
   B. regional differences
   C. lack of natural resources
   D. ethnic differences

____ 6. After unification, relations between Italy and the Roman Catholic Church were
   A. hostile.
   B. friendly.
   C. improving.
   D. no different than before unification.

____ 7. The major threat to the Hapsburg empire came from
   A. national minorities.
   B. the Ottoman empire.
   C. socialist reformers.
   D. the French.

____ 8. How was the Ottoman empire similar to the Austrian empire?
   A. Both were multinational.
   B. Both welcomed nationalism.
   C. Both covered small territories.
   D. Neither gave in to nationalist demands.

____ 9. One obstacle in the way of Russian progress was
   A. a lack of resources.
   B. a small population.
   C. the rigid social structure.
   D. the rapid pace of reforms.

____ 10. The Revolution of 1905 broke out as a result of
   A. persecution of the Jews.
   B. the killing of demonstrators on Bloody Sunday.
   C. the freeing of the serfs.
   D. Napoleon's invasion of Russia.

Growth of Western Democracies (1815–1914)

SECTION 1 ***BRITAIN BECOMES MORE DEMOCRATIC***

◼ TEXT SUMMARY

In 1815, Britain had a monarch. It also had a parliament with two political parties. Still, Britain was not democratic. Parliament was made up of the House of Lords (nobles and high-ranking church leaders) and the House of Commons (men elected by the five percent of the population who could vote). The House of Lords could **veto,** or reject, any bill passed by the House of Commons.

Reformers wanted more democracy. (See diagram below.) In the 1820s, they ended laws that banned some religious groups from voting. Then they turned to another problem. The growth of cities had left some rural **boroughs,** or towns, with few voters. These "rotten boroughs" had more than their fair share of seats in Parliament. The Reform Act of 1832 gave more seats to large towns. It also gave the vote to men who owned a certain amount of property.

Queen Victoria ruled the British empire from 1837 to 1901. The Victorian age was a time for manners, hard work, honesty, and reform. In the 1860s, political parties changed. Nobles and

landowners of the Tory party joined the new Conservative party. The mostly middle-class Whig party grew into the Liberal party. Both parties wanted democracy. A Conservative bill granted the vote to many working-class men. Later, Liberals won the vote for farm workers and most other men. A Liberal bill limited the veto of the House of Lords and gave more power to the House of Commons.

◼ GRAPHIC SUMMARY:

Steps Toward Democracy in Great Britain

1911	• New limits on the power of House of Lords
1880s	• Most men have the vote • Elections now held by secret ballot
1867	• Working-class men can vote
1830s	• Most male property owners can vote • Fair division of seats in Parliament
1820s	• End of bans on voting rights for certain religious groups
1815	• Fewer than five percent of population has right to vote • Politics controlled by wealthy men • Some religions banned from voting

Britain gained democracy through reform rather than revolution.

> ### THE **BIG** IDEA
>
> **In Britain, political change came from gradual reform throughout the 1800s.**

◼ REVIEW QUESTIONS

1. In what way was the British government undemocratic in the early 1800s?

2. Diagram Skills Which British men were allowed to vote in the 1830s?

A CENTURY OF REFORM

◼ TEXT SUMMARY

From 1815 to 1914, British reformers called for change. New laws improved working conditions and allowed trade unions. (See diagram below.) They also provided free elementary schools, reduced harsh punishments for crimes, and ended slavery. Trade reforms lowered **tariffs,** or taxes on imported goods.

In 1900, the trade unions founded a new political party, the Labour party. By the 1920s, the Labour party was stronger than the Liberal party. It pushed through more laws to protect workers.

British women called for the right to vote. They held huge rallies and marches. When peaceful demonstrations failed, some protesters smashed windows and burned buildings. A few went on hunger strikes. In 1918, Parliament gave the vote to women over age 30. Younger women won the right to vote in 1928.

Throughout the 1800s, nationalists in Ireland fought British rule. They demanded change. No longer would the Irish pay high rents to British landlords. No longer would Irish Catholics turn over money to the Church of England. No longer would Irish crops go to England while Irish families starved. In the 1870s, Irish nationalists called for **home rule,** or local self-government. Finally, in 1914, Parliament passed a home rule bill. Counties in the South of Ireland became independent in 1921.

> ### THE **BIG** IDEA
>
> In the 1800s and early 1900s, Parliament passed many reform measures.

◼ GRAPHIC SUMMARY: *Social Reform in Great Britain, 1815–1914*

Between 1815 and 1914, Britain passed laws to abolish slavery, improve working conditions, and extend voting rights.

◼ REVIEW QUESTIONS

1. What actions did British women take to win the vote?

2. **Diagram Skills** How did social reform improve life for children of the British working class?

DIVISION AND DEMOCRACY IN FRANCE

■ TEXT SUMMARY

After the French Revolution of 1848, Louis Napoleon was elected president of the Second Republic. He was nephew to Napoleon Bonaparte, and his famous name won votes. The working class liked his talk of social reform. In 1852, he declared himself Napoleon III, ruler of the Second Empire. (See diagram below.) He ruled like a dictator, censoring the press and choosing officials. However, he did keep his word to workers. He allowed unions and set up free health care.

While Napoleon III made reforms at home, he made mistakes in foreign policy. He tried to take power in Mexico but failed. In 1870, a crushing defeat in the Franco-Prussian War ended the Second Empire.

The Third Republic arose. It had a more democratic two-house legislature. All men could vote for members of the lower house. The two houses elected a president, but real power went to the **premier,** or prime minister. A constitution separated church and state and guarded human rights.

In 1894, a scandal shook the Third Republic. Captain Alfred Dreyfus was jailed for spying for the Germans. Some people thought the army blamed Dreyfus because he was a Jew. In the end, he was freed. The Dreyfus affair, along with **antisemitism** (prejudice against Jews) across Europe, worried Jewish leaders. Some began to call for a separate state where Jews would have the rights and freedoms denied to them in European countries.

> ### THE BIG IDEA
>
> Democratic reforms in France took place under Napoleon III's Second Empire and its successor, the Third Republic.

■ GRAPHIC SUMMARY: *The Rise and Fall of the Second Empire of France*

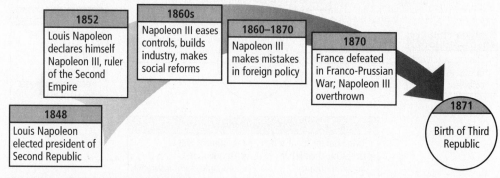

1852
Louis Napoleon declares himself Napoleon III, ruler of the Second Empire

1860s
Napoleon III eases controls, builds industry, makes social reforms

1860–1870
Napoleon III makes mistakes in foreign policy

1870
France defeated in Franco-Prussian War; Napoleon III overthrown

1848
Louis Napoleon elected president of Second Republic

1871
Birth of Third Republic

The defeat of the Second Empire made way for the rise of the Third Republic.

■ REVIEW QUESTIONS

1. How did France become more democratic during the Third Republic?

2. **Diagram Skills** What event directly caused the fall of the Second Empire?

EXPANSION OF THE UNITED STATES

TEXT SUMMARY

The United States grew and changed greatly in the 1800s. Many Americans felt it was their right to settle all the land between the Atlantic Ocean and the Pacific Ocean. They moved west, taking lands from the Native Americans. In 1803, President Jefferson bought land from France. His Louisiana Purchase almost doubled the size of the United States. In 1848, Mexico gave up California and much of the Southwest. In 1867, the United States bought Alaska from Russia. In 1898, it gained Hawaii. War with Spain in 1898 gave the United States control of Puerto Rico, the Philippines, and Guam.

During the 1800s, two movements brought greater democracy. Abolitionists worked to end slavery. Women who worked in the abolitionist movement began to organize a women's rights movement. They called for equality under the law, at work, and in schools.

By 1860, economic conflicts split the nation. The South relied on farming. The North was more industrialized. The regions also disagreed on the issue of slavery. Southern plantations felt they needed slave labor. The South worried when President Lincoln opposed extending slavery into new territories. In 1861, southern states **seceded,** or separated, from the Union. The Civil War began. The North won the war in 1865, and the nation was reunited. It had been the bloodiest war in United States history.

THE BIG IDEA

In the United States, as in much of the world, the 1800s were a time of changing borders, growing industry, and new laws.

GRAPHIC SUMMARY: *Growth of the United States in the 1800s*

New Lands	New Freedoms	New People	New Industries
• Louisiana Territory • Spanish Florida • Oregon Country • Texas • Mexican Cession (California and southwest lands) • Alaska • Hawaii • Puerto Rico, Guam, the Philippines	• End of slavery • All men gain the vote • Growth of women's rights movement • Growth of labor unions	• Waves of immigrants • Many Europeans settle on Atlantic coast • Many Asians settle on Pacific coast	• New inventions (steam locomotive, telegraph, farm machines) • Transcontinental railroad • Growth of big business • United States becomes a world leader of industry

During the 1800s, the United States expanded across the continent to the Pacific Ocean.

REVIEW QUESTIONS

1. What two United States movements of the 1800s worked to gain greater human rights?

2. **Chart Skills** Give one example of how the United States grew in each of these areas in the 1800s: (a) size (b) democratic freedoms (c) economy.

SURVEY CHAPTER 24
MODERN ERA CHAPTER 11   *Test*

◼ IDENTIFYING MAIN IDEAS

Write the letter of the correct answer in the blank provided. (10 points each)

_____ 1. In the early 1800s, the English Parliament represented primarily the interests of
A. everyone in Britain.
B. mainly the middle class.
C. wealthy landowners.
D. the working-class majority.

_____ 2. In England during the 1880s, the vote was extended to farm workers under the leadership of
A. the Conservative party.
B. the Liberal party.
C. the House of Lords.
D. Disraeli.

_____ 3. Which English political party was formed by trade unions?
A. Conservative party
B. Labour party
C. Liberal party
D. Tory party

_____ 4. Which best describes the women's suffrage movement in England?
A. It was entirely peaceful.
B. Few women participated.
C. Peaceful demonstrations gave way to violent protests.
D. It was unsuccessful.

_____ 5. Napoleon III of France appealed to the lower classes mainly because he
A. made France a major industrial power.
B. opposed Prussia.
C. implemented social reforms.
D. extended French influence to Mexico.

_____ 6. The aim of Napoleon III's foreign policy was to
A. reestablish the French as a European power.
B. keep France isolated.
C. establish French neutrality.
D. establish a balance of power with Britain.

_____ 7. The Dreyfus case reflected
A. the growth of religious toleration.
B. the economic security of the lower middle class.
C. the lack of nationalist feelings in Europe.
D. the rise of antisemitism in Europe.

_____ 8. What effect did American westward expansion have on Native Americans?
A. It empowered them.
B. It had no effect on them.
C. It devastated them.
D. It enriched them.

_____ 9. Which movement did the women's rights movement spring from in the United States?
A. the abolition movement
B. the Progressive movement
C. the industrial movement
D. the prohibition movement

_____ 10. One issue the American South was concerned about was the opposition to
A. free trade.
B. the extension of slavery into new territories.
C. voting rights for women.
D. the expansion of the United States.

The New Imperialism (1800–1914)

SECTION 1 A WESTERN-DOMINATED WORLD

▥ TEXT SUMMARY

From 1870 until 1914, the major nations of Europe searched for new colonies. Their industries needed raw materials. They also needed markets in which to sell their goods. (See diagram below.)

Most Europeans favored **imperialism,** or domination by one country of the political and economic life of another country. Soldiers, traders, settlers, and missionaries were most eager to colonize new lands. Still, some Europeans were against empire building. They said it was wrong to seek democracy at home, but take freedom away from others.

The western powers had strong armed forces and new weapons. They gained lands in Africa and Asia with little trouble. Some countries fought the invaders but had little success.

Some western powers set up colonies and chose officials to rule the local people. The French used direct rule. They sent officers from France to run their colonies. The British used indirect rule. They chose local officers. Some powers set up **protectorates.** In a protectorate, the local rulers stayed in place but European advisors controlled trade and sent missionaries. A third form of control was the **sphere of influence.** In this case, an outside power claimed all rights to make investments or conduct trade.

> THE **BIG** IDEA
>
> Economic, political, and military interests spurred European imperialism in the 1800s.

▥ GRAPHIC SUMMARY: *Causes of the New Imperialism*

Economy	Politics and the Military	Society	Science and Invention
• Need for natural resources • Need for new markets • Place for growing populations to settle • Place to invest profits	• Bases for trade and navy ships • Power and security of global empire • Spirit of nationalism	• Wish to spread Christianity • Wish to share western civilization • Belief that western ways are best	• New weapons • New medicines • Improved ships

There were many reasons why western powers built overseas empires.

▥ REVIEW QUESTIONS

1. What is the difference between direct and indirect rule?

2. Chart Skills Give a reason why each of the following would favor the new imperialism: (a) a factory owner (b) a missionary.

THE PARTITION OF AFRICA

◾ TEXT SUMMARY

In the late 1800s, the powers of Europe wanted new colonies. They turned to Africa. By 1914, people in all African lands but Ethiopia and Liberia were subjects of foreign rule.

Europeans of 1800 knew little about Africa. Still, they helped shape its history. Since the 1500s, traders had sold African slaves. At last, in the 1800s, Europe outlawed the slave trade. Christian missionaries came to Africa to convert people to Christianity. They built churches, schools, and clinics. Missionaries intended to help the people they came in contact with, but often tried to replace native culture with their own.

Westerners had long traded on the coasts of Africa. In the 1800s, explorers went inland. The king of Belgium formed a company to trade in the Congo. Soon, other nations of Europe moved deep into Africa. These nations wanted to avoid conflict over African lands. In 1884, they met at a conference in Berlin, Germany. They did not invite any Africans. The Berlin Conference set up rules for colonizing Africa. By 1914, Europe ruled almost all of the continent. France gained large areas in the northwest of Africa. Britain took smaller regions, most of them rich in resources. Belgium, Portugal, Italy, and Germany also gained lands. (See diagram below.)

In many regions, Africans battled the invaders. In 1896, Ethiopia fought off Italian forces. It was the only successful fight for freedom.

THE **BIG** IDEA

In the late 1800s, European powers began colonizing Africa.

◾ GRAPHIC SUMMARY: *The Great Land Grab in Africa*

Africa, 1850

Africa, 1914

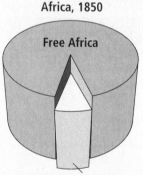

Free Africa

European Possessions
(French, British, Portuguese)

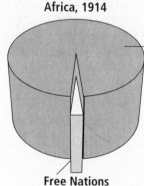

European Possessions
(French, British,
Portuguese,
Belgian, German,
Italian, Spanish)

Free Nations
(Ethiopia and Liberia)

Within about 20 years, European nations divided up the continent of Africa.

◾ REVIEW QUESTIONS

1. Name two groups of Europeans who helped shape the history of Africa.

2. **Diagram Skills** How did Africa in 1850 compare with Africa in 1914?

EUROPEAN CHALLENGES TO THE MUSLIM WORLD

■ TEXT SUMMARY

In the 1500s, huge Muslim empires ruled from western Africa to Southeast Asia. The largest, the Ottoman empire, stretched across the Middle East, North Africa, and part of Eastern Europe.

By 1800, the Ottoman empire faced problems that would soon tear it apart. Regions talked of breaking from the empire. Some Balkan states gained freedom, and Egypt slipped from Ottoman control. Revolts shook Arabia, Lebanon, and Armenia. In the 1890s, Turkish Muslims accused Christian Armenians of supporting plans against the empire. The Turks killed tens of thousands of Armenians. Europe watched the empire crumble, with Britain, France, Germany, and Russia all hoping to gain control.

Egypt in 1800 was on its way to becoming a modern nation. Its Ottoman governor, Muhammad Ali, became known as the "father of modern Egypt." He built up industry, backed irrigation projects, and encouraged world trade. Before Ali died in 1849, Egypt was becoming a major power in the Middle East. Leaders after Ali, however, allowed more foreign control. Britain gained the Suez Canal in 1875. In 1882, it made Egypt a British protectorate.

Like the Ottoman empire, Iran drew interest. Russia gained some power in the north. Britain gained some in the south. In the early 1900s, the discovery of oil in Iran upset the balance. The Russians, the British, and Iranian nationalists all set out to control the oil fields. (See diagram below.)

THE BIG IDEA

During the 1800s, the Ottoman empire was threatened by economic decline, nationalism, and the ambitions of European powers.

■ GRAPHIC SUMMARY: *The Competition for Oil*

Britain	Russia	Iranian Secular Nationalist Group	Iranian Muslim Nationalist Group
• Strongest influence in southern Iran • Anxious to protect its interests in India	• Strongest influence in northern Iran • Anxious to protect its own southern border	• Promotes acceptance of western ways • Supported by urban middle class	• Headed by Muslim religious leaders • Promotes antiwestern feelings

Iran found oil in the early 1900s and set off a struggle for control.

■ REVIEW QUESTIONS

1. What were two problems that the Ottoman empire faced?

2. **Chart Skills** Which two European powers competed for control in Iran?

THE BRITISH TAKE OVER INDIA

▣ TEXT SUMMARY

In the 1800s, a trade group called the British East India Company controlled over half of India. Agents used Indian soldiers, or **sepoys,** to protect their power. They angered the sepoys by ignoring Indian customs and demanding that the soldiers follow rules that were against their religions. In 1857, anger turned into the Sepoy Rebellion. Many lives were lost before Britain crushed the revolt. Britain saw that the East India Company could not keep control. In 1858, it made India a colony.

The British tried to solve problems in India but also caused new ones. Better farming methods and health care sparked a population boom that increased poverty and brought famine. Imported goods put local industries out of business. Top jobs went to the British. It was clear to the Indians that the British looked down on them.

Sons of the upper classes often went to school in Britain. As they learned about democracy, many wanted freedom for their own people. In 1885, they founded the Indian National Congress (or Congress party). The early 1900s brought demands for self-rule. By 1906, Muslims began to fear the Hindu-run Congress party. They formed the Muslim League and talked of a separate Muslim state.

> ### THE **BIG** IDEA
>
> **Following a failed rebellion in 1857, the British government increased its control of India.**

▣ GRAPHIC SUMMARY: *The Effects of British Rule in India*

BRITISH RULE IN INDIA

GOOD EFFECTS	BAD EFFECTS
• New roads and railroads link parts of India. • Telegraph and postal systems unite people. • Irrigation systems improve farming. • New laws mean justice for all classes. • British schools offer education. • Customs that threaten human rights are ended.	• Indian resources go to Britain. • British-made goods replace local goods. • Farms grow cash crops rather than food crops; Indians go hungry. • Top jobs go to the British. • Indians treated as inferiors. • Britain tries to replace Indian culture with western ways.

Britain felt it was helping India, but some policies hurt the colony.

▣ REVIEW QUESTIONS

1. What was one result of the Sepoy Rebellion?

2. Diagram Skills How did British rule help the industries of India? How did it hurt them?

CHINA AND THE NEW IMPERIALISM

SECTION 5

TEXT SUMMARY

Since 1644, rulers of the Qing dynasty had isolated China. They allowed foreign trade only through one small area in southern China. In the 1800s, western nations looked to China for trade rights and new markets for goods. When British merchants brought in opium, the Chinese outlawed the drug. In 1839, the Opium War began. Britain quickly won the war. China had to pay war costs and open ports to British trade. It also had to give Britain the island of Hong Kong.

By the mid-1800s, some Chinese saw a need to import western ideas. Others, including Qing rulers, saw new ideas and Christian missionaries as threats to Confucian traditions.

Wars and rebellions continued to weaken China. (See time line below.) In 1850, peasants rose up in the 14-year Taiping Rebellion. At its end, a weakened Qing dynasty still held power. In 1868, China lost Taiwan and Korea to Japan. The powers of Europe swiftly gained holds in weakened China. The United States called for an "Open Door Policy" that gave it equal rights to trade. In 1900, rebels known as Boxers set out to drive all foreigners out of China. Armies from Japan and the West crushed the uprising, and China had to give up more rights.

Reformers felt only a new government could save China. In 1911, nationalist Sun Yixian led a revolution that ended the Qing empire.

> ### THE **BIG** IDEA
>
> During the 1800s, western powers used diplomacy and war to win favorable trade agreements with China.

GRAPHIC SUMMARY: *Foreign Wars and Chinese Rebellion*

Qing Dynasty

1644
Qing rule begins

1850–1864
Taiping Rebellion

1900
Boxer Uprising

1911
Sun Yixian overthrows Qing empire; becomes president of Chinese Republic

A.D.

| 1600 | 1650 | 1700 | 1750 | 1800 | 1850 | 1900 | 1950 |

1839–1842
Opium War

1894–1895
War with Japan

A series of wars and rebellions weakened China and allowed more foreign control.

REVIEW QUESTIONS

1. Why were westerners interested in China?

2. Time Line Skills Name three wars or rebellions that weakened China between 1800 and 1900.

SURVEY CHAPTER 25
MODERN ERA CHAPTER 12 *Test*

■ IDENTIFYING MAIN IDEAS

Write the letter of the correct answer in the blank provided. (10 points each)

____ 1. How did the Industrial Revolution encourage imperialism?
  A. It made Europeans feel sorry for their "little brothers."
  B. It created a need for land.
  C. It created a need for raw materials and markets.
  D. It made Westerners feel obligated to improve the human species.

____ 2. One advantage European countries had in their imperial expansion was
  A. weak economies.
  B. a lack of resistance on the part of Africans and Asians.
  C. poorly organized governments.
  D. powerful armies and navies.

____ 3. Why did Christian missionary groups go to Africa?
  A. to gather slaves
  B. to study African culture
  C. to win souls to Christianity
  D. to map out the course of rivers

____ 4. Which European country gained large territories in the northwest of Africa?
  A. France
  B. Britain
  C. Germany
  D. Italy

____ 5. Which countries sought to benefit from the slow crumbling of the Ottoman empire?
  A. Britain and Italy
  B. France and Germany
  C. Russia, Italy, and Britain
  D. Britain, France, Russia, and Germany

____ 6. How did the discovery of oil in Iran affect imperialist interests in the region?
  A. Russia lost interest in Iran.
  B. Britain and Russia maneuvered for control of the oil fields.
  C. Iranian nationalists invited the British to take control.
  D. Russia and Britain moved their troops out of the region.

____ 7. Which of the following was a result of the Sepoy Rebellion?
  A. India gained its independence.
  B. India became a protectorate of Britain.
  C. Britain began to rule India as a colony.
  D. The East India Company took over the rule of India.

____ 8. The Indian National Congress wanted
  A. eventual self-rule for India.
  B. a revolution to end British rule.
  C. a tax on British goods.
  D. control of India.

____ 9. What was the result of the Taiping Rebellion?
  A. The rebels overthrew the Qing dynasty.
  B. Land reforms were passed.
  C. The Qing dynasty was weakened.
  D. Western powers took over China.

____ 10. What was the goal of the rebels known as Boxers?
  A. to work with Christian missionaries
  B. to set up protected communities
  C. to drive foreigners out of China
  D. to adopt western ideas

New Global Patterns (1800–1914)

SECTION 1 JAPAN MODERNIZES

■ TEXT SUMMARY

Since 1638, shoguns had closed Japan to visitors and trade. In 1853, United States warships sailed into Tokyo Bay. Commodore Perry carried a letter demanding that Japan open its ports. Japan could not fight the American navy. It soon signed the first of many trade treaties.

Some Japanese said the shogun showed weakness against the foreigners. In 1867, revolt ended shogun control. A young emperor began a long reign. (See diagram below.) The Japanese were ready to accept the western world and learn what they could.

By the 1890s, Japan had developed a modern army and navy. It had steel mills and railroads. The quick success was due to a number of causes. A common culture and language helped people get along. Also, the Japanese had a history of economic growth and of learning from foreigners. Finally, the Japanese were determined to resist foreign rule.

As industry grew, Japan needed colonies to supply raw materials. Gaining such colonies meant war. In 1894, Japan defeated China and gained claims in Korea. When Russia showed interest in Korea, Japan declared war. For the first time in modern history, an Asian nation defeated a European power. By 1910, Japan held complete control of Korea. An age of Japanese imperialism had begun.

> ### THE BIG IDEA
>
> To avoid domination by the West, Japan opened its doors to foreign influences and became a modern industrialized power.

■ GRAPHIC SUMMARY: *Japan During the Meiji Period*

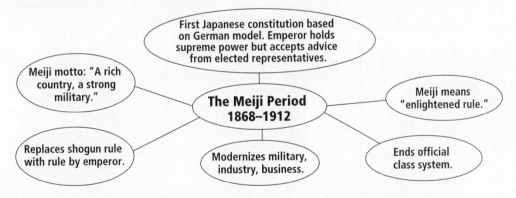

First Japanese constitution based on German model. Emperor holds supreme power but accepts advice from elected representatives.

Meiji motto: "A rich country, a strong military."

The Meiji Period 1868–1912

Meiji means "enlightened rule."

Replaces shogun rule with rule by emperor.

Modernizes military, industry, business.

Ends official class system.

Meiji leaders based new political, military, economic, and social systems on western models.

■ REVIEW QUESTIONS

1. What event urged Japan to open its ports to foreign trade?

2. **Diagram Skills** What were two ways Japan changed during the Meiji period?

SOUTHEAST ASIA AND THE PACIFIC

■ TEXT SUMMARY

In the 1800s, industrial powers looked to Southeast Asia for resources and markets. Christians saw a place to spread their religions. Just as it had in Africa, Europe began to grab land. The Dutch East India Company controlled the Spice Islands, and the Dutch set up colonies to grow coffee and spices. The people of Burma (now called Myanmar) did not realize the might of British forces. They lost many wars before falling to Britain in the 1880s. In Vietnam, leaders also failed to understand western might. The French gained Vietnam, Laos, and Cambodia. They called their holdings French Indochina. By the 1890s, Europeans controlled most

> ### THE **BIG** IDEA
>
> **Western industrialist powers divided up Southeast Asia in pursuit of raw materials, new markets, and Christian converts.**

of Southeast Asia.

The king of Siam (now called Thailand) did not underestimate western powers. He decided to learn from the West and build his own strength. Siam granted some rights to the West but remained a free kingdom. (See diagram below.)

The United States became an imperialist nation by reaching into the Pacific. In 1878, it gained rights in Samoa. In 1898, success in the Spanish-American War gave the United States the Philippines. In 1893, the queen of Hawaii tried to reduce foreign holdings. American sugar planters led a revolt. The United States annexed Hawaii in 1898.

By 1900, western powers held nearly every island in the Pacific. Soon Japan wanted its share, too.

■ GRAPHIC SUMMARY: *How Siam (Thailand) Remained Free*

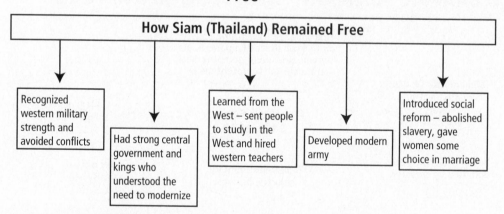

King Mongkut and his son brought new ways to Siam and kept out foreign rule.

■ REVIEW QUESTIONS

1. Which three European powers gained colonies in Southeast Asia?

2. **Diagram Skills** Why do you think Siam was able to remain free while Burma and Vietnam failed?

 **SECTION 3**

SELF-RULE FOR CANADA, AUSTRALIA, AND NEW ZEALAND

◾ TEXT SUMMARY

In the British colonies of Canada, Australia, and New Zealand, white settlers quickly outnumbered the natives. (See diagram below.) The British freed these colonies easily. They felt that whites were more able to govern themselves than the nonwhites of India and Africa.

Britain gained Canada from France in 1763. Following the American Revolution and a revolt in Upper and Lower Canada in 1837, Britain created the free Dominion of Canada in 1867. The new nation kept close ties with Britain.

The first Australians probably came from Southeast Asia. They became known as Aborigines. In 1770, British Captain James Cook claimed Australia. Britain first used the land as a **penal colony,** a place to send people convicted of crimes. A gold rush and fine sheep ranches brought new settlers. They moved into the rugged interior known as the **Outback,** pushing out or killing the Aborigines. In 1901, Britain granted self-rule. The new country still honored the British monarch as head of state.

In 1769, Captain Cook claimed New Zealand. In 1840, Britain annexed New Zealand and white settlers began to claim land. The local Maori people fought back. By 1870, most Maoris had died in wars or from disease. New Zealand gained self-rule in 1907. New Zealand, too, kept close ties to Britain.

THE **BIG** IDEA

The British colonies of Canada, Australia, and New Zealand won independence faster and with greater ease than territories in Africa or Asia.

◾ GRAPHIC SUMMARY: *Effects of Colonization*

COUNTRY	ORIGINAL PEOPLE	WAY OF LIFE	RESULTS OF COLONIZATION
Canada	Native Americans	• Many groups • Live throughout Canada	• Sign treaties giving up lands • Lose much of their culture • Government troops put down their uprisings
Australia	Aborigines	• Live in small hunting and gathering bands throughout continent • Speak over 250 languages	• Most pushed off their lands • Many killed • Give little resistance
New Zealand	Maoris	• Farmers • Live in one small area • Warlike	• Many die defending their lands • Many die from new diseases brought by settlers • By 1870, Maori population drops from 250,000 to less than 50,000

Europeans quickly pushed out the original people of Canada, Australia, and New Zealand.

◾ REVIEW QUESTIONS

1. Why do you think Britain granted self-rule to Canada, Australia, and New Zealand more easily than to its colonies in Asia or Africa?

2. **Chart Skills** What were two ways the Maoris of New Zealand differed from the Aborigines of Australia?

ECONOMIC IMPERIALISM IN LATIN AMERICA

◼ TEXT SUMMARY

> ### THE **BIG** IDEA
>
> **The economy of Latin America became dependent on industrial nations for investment, technology, and manufactured goods.**

Most of Latin America gained independence in the 1800s. Yet, life did not improve for most people. There were revolts and civil wars. Prejudice and poverty continued. A ruling class and the Catholic Church still controlled lands. Local strongmen known as **caudillos** put together armies and made themselves dictators. Revolts often overthrew the caudillos. Still, power stayed with a small ruling class.

Colonial economies had depended on Spain and Portugal. The colonies sent raw materials to their ruling lands. They bought finished goods from them. Later, Britain and the United States became trading partners with the freed nations. They took control of prices and set rules regulating trade. Latin America came to depend on them.

British and American companies wanted to guard their employees and investments in Latin America. They claimed the right to act when events threatened their interests. In 1823, United States President Monroe issued the Monroe Doctrine. (See diagram at right.) It said that the Americas were closed to further colonization and that the United States would oppose any European efforts to reestablish colonies.

In 1903, the United States wanted to build a canal across the Central American land of Panama. Colombia, which ruled Panama, refused to grant land for the canal. The United States backed a revolt against Colombia. Panama won freedom and gave the United States land to build the canal. Many Latin Americans saw the United States actions as interference and an example of Yankee imperialism.

◼ GRAPHIC SUMMARY:

The Monroe Doctrine

The Monroe Doctrine

The American continents are henceforth not to be considered as subjects for future colonization by any European powers.

- Issued by President James Monroe in 1823

- Prompted by Spanish plot to regain American colonies

- Backed by British naval power

The United States said it would stay out of European affairs and warned Europe to stay out of the Americas.

◼ REVIEW QUESTIONS

1. Describe three problems that troubled Latin American nations after independence.

2. Diagram Skills Why do you think the United States wanted to keep European interests out of the Americas?

IMPACT OF IMPERIALISM

◼ TEXT SUMMARY

The Age of Imperialism changed the West and its colonies. The industrial nations of Britain, France, Germany, and the United States controlled a new global economy. They sent goods, investment money, and knowledge to the rest of the world. In return Africa, Asia, and Latin America supplied natural resources, farm crops, and cheap labor. (See diagram below.)

In many ways, colonies suffered greatly under foreign rule. Imported goods wiped out local craft industries. Famines swept lands where farms grew export crops in place of food. Yet, foreign rule also moved countries into the modern age.

Imperialism brought an exchange of cultures. Europeans made it their mission to spread western ways. Many conquered peoples accepted new ways. They spoke western languages. They wore western styles. Some lost touch with their own cultures. However, others held on to their customs. In the end, most colonies blended old and new ideas. Imperialism enriched the West. Ties with Africa, Asia, and Latin America brought new art, music, fashions, and foods.

At times, more than one European nation tried to gain the same colony. Tensions rose as each feared the other would build a stronger empire. Conflicts sometimes threatened to end in war.

> ### THE **BIG** IDEA
>
> The Age of Imperialism brought an exchange of goods, money, materials, and ideas.

◼ GRAPHIC SUMMARY: *Imperialism Brings Great Change*

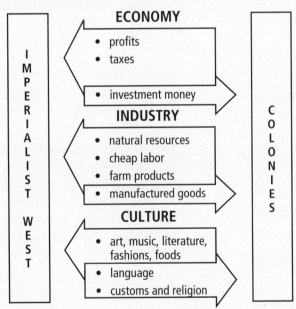

IMPERIALIST WEST

ECONOMY
- profits
- taxes
- investment money

INDUSTRY
- natural resources
- cheap labor
- farm products
- manufactured goods

CULTURE
- art, music, literature, fashions, foods
- language
- customs and religion

COLONIES

The Age of Imperialism produced a global economy.

◼ REVIEW QUESTIONS

1. Describe two ways colonial subjects reacted to the arrival of western culture.

2. Diagram Skills What were three things colonies supplied to the imperialist West?

SURVEY CHAPTER 26
MODERN ERA CHAPTER 13   *Test*

■ IDENTIFYING MAIN IDEAS

Write the letter of the correct answer in the blank provided. (10 points each)

____ 1. Which of the following results followed Perry's expedition to Japan in 1853?

A. Japan allowed the Dutch to trade at Nagasaki.

B. Japan opened its ports to American trade.

C. Japan closed its ports to all foreigners.

D. Japan defeated Perry's naval forces.

____ 2. Japan became an imperialist power by gaining control of

A. Russia.

B. Thailand.

C. Indochina.

D. Korea.

____ 3. Thailand remained independent partly because its rulers

A. sought protection from China.

B. did not modernize.

C. did not underestimate western power.

D. did not accept unequal treaties.

____ 4. American sugar planters asked the United States to annex

A. Samoa.

B. Hawaii.

C. the Philippines.

D. Japan.

____ 5. What did Britain first use Australia for?

A. as a market for goods

B. as a navy base

C. as an outlet for a growing population

D. as a place to send criminals

____ 6. How did independent Australia keep its ties to Britain?

A. by recognizing the British monarch as head of state

B. by keeping women from voting

C. by importing exclusively from Britain

D. by granting British citizens free land

____ 7. The United States intervened in Latin American countries in the early 1900s to

A. spread western civilization.

B. gain additional colonies.

C. protect American lives and investments.

D. grant independence.

____ 8. How did many Latin Americans view the Panama Canal?

A. as a hindrance to trade and shipping

B. as an opportunity for Panama to increase trade

C. as an engineering disaster

D. as an example of Yankee imperialism

____ 9. Western imperialist nations tried to modernize the lands they conquered by

A. adopting the cultural traditions of subject people.

B. imposing western culture on subject people.

C. encouraging subject people to keep their own traditions.

D. showing no interest in the cultures of subject people.

____ 10. The competition among western powers for global empires caused

A. Germany and France to unite.

B. increasing political tensions.

C. nationalist movements to die off.

D. the collapse of the British empire.

World War I and Its Aftermath (1914–1919)

SECTION 1 — *THE STAGE IS SET*

■ TEXT SUMMARY

In the early 1900s the world seemed at peace. People joined anti-war groups. Leaders met to talk. At the same time, however, other forces pushed Europe toward war. (See diagram below.)

One of these forces was **nationalism**— a strong loyalty to a nation and culture. Pride of country and fierce religious and ethnic bonds divided much of Europe.

Nations also wanted economic power. Britain had been a leader of industry. Now it had to keep up with modern German factories. Industrialized countries needed raw materials. France, Britain, and Germany all competed for lands in Africa.

Fearful of losing their colonies, nations built up military power. This **militarism,** or glorification of the military, led to an arms race. No one wanted war, but everyone was getting ready to fight.

Fear and distrust grew. Nations formed alliances, promising to protect each other against attack. By 1914, there were two big alliances. One was the Central Powers, including Germany, Austria-Hungary, and, for a short time, Italy. The other group was the Allies, consisting of Britain, France, and Russia. More nations soon joined the alliances. Each country promised to help its friends if war broke out in Europe. The stage was set so that a small conflict could easily become a huge war.

> ### THE **BIG** IDEA
>
> Aggressive nationalism, economic and imperial rivalries, and militarism pushed Europe toward war.

■ GRAPHIC SUMMARY: *The Push Toward War*

NATIONALISM	ECONOMIC CONFLICTS	MILITARISM	ALLIANCES
• German pride in military and industry • French anger toward Germany for earlier losses • Russian loyalty to all Slavic peoples	• Rivalries among Britain, Germany, and France • Desire to be leader of industry • Competition for colonies	• Race to build bigger armies and navies • Need to be ready for war • Image of war as glorious • Growing power of military leaders	• Uniting of Central Powers • Uniting of Allies • Russian agreements with smaller Slavic nations • Agreements to defend each other

WORLD WAR I

These forces crushed peace efforts and set the stage for war.

■ REVIEW QUESTIONS

1. How could strong alliances between nations turn a small conflict into a large-scale war?

2. Chart Skills Describe one force that pushed Europe toward war.

THE GUNS OF AUGUST

▥ TEXT SUMMARY

By June of 1914, Europe was tense. In an eastern region known as the Balkans, things were about to explode. Archduke Ferdinand of Austria-Hungary was going to visit the province of Bosnia. Many Serbs lived there. Some thought Bosnia should belong to Serbia rather than to Austria-Hungary.

As the archduke planned his trip, Serb terrorists made plans too. Gavrilo Princip was part of a group known as the Black Hand. Their goal was to join all South Slavic people in one nation. Now they plotted to kill the archduke.

On June 28, the archduke and his wife drove through the Bosnian city of Sarajevo. Acting on a Black Hand plan, Gavrilo Princip shot them.

Austria-Hungary blamed Serbia for the murders. On July 28, 1914, it declared war.

Alliances came into play. Germany stood by Austria-Hungary. Russia, a Slavic nation, backed Serbia. France came to the aid of Russia. On August 3, 1914, Germany attacked Belgium as a path to France. An angry Britain declared war on Germany. World War I had begun.

The **assassination,** or murder, of Archduke Ferdinand sparked trouble. However, most historians agree that all the nations involved must share the blame for the war no one wanted. (See diagram below.)

> ### THE **BIG** IDEA
>
> The murder of Archduke Francis Ferdinand of Austria-Hungary led to World War I.

▥ GRAPHIC SUMMARY: *World War I: Who Was to Blame?*

After the murder of Archduke Francis Ferdinand, each nation believed it had reasons for going to war.

▥ REVIEW QUESTIONS

1. How did Austria-Hungary react to the assassination of Archduke Ferdinand?

2. **Diagram Skills** Why did Germany get involved in the conflict? Why did Russia?

A New Kind of Conflict

◾ TEXT SUMMARY

Some have called World War I "The Great War." More troops fought and died than ever before in history.

Heavy fighting took place on the **Western Front,** a 600-mile stretch from the English Channel to Switzerland. The Germans hoped for an early victory there. However, French and British troops stopped them. For four years, neither side advanced.

Troops dug trenches along the front. When they came out to fight, many were killed. Neither side won much ground.

There was also an Eastern Front in Europe. One part ran from the Baltic Sea to the Black Sea. The other part ran between Italy (which joined the Allies in 1915) and Austria-Hungary.

This was the first war to make use of modern technology and machinery. Warplanes flew the skies. Submarines sailed under the sea. Machine guns, tanks, and poison gas made battles deadly.

World War I became a global conflict. Its effects were felt worldwide. (See chart below.) The powers of Europe looked to their colonies for soldiers, workers, and supplies. In the Middle East, the Ottoman empire joined the Central Powers. Japan, allied to Britain, took German colonies in China and islands in the Pacific. The United States would soon join the battle as well.

THE BIG IDEA

Modern weapons resulted in a huge number of casualties and stopped either side from gaining an advantage.

◾ GRAPHIC SUMMARY: *Technology Changes Warfare*

Invention	Description	Use in World War I
Automatic machine gun	Mounted gun that fires a rapid, continuous stream of bullets.	Made it possible for a few gunners to mow down waves of soldiers.
Tank	Armored vehicle that travels on a track allowing it to cross many kinds of land.	Protected advancing troops as they broke through enemy defenses. Early tanks were slow and clumsy.
Submarine	Underwater ship that can launch torpedoes, or guided underwater bombs.	Used by Germany to destroy Allied shipping. Submarine attacks helped bring United States into war.
Airplane	One- or two-seat propeller plane equipped with machine gun or bombs.	At first, mainly used for observation. Later, flying "aces" engaged in air combat.
Poison gas; gas mask	Gases that cause choking, blinding, or severe skin blisters; gas masks protect soldiers from poison gas.	Lobbed into enemy trenches, killing or disabling troops. Gas masks lessened the importance of poison gas.

World War I was the first modern, fully industrialized war.

◾ REVIEW QUESTIONS

1. Name three ways that World War I was different from earlier wars.

2. Chart Skills Which new weapon was partly responsible for bringing the United States into the war?

WINNING THE WAR

■ TEXT SUMMARY

World War I was what we call a **total war.** In a total war, all of a nation's resources go into the war effort. Governments drafted men to fight the war. They raised taxes to pay the costs of fighting. They **rationed**, or limited the supply of goods, so that they could supply the military. They used the press to publish **propaganda** that made the enemy look bad. Propaganda is the spreading of ideas to promote a cause or damage an opposing cause.

Women played a major part in total war. Many took jobs that soldiers left behind. Some joined the armed services. Others went to the fronts as nurses.

By 1917, Europe had seen too much death and ruin. In Russia, low **morale,** or spirits, led to revolution. Early in 1918, the new leader signed a treaty with Germany that took Russia out of the war.

Russia's withdrawal was good news for the Central Powers. However, there was good news for the Allies too. (See diagram below.) The United States was no longer neutral. In April 1917, the United States declared war on Germany.

With new soldiers and supplies from the United States, the Allies gained control. The other Central Powers had given up, and the Germans stood alone. They asked for an end to the fighting. On November 11, 1918, an **armistice,** or agreement to end fighting, was declared. The Great War was over.

> ### THE **BIG** IDEA
>
> In their efforts to win World War I, governments engaged in total war, committing all of their nation's resources to the effort.

■ GRAPHIC SUMMARY: *Events Change the Balance of Power*

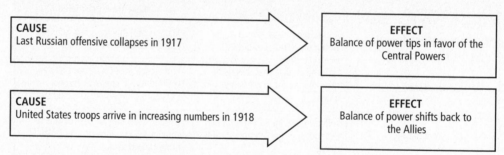

CAUSE	EFFECT
Last Russian offensive collapses in 1917	Balance of power tips in favor of the Central Powers

CAUSE	EFFECT
United States troops arrive in increasing numbers in 1918	Balance of power shifts back to the Allies

Events in Russia and the United States changed the balance of power.

■ REVIEW QUESTIONS

1. What did the warring nations do to support their war effort?

2. Diagram Skills How did the actions of Russia and the United States affect World War I?

MAKING THE PEACE

◪ TEXT SUMMARY

As World War I ended, Europe faced huge losses. (See diagram below.) Millions had died. More had been wounded. Hunger threatened many lands. In addition, a deadly epidemic of influenza swept the world in 1918.

Much of the European continent was in ruins. Cities had to be rebuilt. Governments had fallen in Russia, Germany, Austria-Hungary, and the Ottoman empire.

United States President Wilson and British Prime Minister David Lloyd George joined French leader Georges Clemenceau in Paris. They were the "Big Three" of the Paris Peace Conference. Each had his own goals. Wilson stressed **self-determination,** by which people choose their own government. Britain and France wanted to punish Germany.

By June 1919, the conference had drawn up the Treaty of Versailles. The document blamed the Germans for the war. They had to pay over $30 billion in **reparations** (payment for war damages), give up colonies and some European lands, and cut back their military.

There were other changes as well. New nations formed on land that had belonged to Russia, Austria-Hungary, and Germany. The treaty also set up the League of Nations. This group of over 40 countries hoped to settle problems without war. Though the league was Wilson's plan, the United States never joined.

> ### THE **BIG** IDEA
>
> **As Europe struggled to recover from the devastation of the war, world leaders met in Paris to craft a peace treaty.**

◪ GRAPHIC SUMMARY: *The Costs of War*

Human Costs	Political Costs	Financial Costs
• More than 8.5 million dead • More than 17 million wounded • Famine	• Collapse of governments • Unrest in colonies • Rising threat of communism	• War loans to repay • Factories, farms, homes, and roads destroyed • German reparations • Loss of economic and industrial power in Great Britain

In the years ahead, Europe would continue to pay the costs of war.

◪ REVIEW QUESTIONS

1. Why do you think Britain and France were concerned with punishing Germany?

2. Chart Skills Which financial cost applied only to Germany?

SURVEY CHAPTER 27
MODERN ERA CHAPTER 14
Test

◼ IDENTIFYING MAIN IDEAS

Write the letter of the correct answer in the blank provided. (10 points each)

_____ 1. What was one result of militarism?
   A. economic rivalry
   B. imperialism
   C. an arms race
   D. war in the Balkans

_____ 2. What was the main intention of the alliances formed among European nations?
   A. to create trading opportunities
   B. to discourage outside attacks
   C. to isolate the United States
   D. to increase tensions in Europe

_____ 3. Which of the following helped to start World War I?
   A. a poor economy
   B. the United States
   C. an environmental disaster
   D. an assassination

_____ 4. Why did the British declare war on Germany?
   A. to protect Belgium
   B. to punish Serbia
   C. to challenge Italian neutrality
   D. to gain territory

_____ 5. World War I was the first
   A. mechanized war.
   B. weaponless war.
   C. European war.
   D. British war.

_____ 6. The Allies used their colonies for
   A. a buffer zone.
   B. bargaining chips.
   C. financial support.
   D. soldiers, workers, and supplies.

_____ 7. How did governments pay for the war?
   A. raising taxes and borrowing money
   B. selling weapons to the enemy
   C. selling land to other countries
   D. spending less than they took in

_____ 8. Which of the following statements is true regarding the roles of women during World War I?
   A. They contributed little to the war effort.
   B. Their roles differed very little from their roles during peace time.
   C. They kept their nations' economies going during the war.
   D. They focused their efforts on ending the war.

_____ 9. In 1918, Europe was
   A. an economic giant.
   B. gearing up for war.
   C. in ruins.
   D. rebuilding itself.

_____ 10. What goal for the postwar peace was shared by the British and French leaders?
   A. to punish Germany
   B. to fashion "peace without victory"
   C. to establish a League of Nations
   D. self-determination for former colonies

Revolution in Russia (1917–1939)

 **SECTION 1** *TWO REVOLUTIONS IN RUSSIA*

■ TEXT SUMMARY

In 1917, Russia was in trouble. Millions of Russians had died in World War I. There was not enough food, and citizens were starving. Many people blamed Czar Nicholas II for the problems. A strike of workers began a revolution in March. A new government seized power and promised to be democratic. However, this government decided to continue the war against Germany. This decision drained more men, money, and food.

Vladimir Lenin, an enemy of the czar, returned to Russia in April from exile in Switzerland. He and his followers, the Bolsheviks, started a second revolution. Lenin called for a classless society based on socialist teachings of the German Karl Marx. He and his Bolsheviks promised "Peace, Land, and Bread" and won control of the government in November 1917. They set up councils, called **soviets,** to govern the nation. Lenin made peace with Germany, but for the next three years faced unrest in Russia.

Russians had expected democracy. But they found that the Bolsheviks, now called Communists, ran the soviets. A civil war erupted when rebel forces fought against Lenin's Red Army. By 1921, the Communists had defeated the rebels.

> ### THE **BIG** IDEA
>
> **Two revolutions rocked Russia in 1917.**

■ GRAPHIC SUMMARY: *Russia, 1917*

THE MARCH REVOLUTION

Causes
- Heavy loss of lives in WWI
- Food shortages
- Military defeats
- Power-hungry rulers

Goals
- Overthrow the czar
- Set up new Russian republic

Results
- End of czarist rule
- Beginnings of a constitution
- Continued war with Germany

THE NOVEMBER REVOLUTION

Causes
- Continued loss of lives in WWI
- Continued food shortages
- Continued military defeats
- Return of Lenin

Goals
- Bolshevik overthrow of government
- Ideals of Karl Marx applied to Russia

Results
- Bolshevik-run soviets control government
- End of private ownership of land
- Peace with Germany
- Outbreak of civil war

In 1917, there were two revolutions in Russia.

■ REVIEW QUESTIONS

1. Why were the Russians ready to revolt in 1917?

2. Diagram Skills What continuing problems caused both the March and November revolts?

FROM LENIN TO STALIN

◾ TEXT SUMMARY

In 1922, Lenin and the Communists controlled much of the old Russian empire. They called it the Union of Soviet Socialist Republics (USSR). The USSR, or Soviet Union, was made up of many **republics,** or states. Russia was the largest republic and it controlled the others.

Under Communist party control, the economy slowed. Lenin had said he wanted to put all factories and lands in the hands of the people. In truth, the party, not the people, was in charge. Lenin had to give up some of his socialist ideals. His New Economic Policy (NEP) allowed some private profit. It let peasants own plots of land. The NEP improved business and the standard of living.

When Lenin died in 1924, Joseph Stalin became head of the USSR. (See diagram below.) "Stalin" meant "man of steel," and this new leader was, indeed, cold and hard. Stalin destroyed all those he thought were against him. His police arrested millions and had them shot or sent to labor camps. He brought all factories and farms under government control. In his **command economy** government officials made all basic economic decisions. Workers who met their production goals were rewarded. Those who did not were punished. Some production levels went up. Still, most Russians were poor. Their standard of living and spirits were low. Stalin built up Soviet trade. Yet, many nations did not fully trust the USSR.

THE **BIG** IDEA

Lenin and Stalin were the first leaders of the USSR.

◾ GRAPHIC SUMMARY: *First Leaders of the USSR*

Lenin
(Soviet leader 1917–1924)
- *Chief goal: to create a classless society with production in the hands of the people*
- Allows some private business; lets some peasants hold land
- Standard of living rises for many workers and peasants

- Spent time in Siberian exile before 1917 revolution
- Became Communist party leader
- Uses secret police to enforce Communist will
- Wants to bring about a worldwide Communist revolution

Stalin
(Soviet leader 1924–1953)
- *Chief goal: to make USSR into a modern industrial power with all production under government control*
- Creates a command economy
- Brings all agriculture under government control; forces peasants to live on group farms
- Standard of living falls for most workers and peasants

Lenin established the Soviet Union under the Communist party. After Lenin's death, Joseph Stalin gained absolute power over the nation.

◾ REVIEW QUESTIONS

1. Who controlled farms under Stalin?

2. Diagram Skills How did the main goal of Lenin differ from that of Stalin?

LIFE IN A TOTALITARIAN STATE

◼ TEXT SUMMARY

Joseph Stalin turned the Soviet Union into a **totalitarian state.** In this form of government, a one-party dictatorship attempts to regulate every aspect of the lives of its citizens.

Stalin used propaganda to make himself a hero. His pictures appeared everywhere. Stalin **censored,** or withheld, news from inside and outside the USSR. The news said only what he wanted people to know. It spoke of the evils of capitalism, never of problems at home. He controlled all art so it showed only the good side of communism.

Fear taught Russians to be obedient and loyal. The Communists used secret police to silence all critics. They closed churches and synagogues and tried to replace religion with communism.

The totalitarian state changed Soviet life. (See diagram below.) The classless society did not happen. Members of the Communist party made up a new upper class. The Communists offered free schooling and health care. New laws gave women training and jobs. Still, the standard of living stayed low for most people. Housing, meat, fresh foods, and clothes were scarce.

When Stalin died in 1953, the Soviet Union had become a modern military and industrial power. However, it had gained that power through a strict program of censorship, propaganda, and fear.

THE **BIG** IDEA

Under Stalin, the Soviet government used propaganda, censorship, and terror to establish a totalitarian state.

◼ GRAPHIC SUMMARY: *Life in a Totalitarian State*

Economics	Politics	Arts	Religion	Society
• Growth of industry • Growth of military • Low standard of living • Shortage of foods and consumer goods	• One-party dictatorship • Total government control of citizens • Total government control of industry and agriculture • Use of propaganda to win government support	• Censorship of books, music, art • Purpose of all art to praise communism • Observation of artists, writers, and musicians by secret police	• Government war on religion • Takeover of houses of worship • Secret police control religious worship • Communist ideals replace religious ideals	• Fear of secret police • An upper class of Communist party members • Free education and health care • Public transportation and recreation • Jobs for women

From 1924 until 1953, Stalin controlled life in the Soviet Union.

◼ REVIEW QUESTIONS

1. What was one way Stalin made sure his people were loyal?

2. Chart Skills Describe one of the bad sides of life under Stalin. Describe one of the good sides.

SURVEY CHAPTER 28
MODERN ERA CHAPTER 15 *Test*

▪ IDENTIFYING MAIN IDEAS

Write the letter of the correct answer in the blank provided. (10 points each)

____ **1.** One cause of the March 1917 revolution in Russia was
   A. the death of Rasputin.
   B. food shortages.
   C. Lenin's return to Russia.
   D. the Treaty of Brest-Litovsk.

____ **2.** Lenin and the Bolsheviks promised the people
   A. "Victory and Recovery."
   B. "Peace, Land, and Bread."
   C. "Equality, Liberty, and Fraternity."
   D. "Prosperity and Brotherhood."

____ **3.** Which of the following was a result of the Bolshevik Revolution?
   A. civil war in Russia
   B. World War I
   C. war between Russia and Japan
   D. fighting between the Bolsheviks and the Red Army

____ **4.** What did Lenin call his economic program?
   A. the Great Purge
   B. the Five-Year-Plan
   C. the New Economic Policy
   D. Comintern

____ **5.** Which of the following statements is true regarding the Soviet Union under Lenin?
   A. It was a classless society.
   B. The government was democratic.
   C. The Communist party held absolute control over the government.
   D. Capitalism was completely abolished.

____ **6.** Stalin became the Soviet leader as the result of
   A. Lenin's death.
   B. Trotsky's assassination.
   C. a popular uprising.
   D. a free election.

____ **7.** Stalin mainly used propaganda to
   A. promote militarism.
   B. increase support for communism.
   C. wage a war against illiteracy.
   D. wage a war against smallpox.

____ **8.** By what means did Stalin's Communist party ensure obedience?
   A. persuasion and negotiation
   B. fair laws for all citizens
   C. secret police, censorship, and terror
   D. open warfare

____ **9.** What is one change that occurred in women's lives under the Communist party?
   A. New laws meant jobs for women.
   B. Women were kept out of most jobs.
   C. Women became leaders of the party.
   D. All women became full-time mothers.

____ **10.** Which of the following is a true statement regarding Soviet society?
   A. There were no social classes.
   B. Farm workers made up a new elite.
   C. Communist party members made up a privileged group.
   D. Landowners remained at the top of the social order.

Nationalism and Revolution Around the World (1910–1939)

SURVEY CHAPTER

29

MODERN ERA CHAPTER 16

 **SECTION 1**

STRUGGLE FOR CHANGE IN LATIN AMERICA

■ TEXT SUMMARY

After World War I, people all over the world wanted to control their own nations. Leaders spoke of self-determination. In some lands, they called for revolution.

Mexico was ruled by a dictator who welcomed foreign investors. They developed mines, built railroads, and drilled for oil. However, all the wealth and profits went to land and business owners. Most Mexicans were poor and had no land. In 1910, the people rebelled. They forced out the dictator, but the fight for sound government and freedom from foreign control lasted for years.

In 1917, a new constitution sought to reform laws governing land, religion, and workers. (See diagram at right.) In the 1920s, Mexican people became the first in Latin America to see real social and economic reform. Social change helped Indians regain land, supported labor unions, and spread education.

Nationalism swept throughout Latin America. By the 1920s, countries wanted economic independence from foreign nations, especially the United States. In response, the "Good Neighbor Policy" of the 1930s promised Latin America that

the United States would keep out of its affairs. Nationalism affected artists and writers as well. Art, books, and music showed a new pride in native culture.

THE **BIG** IDEA

Desires for land, better wages, and democratic reforms led to the Mexican Revolution.

■ GRAPHIC SUMMARY:

Mexico's Constitution

THE CONSTITUTION OF 1917
- Permits breakup of large estates
- Limits foreign ownership of Mexican land
- Returns some Indian lands
- Allows government takeover of natural resources
- Gives government control of church land
- Sets minimum wage for workers
- Protects the right of workers to strike
- Gives all men the right to vote
- Grants women some new rights

The constitution implemented reforms that were meant to serve all groups of society.

■ REVIEW QUESTIONS

1. Why were Mexicans unhappy with their government in 1910?

2. **Chart Skills** Identify three ways that the new constitution helped Mexican workers.

 **SECTION 2**

NATIONALIST MOVEMENTS IN AFRICA AND THE MIDDLE EAST

TEXT SUMMARY

As World War I ended, the people of Africa were growing tired of their colonial status. They paid taxes to foreign nations, fought their wars, and worked their farms. During the 1920s and 1930s, nationalists spoke of returning Africa to the Africans. There were few total revolts, but many protests. (See chart below.) Only Egypt won its independence.

Nationalist movements also grew in the Middle East. After World War I, the Allies had divided the lands of the defeated Ottoman empire. The Turks, however, would not accept foreign control. In 1923, they made Turkey a republic and replaced old Muslim traditions with western ideas. Nationalists in Iran followed Turkey's lead.

During World War I, many Arabs had helped the Allies. In return, they had been promised independence. Instead, Britain and France took over territories, or **mandates,** throughout the Middle East. In the 1920s and 1930s, Arab nationalists sought to be free of foreign control. They hoped to unite all Arabs in their own state.

There was great conflict in the British mandate of Palestine. The Allies had promised Arabs land that included Palestine. They had also pledged to set up a Jewish nation in the same region. Even now, Arab and Jewish nationalists battle over this same land.

> **THE BIG IDEA**
>
> Following World War I, nationalist movements grew in Africa and the Middle East.

GRAPHIC SUMMARY: *African Nationalism in the 1920s and 1930s*

Kenya	South Africa	Nigeria
Leadership: Jomo Kenyatta	Leadership: African National Congress (ANC)	Leadership: Ibo women
Protests against: • Loss of land • Forced labor • Heavy taxes • Laws forcing Africans to carry passes	Protests against: • System of apartheid that separates races • White control of best jobs, lands, schools, etc. • Laws forcing black Africans to carry passes	Protests against: • Loss of rights for women • No voice in government
Results: • Jailing of nationalist leaders • Continuing protests	Results: • Harsher system of apartheid	Results: • Protests silenced by British guns

In the 1920s and 1930s, Africans protested their treatment under foreign rule.

REVIEW QUESTIONS

1. What were two goals of Arab nationalists?

2. **Chart Skills** Name two reasons African nationalists protested foreign control.

INDIA SEEKS SELF-RULE

TEXT SUMMARY

In 1858, India became officially a British colony. As time passed, Indians called for more freedom. (See time line below.) In 1885, nationalists set up the Indian National Congress (later called the Congress party). They worked to give Indians a voice in running their land.

World War I made the nationalist movement stronger. Indian soldiers had fought for Britain, yet they had few rights at home. Britain failed to fulfill its promise to grant India greater self-government. Post-war anger led to protest. On April 13, 1919, British troops killed nearly 400 protesters in the city of Amritsar.

In the 1920s and 1930s, Mohandas Gandhi led the nationalist movement in India. He taught that nonviolent resistance and **civil disobedience** (the refusal to obey unjust laws), not bloodshed, were the way to win rights. His followers did not buy British goods or follow their laws. Peaceful resistance won some new rights. However, India did not gain total independence until 1947, one year before Gandhi died.

As India struggled to be free, tensions grew between two religious groups. Muslims worried that the Hindu majority would rule a free India. Some wanted their own Muslim state, called Pakistan. This conflict would divide India for years.

> ## THE **BIG** IDEA
>
> **After fighting for the British in World War I, Indian nationalists began demanding self-government.**

GRAPHIC SUMMARY: *India and the Road to Self-Rule*

1858
India becomes officially a British colony.

1918
WWI ends.

1920
Gandhi begins nonviolent resistance.

1947
India gains its independence.

1850 — 1900 — 1950

1885
Indian National Congress (Congress party) forms.

1919
British troops fire on protesters in Amritsar.

1930
Gandhi leads salt march to the sea.

1948
Gandhi is killed.

India was a British colony for almost 90 years.

REVIEW QUESTIONS

1. Why were Indians angry after World War I?

2. **Time Line Skills** When did Gandhi begin leading peaceful protests against British rule?

UPHEAVALS IN CHINA

◪ TEXT SUMMARY

The new republic in China faced problems. There was upheaval in 1912 when Sun Yixian stepped down as president. The new leader tried to rule like an emperor. When he died in 1916, warlords from the provinces fought for power.

On May 4, 1919, students protested Japanese control of colonies in China. This began the May Fourth Movement. Its supporters aimed to make China stronger through modernization. Other groups looked to the revolutionary ideas of Marx and Lenin for answers.

By 1921, Chinese Communists had

formed their own party. Meanwhile, Sun Yixian had formed a Nationalist party, the **Guomindang.** At first, the two parties worked together to beat the warlords and unite China.

When Sun died in 1925, Jiang Jieshi, the new head of the Guomindang, saw the Communists as a threat. He began a fierce, 22-year war. A new Communist leader, Mao Zedong, turned to the peasants for support. He saw strength in their large numbers.

As the Nationalists and Communists waged civil war, Japan attacked. Until 1945, the Guomindang, the Communists, and the Japanese fought to control China.

> ### THE **BIG** IDEA
>
> **The new republic of China was troubled by civil war and foreign invasion.**

◪ GRAPHIC SUMMARY: *Struggle for Control in China, 1931–1945*

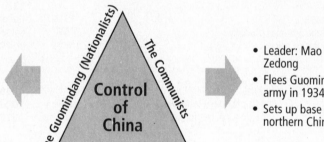

- Leader: Jiang Jieshi
- Forces Communists into northern China in 1934
- Loses capital city to Japanese in 1937; moves inland to new capital

The Guomindang (Nationalists)

Control of China

The Communists

- Leader: Mao Zedong
- Flees Guomindang army in 1934
- Sets up base in northern China

The Japanese

- Invades Manchuria in 1931
- Attacks China in 1937 and seizes Nationalist capital

The Guomindang, the Communists, and the Japanese all struggled for control of China.

◪ REVIEW QUESTIONS

1. When did civil war begin in China? What two parties fought for control?

2. **Chart Skills** Why did the Nationalist Guomindang move their capital in 1937?

EMPIRE OF THE RISING SUN

◾ TEXT SUMMARY

World War I helped expand the economy of Japan. The Japanese exported goods to the Allies. However, the economy slowed in the 1920s. Peasants were poor, and workers earned low wages.

Looking for change, Japan moved toward greater democracy. By 1925, all men could vote. Political parties were strong. The young Japanese backed the changes. They refused to follow traditions. They dressed in western styles and called for new rights.

In 1929, the world faced the **Great Depression.** During this period of economic downturn, nations could not afford to buy Japanese exports. Factories in Japan closed. Some Japanese blamed the democracy movement for the economic problems. Japan, they said, must expand its military and its empire.

Through the 1930s, these militarists gained power. (See diagram at left.) By 1937, democracy ended. Militarists demanded citizens serve the state and honor the emperor as a god. Schools encouraged nationalism and anti-western feelings.

During the 1930s, civil war raged in China. Seeing the chance to win lands, Japan attacked the weakened nation. (See Survey Chapter 29 and Modern Era Chapter 16, Section 4.) In 1939, as Japan fought for control in China, World War II broke out in Europe.

◾ GRAPHIC SUMMARY:

Japanese Militarists of the 1930s

CAUSES
- Unhappiness over loss of traditions
- Loss of foreign markets due to Great Depression
- Unemployment
- Poverty among peasants
- Feelings of nationalism
- Demand for expansion of Japanese empire

Rise of Militarists in Japan

EFFECTS
- 1931 attack on Chinese province of Manchuria
- Withdrawal from League of Nations
- Anti-western feelings
- End of many democratic freedoms
- Renewed practice of traditions
- Increased honor for emperor
- Renewed expansion and efforts to control China

The militarists gained power in Japan during the 1930s.

> ## THE **BIG** IDEA
>
> By the 1930s, the Japanese military dominated a government that emphasized service to the nation and a policy of imperialist expansion.

◾ REVIEW QUESTIONS

1. Why did the Great Depression cause problems in Japan?

2. Chart Skills What were two reasons the militarists were able to gain power in Japan?

SURVEY CHAPTER 29
MODERN ERA CHAPTER 16 *Test*

▪ IDENTIFYING MAIN IDEAS

Write the letter of the correct answer in the blank provided. (10 points each)

_____ **1.** The main cause of revolution in Mexico in 1910 was
   A. a repressive government.
   B. food shortages.
   C. the unequal distribution of land.
   D. high taxes.

_____ **2.** What was the goal of economic nationalism in Latin America?
   A. to encourage foreign investors to buy Latin American industries
   B. to remove the president from power
   C. to raise the value of oil and other resources
   D. to end foreign control of Latin American economies

_____ **3.** Why did the Arabs feel betrayed by the West following World War I?
   A. They wished to be given colonies in Africa.
   B. They had no voice in the League of Nations.
   C. They were promised independence but instead were carved into mandates.
   D. They believed the West owed them reparations from the war.

_____ **4.** When World War I ended, many Indians expected
   A. to gain more territory.
   B. to become citizens of Britain.
   C. separate states for Hindus and Muslims.
   D. greater self-government.

_____ **5.** What method did Gandhi adopt in his struggle against British injustice?
   A. guerrilla warfare
   B. nonviolence
   C. holy wars
   D. political action

_____ **6.** Which of the following was a protest urged by Gandhi?
   A. rioting
   B. attacks on British residents
   C. refusal to buy British goods
   D. refusal to wear cloth made in India

_____ **7.** The ultimate aim of the May Fourth Movement was to
   A. strengthen China by modernizing it.
   B. make China a military power.
   C. win equal rights for women.
   D. install a Communist government in China.

_____ **8.** Who believed the Communists should seek support among the peasants in China?
   A. Mao Zedong
   B. Sun Yixian
   C. Jiang Jieshi
   D. the Guomindang

_____ **9.** One effect of the Great Depression in Japan was that
   A. civil war broke out.
   B. ultranationalists demanded expansion.
   C. Japan gave up its claim on China.
   D. Japan went bankrupt.

_____ **10.** Under the militarists, the Japanese government taught schoolchildren
   A. western ideas.
   B. independent thinking.
   C. communist ideology.
   D. service to the state.

Crisis of Democracy in the West (1919–1939)

SECTION 1 — THE WESTERN DEMOCRACIES

TEXT SUMMARY

In 1919, Britain, France, and the United States were major world powers, but they and other nations faced serious problems. Soldiers returning from World War I needed jobs. Nations had war debts to pay and cities to rebuild.

Nations had seen the horrors of war. Now they looked for ways to keep peace. (See chart below.) During the 1920s, the League of Nations worked hard to resolve conflicts. In 1925, treaties signed in Locarno, Switzerland, settled German borders. The Kellogg-Briand Pact, signed in 1928, tried to limit arms. Sadly, these efforts could not protect the peace.

The United States was the leading economic power of the 1920s. When things went wrong there, the whole world was affected. In 1929, many Americans lost money in the stock market crash. Banks failed. Businesses closed. As a result, foreign trade almost stopped. The United States demanded that nations repay loans. The Great Depression of the 1930s began.

Worldwide depression left millions out of work. Across Europe, people lost faith in their governments. In France and Britain, democracy survived. In other nations, hungry, hopeless people turned to leaders who demanded absolute power.

THE BIG IDEA

Following World War I, the leading democratic powers faced difficult political and economic challenges both at home and abroad.

GRAPHIC SUMMARY: *Working Toward Peace*

	LEAGUE OF NATIONS	LOCARNO TREATIES	KELLOGG-BRIAND PACT
When?	1920	1925	1928
Where?	• Geneva, Switzerland	• Locarno, Switzerland	• Paris, France
Who?	• Organization of more than 40 nations	• Signed by seven European nations	• Signed by most nations of the world
What?	• Aimed to settle conflicts without violence • Aimed to protect smaller nations against attack by stronger ones	• Settled German borders with France, Belgium, Czechoslovakia, and Poland • Became symbol of era of peace	• Outlawed war • Agreed to solve problems by peaceful means • Promised to limit size of many navies
Why Failed?	• United States did not join • No power to stop attacks or prevent war	• Did not permanently end German attacks beyond its borders	• No agreements about limiting the size of armies • No means to enforce

After the horrors of World War I, nations wanted a lasting peace.

REVIEW QUESTIONS

1. Why did the Great Depression make some people want a change in government?

2. **Chart Skills** Give two reasons why the League of Nations failed.

A CULTURE IN CONFLICT

◼ TEXT SUMMARY

THE BIG IDEA

Western culture experienced great changes in the years following World War I.

After World War I, new ideas and discoveries created change. Scientists of the early 1900s questioned past ideas. Marie Curie found that some atoms change and give off energy. Albert Einstein presented surprising **theories,** or ideas, about measuring time and space. Sigmund Freud studied dreams to understand the human mind.

Post-war writers, artists, and musicians developed new styles. Many writers expressed a loss of hope in western civilization. Writers Virginia Woolf and James Joyce described the thoughts of their characters in a style called **stream of consciousness.** In this technique, a writer explores a character's thoughts without providing any logic or order. Many painters stopped trying to make art look like real life. Their designs used color and shape in unusual ways. African American musicians introduced jazz. The new music mixed western sounds with African rhythms.

Many young people of the 1920s liked the changes. In America, bold young women cut their hair short and wore short skirts. They called themselves **flappers.** Their styles soon spread to Europe.

Postwar years brought the right to vote to women in many western countries. Women began careers that had once been for men only. Some even held public office. Many fields, however, remained closed to women, and women doing the same work as men earned much less.

◼ GRAPHIC SUMMARY: *Revolution in Art, Early 1900s*

ARTIST	COUNTRY	STYLE
Henri Matisse (1869–1954)	France	Paintings unlike real life
Pablo Picasso (1881–1973)	Spain	Objects shown in new shapes and angles
Paul Klee (1879–1940)	Switzerland	Abstract paintings
Vasily Kandinsky (1866–1944)	Russia	Abstract paintings
Salvador Dali (1904–1989)	Spain	Dream-like paintings

Scientists, writers, artists, and musicians of the early 1900s experimented with new, sometimes startling, ideas.

◼ REVIEW QUESTIONS

1. Give two examples that show how the post-World War I era was a time of change.

2. Chart Skills How did Pablo Picasso's paintings offer a new view of reality?

FASCISM IN ITALY

TEXT SUMMARY

Italy was a troubled nation after World War I. The Paris Peace Treaties gave away lands the Italians had expected to control. Many war veterans could not find jobs. Trade was slow. Taxes were high. Workers held strikes. Officials argued among themselves, and the government seemed powerless. People wanted change.

Benito Mussolini took advantage of the unrest. In 1919, he gathered war veterans and other unhappy Italians. He called his group the Fascist party. Mussolini pledged to end unemployment. He promised to gain more lands and make the nation strong. The Fascists, he declared, would outlaw rebellion among workers and stamp out all threats of communism.

By 1925, the Fascists had used force and terror to gain control. They ended free elections, free speech, and the free press. They killed or jailed those who were against them. Desperate Italians accepted violence in exchange for order. They learned to put the goals of the state above individual rights.

Mussolini had promised change, and life did change in Italy. The economy and industry grew under state control. However, wages for workers fell. Men were expected to fight for glory. Women were expected to be mothers. Boys learned to be soldiers, ready to help Italy gain power.

THE BIG IDEA

Angered by political and economic problems, many Italians turned to Benito Mussolini and fascism for solutions.

GRAPHIC SUMMARY: *The Fascist State*

Fascism promised a strong government, but it took away freedoms.

REVIEW QUESTIONS

1. Why was Mussolini able to take control of Italy? Give two reasons.

2. **Diagram Skills** Name three characteristics of fascism.

HITLER AND THE RISE OF NAZI GERMANY

TEXT SUMMARY

At the end of World War I, the Kaiser stepped down, and Germany was in chaos. Moreover, the new government, called the Weimar Republic, had troubles. It took the blame for the terms of the Versailles peace treaty that left Germany weak. Political parties fought with one another. In 1923, inflation raised prices. When the Great Depression hit, Germans demanded a leader who could provide jobs and build pride.

That leader was Adolf Hitler. In 1921, the ex-soldier headed the National Socialist German Workers, or Nazi, party. Hitler said that Germans were a superior race who should build a new empire. The Nazis won many followers. In 1933, Hitler was appointed chancellor of Germany.

Like Mussolini, Hitler was a dictator. He built a one-party state, ended civil rights, and silenced enemies with force. Hitler put businesses under government control and raised the standard of living. Most Germans accepted the loss of freedoms. They did not question Nazi racism. They let Hitler blame troubles on the Jews. No one stopped his military buildup, an act outlawed by the Versailles treaty.

Poverty and civil conflicts let fascism take hold in new nations of Eastern Europe. As ethnic and religious groups fought for control, Fascist rulers promised to bring order. They took power in most Eastern European countries.

THE BIG IDEA

Under Adolf Hitler, the Nazi government used terror, repression, and one-party rule to establish a totalitarian state.

GRAPHIC SUMMARY: *Rise of the Nazis*

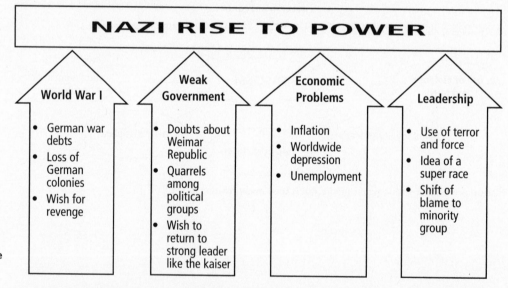

NAZI RISE TO POWER

World War I
- German war debts
- Loss of German colonies
- Wish for revenge

Weak Government
- Doubts about Weimar Republic
- Quarrels among political groups
- Wish to return to strong leader like the kaiser

Economic Problems
- Inflation
- Worldwide depression
- Unemployment

Leadership
- Use of terror and force
- Idea of a super race
- Shift of blame to minority group

By 1933, the Nazis had gained complete control of Germany.

REVIEW QUESTIONS

1. How was Hitler similar to the Italian leader Mussolini?

2. Diagram Skills Describe two factors that led to the rise of the Nazis.

SURVEY CHAPTER 30
MODERN ERA CHAPTER 17 *Test*

▣ IDENTIFYING MAIN IDEAS

Write the letter of the correct answer in the blank provided. (10 points each)

_____ 1. One effect of the Kellogg-Briand Pact was
   A. the pursuit of disarmament.
   B. the establishment of the League of Nations.
   C. the formation of new alliances.
   D. the end of war.

_____ 2. What is one way that the Great Depression affected the world economy?
   A. Governments lowered their tariffs.
   B. Standards of living rose in Britain.
   C. Workers staged a general strike in Britain.
   D. American banks demanded repayment of foreign loans.

_____ 3. Literature in the postwar period reflected writers' loss of faith in
   A. stream of consciousness.
   B. the Jazz Age.
   C. western civilization.
   D. women's rights.

_____ 4. What right did many women in western countries gain in the 1920s?
   A. the right to hold a job
   B. the right to vote
   C. the right to own property
   D. the right to speak freely

_____ 5. Problems in postwar Italy included
   A. overproduction of goods.
   B. economic hard times.
   C. famine.
   D. overcrowding in the cities.

_____ 6. Why were Italians attracted to fascism in the 1920s?
   A. It promised order in a time of uncertainty.
   B. It guaranteed a job for everyone.
   C. It promised to restore "rule by reason" to Italy.
   D. It restored the Church as the most important institution in Italy.

_____ 7. Which of the following describes fascism?
   A. It was democratic.
   B. It glorified blind loyalty to the state.
   C. It promoted Communist ideas.
   D. It condemned warfare.

_____ 8. For what did many Germans blame the Weimar Republic?
   A. the Versailles treaty
   B. its parliamentary government
   C. peasant uprisings
   D. the Dawes Plan

_____ 9. What changes in Germany biased people's judgment of Hitler?
   A. the economy improved
   B. women won equal rights
   C. freedom of religion was allowed
   D. the Versailles treaty was nullified

_____ 10. Which of the following helped Fascist leaders to gain power in Eastern Europe?
   A. a dislike for democracy
   B. an uneducated population
   C. large amounts of capital
   D. poverty and civil conflict

World War II and Its Aftermath (1931–1955)

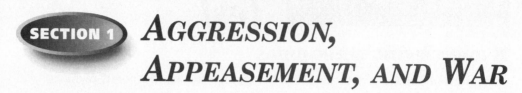

SECTION 1 AGGRESSION, APPEASEMENT, AND WAR

◼ TEXT SUMMARY

In the 1930s, Italy, Germany, and Japan wanted to build new empires. The three nations formed an alliance known as the Rome-Berlin-Tokyo Axis. They agreed to let each other attack and take over new lands. The League of Nations had no power to stop them. Most other countries avoided conflict out of fear of war. The world was busy recovering from the Great Depression. No one halted the acts of aggression that led to World War II. (See diagram below.)

In 1936, civil war broke out in Spain. Italy and Germany helped General Franco gain control. Both sides used new weapons and committed horrible acts of violence. The brutal war showed how much destruction a modern war could cause.

German aggression continued. Britain and France still tried to keep peace through a policy of **appeasement,** or giving in to the demands of an aggressor. The United States remained neutral. By 1939, Hitler had taken all of Austria and Czechoslovakia. It was clear that appeasement

had failed. Britain and France promised to protect Poland from Nazi attack.

In August of 1939, Hitler made a pact with Joseph Stalin, leader of the Soviet Union. The long-time enemies agreed not to fight each other. One week later, German armies invaded Poland. Britain and France kept their promise. On September 3, 1939, they declared war on Germany. World War II had begun.

◼ GRAPHIC SUMMARY:

Aggressive Steps to World War II

1939	Germany invades Poland; Britain and France declare war.
1939	Italy takes over Albania.
1938	Germany takes Sudetenland (a border region of Czechoslovakia).
1938	Germany makes Austria part of its empire.
1937	Japan takes over much of eastern China.
1936	Germany sends troops into Rhineland just outside French border.
1935	Italy invades Ethiopia.
1931	Japan invades Manchuria.

Throughout the 1930s, nothing stopped the acts of aggression that finally led to war.

> ### THE **BIG** IDEA
>
> **During the 1930s, dictators undermined peace by committing acts of aggression and taking foreign lands.**

◼ REVIEW QUESTIONS

1. What kept nations from stopping aggressive attacks by Japan, Germany, and Italy?

2. Diagram Skills What act finally forced Britain and France to declare war? In what year did that act take place?

THE GLOBAL CONFLICT: AXIS ADVANCES

◼ TEXT SUMMARY

During World War II, the Axis powers of Germany, Italy, and Japan were on one side. Allied powers of France and Britain were on the other. The Allies were soon joined by the Soviet Union, China, and the United States.

Axis powers wanted to conquer Europe. The Germans used a type of warfare called **blitzkrieg,** or "lightning war." Planes and new, faster tanks swiftly took Poland. The blitzkrieg overran most of Europe. France fell in June 1940. Britain stood alone against the Axis.

In September 1940, Hitler began a bombing, or **blitz,** of London. The British Royal Air Force used newly developed radar that detected approaching aircraft. They held off the Germans. The British, led by Prime Minister Churchill, would not give up. In June 1941, Hitler ended the bombing.

Then Germany turned to attack the Soviet Union for its many natural resources. The Russians fought back with great spirit. German troops suffered in the icy winter. In the end, the assault made Britain and the Soviet Union allies.

The Japanese wanted control of the Pacific but felt that the United States stood in their way. On December 7, 1941, Japanese planes bombed a naval base at Pearl Harbor, Hawaii. The next day, the United States declared war on Japan. Three days later, Germany and Italy declared war on the United States.

THE **BIG** IDEA

Armed with modern technology, the Axis powers rolled over much of Europe in the early years of World War II.

◼ GRAPHIC SUMMARY: *Modern Warfare of World War II*

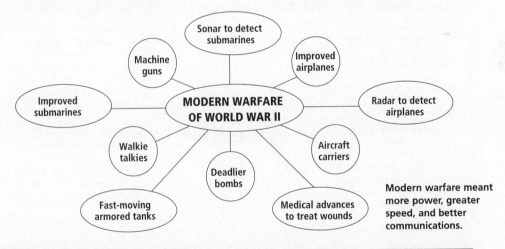

Modern warfare meant more power, greater speed, and better communications.

◼ REVIEW QUESTIONS

1. Why did Japan attack the United States, and what was the result of the attack?

2. Diagram Skills Which invention would have allowed (a) officers to keep in touch with their soldiers (b) planes to take off from the middle of the ocean?

THE GLOBAL CONFLICT: ALLIED SUCCESSES

■ TEXT SUMMARY

Germany and Japan wanted to establish total control of the people they conquered. The Germans robbed occupied lands of art and resources. Hitler planned to kill all people he thought were "racially inferior." Nazi racism was aimed most directly at the Jews. The Nazis built **concentration camps,** or detention centers for civilians, where Jews were starved, shot, or gassed to death. By 1945, over six million Jews had died in what became known as the **Holocaust.** Gypsies, Slavs, and the mentally ill were victims, too. The Japanese were also brutal rulers. They killed and tortured prisoners. They stole food crops and forced conquered people into slave labor.

> ### THE **BIG** IDEA
>
> From 1939 until mid-1942 the Axis had a string of successes. The tide began to turn when the Allies won key victories in 1942 and 1943.

Up until 1942, it looked like the Axis was winning the war. However, the Allied nations began to wage total war. Factories made tanks instead of cars. The Allies rationed goods to supply their troops. Women aided the war effort. They replaced men in jobs, served in the armed forces, and joined resistance groups. Even democratic countries limited civil rights during wartime. A fear of spies led the United States to force many Japanese Americans to live in special camps.

By 1942, Allied victories turned the tide of war. (See diagram below.) The first turning points came in North Africa, Italy, and the Soviet Union. On June 6, 1944 (D-Day), Allied soldiers landed at Normandy in France. They broke through the German lines and freed Paris. By the end of September 1944, all of France was free.

■ GRAPHIC SUMMARY: *Allied Victories of 1942–1943*

Battle of El Alamein 1942 British drive back German advances. This leads to German surrender of African lands.		**Battle of Stalingrad 1942–1943** Germans try to take Stalingrad. Russian troops and freezing weather force their surrender.
Invasion of Italy 1943 British and American forces land in Sicily and go on into Italy. Italian government surrenders. Hilter sends in Geman troops and fighting continues in northern Italy.	**TURNING POINTS IN WORLD WAR II**	**Invasion of Normandy (D-Day) 1944** Allied troops land on beaches of Normandy. They go on to free France from German control.

In 1942 and 1943, Allied victories turned the tide of war in their favor.

■ REVIEW QUESTIONS

1. How did the Germans and the Japanese treat the people they conquered?

2. Diagram Skills Give two reasons why the Germans were forced to surrender at Stalingrad.

TOWARD VICTORY

▨ TEXT SUMMARY

After their attack on Pearl Harbor, the Japanese won battle after battle. However, the tide of war turned in 1942. In the battles of the Coral Sea and Midway Island, American victories stopped the Japanese advance. Successful attacks moved United States forces closer to Japan. By 1944, their planes were bombing Japanese cities. Still, Japan would not **surrender,** or give up.

In Europe, Hitler fought to stop an Allied invasion of Germany. The bloody Battle of the Bulge in Belgium was the last real German effort. Air attacks pounded Germany day and night. Early in 1945, the Soviets moved in from the east, while the other Allied forces closed in from the west. As Soviet troops fought their way into Berlin,

Hitler committed suicide. Berlin fell on May 2, 1945. On May 7, Germany surrendered.

The Allies still had to defeat Japan. United States scientists had created an atomic bomb, more powerful than any yet known. President Harry Truman decided this bomb would bring the quickest end to the war. (See diagram below.) Truman warned the Japanese, but they would not surrender. So, on August 6, 1945, a United States plane dropped an atomic bomb on Hiroshima, Japan. Still, Japan did not give up. Three days later, a second bomb hit the city of Nagasaki. On August 10, the Japanese asked for peace. World War II was over.

THE **BIG** IDEA

The Axis powers finally fell in 1945, with the surrender of Germany in May and Japan in August.

▨ GRAPHIC SUMMARY: *The Atomic Bomb: A Difficult Decision*

PROBLEM
Should U.S. President Truman use the atomic bomb against Japan?

Reasons FOR	Reasons AGAINST
• It would save American lives. • It would bring a quick end to the war. • It would show the power of the United States to any future enemies.	• It would cause massive destruction. • Once used, it would more likely be used again. • It would release deadly radioactivity.

Decision
Truman orders atomic bomb dropped on Hiroshima and Nagasaki.

RESULTS
• More than 110,000 die. • Japan surrenders.

People continue to discuss whether or not the United States should have used the atomic bomb against Japan.

▨ REVIEW QUESTIONS

1. What two battles were turning points in the Pacific war?

2. **Chart Skills** Do you think the United States should have used the atomic bomb? Explain your answer.

FROM WORLD WAR TO COLD WAR

◼ TEXT SUMMARY

As the Allies celebrated victory, the costs of war began to come clear. The war killed as many as 75 million people. The Soviet Union had the most casualties, with more than 22 million dead. Cities were in ruins. Survivors faced hunger and disease. To keep the peace, 50 countries set up the United Nations (UN). The UN aimed to stop war, guard rights, and improve health and education.

> ### THE **BIG** IDEA
>
> **The United States and the Soviet Union emerged from World War II as dominant new superpowers.**

After World War II, the United States and the Soviet Union created the strongest military forces on Earth. Many Eastern European countries and part of Germany came under Soviet domination. The Soviet leader Stalin wanted to spread communism and create a **buffer** zone to prevent attacks from the West. The United States and other democratic countries opposed Stalin's plan. Tension between the two powers led to the **Cold War,** a state of conflict without armed battle. The "iron curtain" that separated Eastern Europe and free nations in the West became a symbol of the Cold War.

The United States took steps to stop the spread of communism. (See diagram below.) In 1949, the free nations of the West set up the North Atlantic Treaty Organization (NATO). To counter NATO, the Soviet Union formed the Warsaw Pact, joining the Soviet Union and its satellite nations in Eastern Europe.

◼ GRAPHIC SUMMARY: *Cold War Efforts to Halt Communism*

Truman Doctrine (1947)	Marshall Plan (1947)	North Atlantic Treaty Organization (NATO) (1949)
• U.S. program to stop the spread of communism • Formed by U.S. President Harry Truman • Offered to poor nations likely to fall to communism • States that United States would give military and economic aid to any country fighting communism • Aid given to Greece and Turkey	• Gave U.S. financial aid to rebuild Europe • Named after U.S. Secretary of State George C. Marshall • Gave over $17 billion in aid, including food, machinery, and raw materials • Welcomed by all nations of Europe except the Soviet Union and its Communist allies	• Joined United States, Canada, Britain, France, Italy, and six smaller nations in a military alliance • Formed to stop Communist takeovers in Europe • Maintained troops, military equipment, and weapons • Considered an attack against one member an attack against all

After World War II, the United States acted to stop the spread of communism.

◼ REVIEW QUESTIONS

1. What was the Cold War? Why did it begin?

2. Chart Skills How much aid did the United States send Europe under the Marshall Plan?

SURVEY CHAPTER 31
MODERN ERA CHAPTER 18 *Test*

■ IDENTIFYING MAIN IDEAS

Write the letter of the correct answer in the blank provided. (10 points each)

____ **1.** What position did the United States take as conflict engulfed Europe?
  A. sided with Germany
  B. sided with Britain
  C. declared war on Germany
  D. remained neutral

____ **2.** What German action finally caused Britain and France to declare war?
  A. the annexation of Austria
  B. the invasion of Poland
  C. the seizing of Czechoslovakia
  D. the invasion of Ethiopia

____ **3.** What new invention detected aircraft?
  A. sonar
  B. radar
  C. radioactivity
  D. the blitzkrieg

____ **4.** Japan attacked Pearl Harbor, Hawaii, to
  A. bring the war to an end.
  B. bring the United States into the war.
  C. end the United States presence in Asia and the Pacific.
  D. test the destructive power of its bombers.

____ **5.** The term *Holocaust* refers to the
  A. bombing of Britain.
  B. mobilization for total war.
  C. massacre of more than six million Jews.
  D. turning point of the war in North Africa.

____ **6.** As men went off to war, who took their place in factories and offices?
  A. prisoners of war
  B. soldiers
  C. foreigners
  D. women

____ **7.** What was the importance of the battles of the Coral Sea and Midway Island?
  A. They won the war.
  B. They were the last Allied successes.
  C. They stopped the Japanese advance.
  D. They stopped the German advance.

____ **8.** Which of the following was one reason that Truman decided to drop the atomic bomb on Japan?
  A. He had no other alternatives.
  B. He harbored ill feelings toward the Japanese.
  C. Experts had underestimated the bomb's capabilities.
  D. An invasion of Japan would have resulted in an enormous loss of American lives.

____ **9.** Which nation suffered the highest number of casualties in World War II?
  A. Germany
  B. the United States
  C. the Soviet Union
  D. Japan

____ **10.** The state of tension between nations without armed conflict was known as the
  A. iron curtain.
  B. Marshall Plan.
  C. Cold War.
  D. world war.

The World Since 1945: An Overview (1945–Present)

SECTION 1 · THE CHANGING POLITICAL CLIMATE

TEXT SUMMARY

Soon after World War II, empires of Europe crumbled as colonies in Africa, Asia, and the Middle East called for self-rule. At first, Britain, France, and others tried to hold on to their colonies. However, the war had used up their military and financial resources. Nearly 100 nations gained freedom during the era known as the "The Great Liberation."

Cold War tensions increased because both the United States and the Soviet Union wanted to make the new countries their allies. Each offered aid to developing nations. In addition, the new nations faced other problems. Some groups wanted free elections.

Some leaders wanted one-party rule. People of different ethnic groups quarreled. Countries struggled through civil wars and revolutions.

New transportation and communication systems have made the world more interdependent. Nations count on each other for goods and information. Nations also share troubles. Nuclear weapons are a threat to peace. **Terrorism,** the deliberate use of violence to achieve political goals, spreads fear throughout the world. The United Nations (UN) has expanded to deal with global issues. It must decide if it should step in when human rights are in danger. The UN and other groups do their best to solve global problems. (See chart below.)

> ### THE **BIG** IDEA
>
> The balance of world power shifted after World War II, with the United States and the Soviet Union emerging as superpowers.

GRAPHIC SUMMARY: *Global Problem Solvers*

INTERNATIONAL ORGANIZATIONS	
Health, Welfare, and International Relations	**International Economics**

• United Nations (UN)
    –Settles disagreements
 	
 • World Health Organization (WHO)
    –A UN agency; provides health services
 	
 • International Olympic Committee
    –Promotes good relations through
     international athletic games
 	
 • International Red Cross
    –Provides emergency relief worldwide
	• European Community
	    –Promotes and controls trade among nations
	     of Europe
	
	 • Association of Southeast Asian Nations (ASEAN)
	    –Promotes and controls trade among nations
	     of Southeast Asia
	
	 • World Bank
	    –Makes loans to developing nations

International organizations strengthen ties between nations and solve problems.

REVIEW QUESTIONS

1. What happened during the Great Liberation?

2. **Chart Skills** Describe a goal of each of the following: (a) World Bank (b) International Red Cross.

GLOBAL ECONOMIC TRENDS

■ TEXT SUMMARY

The world is made up of rich nations and poorer ones. A land with strong industries and trade is known as a **developed nation.** Most of its people can read and write. The birthrate is low. Health services are good. A developed nation has a high standard of living. In **developing nations,** most people are poor. They do not have good schools or roads. Farming is the most common type of work.

Most developed nations lie in a zone known as the global North. It includes all of Western Europe and North America, as well as Japan and Australia. Since most poor nations lie south of the Equator, the developing world is called the global South. Much of Asia, Africa, and Latin America are in this zone.

Certain problems are common to the global South. Many developing nations are held back by unfavorable climate, civil war, and dense population. They depend on the help of other countries. All these problems block progress.

In both rich and poor nations, economic growth can harm the environment. Industries use up natural resources. Factories pollute water, air, and soil. Accidents and errors threaten crops, animals, and people. These are global concerns.

> ### THE **BIG** IDEA
>
> **The global North includes many wealthy industrial nations. The global South includes many developing nations.**

■ GRAPHIC SUMMARY: *Hurdles to Development*

Geography	Population and Poverty	Economic Dependence	Economic Policies	Political Unrest
• Difficult climate (dry spells, floods, wind storms) • Few natural resources • Poor soil for farming	• High birthrate • Traditions encourage large families • Not enough food, housing, jobs, medical care	• Dependence on developed nations for manufactured goods and technology • Dependence on one crop • Heavy borrowing from foreign banks, high interest rates	• Unsuccessful attempts to follow socialism • Inability of government to pay for big projects • Spending on weapons instead of health care, education, housing	• Quarrels among religious groups • Civil wars • Conflict between Soviet efforts to encourage communism and U.S. efforts to encourage democracy

Developing nations face many difficult problems.

■ REVIEW QUESTIONS

1. What is the difference between a developed nation and a developing nation?

2. Chart Skills What is one way geography can get in the way of economic development?

CHANGING PATTERNS OF LIFE

◼ TEXT SUMMARY

During this century, much of the world has changed from a rural lifestyle to an urban one. Most people have moved in search of jobs. This **migration,** or movement, to the cities has changed both *where* and *how* people live. Children learned new values in city schools. Some grew up speaking a new language. Urban families tended to be small. Extended family members lived miles apart.

> ### THE **BIG** IDEA
> **Urbanization has changed the lives of people in the developing world.**

Most modern societies work to provide equal rights for men and women. Women continue to gain better education, jobs, and pay. Yet, change does not always bring an easier life. While taking on new roles, many women still have the full responsibility for child care and housework.

Since 1945, technology has improved the standard of living for much of the world. Satellites, computers, and fax machines spread ideas rapidly and link nations. People share fashion styles, music, art, and foods. Countries not only depend on each other for economic success. They also enjoy a new global culture.

However, each breakthrough has its limits. (See chart below.) Many developing nations cannot pay for new technology. For example, those most in need of food cannot afford to buy farm machines. So, poor countries fall farther behind. In some ways, technology has widened the gulf between the global North and the global South.

◼ GRAPHIC SUMMARY: *New Technology: Benefits and Limits*

TECHNOLOGY	BENEFITS (+)	LIMITS (–)
The computer revolution	• Creates new jobs • Links people, businesses, nations • Makes more information available	• Threatens some jobs • Available only to those who can afford equipment • Widens gap between global North and global South
Medical breakthroughs	• Prevents illnesses • Wipes out diseases • Makes surgery safer	• Available only to nations and people who can afford them • Presents new problems with genetic engineering
Revolution in agriculture (The Green Revolution)	• Increases food production • Develops new food products	• May succeed only where rainfall is regular • Requires costly chemicals • High cost may force out small farmers

Since 1945, technology has greatly changed human life.

◼ REVIEW QUESTIONS

1. Give an example of how urbanization changed older ways of life.

2. **Chart Skills** How has new technology widened the gap between wealthy nations and poorer ones?

SURVEY CHAPTER 32
MODERN ERA CHAPTER 19 *Test*

◼ IDENTIFYING MAIN IDEAS

Write the letter of the correct answer in the blank provided. (10 points each)

_____ **1.** The United States and the Soviet Union competed for influence in the developing world by offering
   A. independence.
   B. an end to the Cold War.
   C. military and economic aid.
   D. resolution of old border disputes.

_____ **2.** One organization that has expanded to deal with issues of global interdependence is the
   A. Senate.
   B. Communist party.
   C. United Nations.
   D. World Bank.

_____ **3.** Many nations wonder whether the world community has a right to intervene to stop
   A. the Cold War.
   B. terrorism.
   C. human rights abuses in other countries.
   D. global interdependence.

_____ **4.** Which of the following best describes the global North?
   A. poor
   B. developing
   C. rich
   D. Third World

_____ **5.** Which of the following best describes the global South?
   A. poor
   B. rich
   C. industrial
   D. north of the equator

_____ **6.** Which of the following poses the most immediate challenge to many developing nations?
   A. population growth
   B. nuclear proliferation
   C. migration
   D. global warming

_____ **7.** Many people in developing nations have moved to the city to find
   A. movies, stores, and sports.
   B. a traditional village life.
   C. religion.
   D. jobs.

_____ **8.** Across the world, women have continued to bear most of the burden for
   A. child-rearing.
   B. participating in government.
   C. filling high-paying jobs.
   D. developing new technologies.

_____ **9.** Technology has helped form a global culture by
   A. making all cultures alike.
   B. spreading ideas rapidly.
   C. mass-producing works of art.
   D. giving all people everywhere access to computers.

_____ **10.** While computers led to an information revolution, they also added to the gap between
   A. science and the arts.
   B. men and women.
   C. socialism and capitalism.
   D. the global North and South.

Europe and North America (1945–Present)

SECTION 1

THE WESTERN WORLD: AN OVERVIEW

◼ TEXT SUMMARY

For more than 40 years, the Cold War divided Europe. Berlin, Germany, was a Cold War trouble spot. After World War II, the city was divided into the democratic West and the communist East. In 1961, the communists built a wall to stop East Germans from fleeing into West Berlin. In addition, distrust led both the United States and the Soviet Union to build more nuclear weapons. However, Soviet and American leaders knew an arms race could bring disaster. In the 1970s, a joint effort called **détente,** or lessening of bad feelings, aimed to ease tensions and limit arms.

As Western Europe recovered after World War II, the economy grew. Nations set up **welfare,** or government aid programs, to aid the needy. In 1957, much of Western Europe joined the Common Market (later called the European Community and European Union). This powerful trade alliance worked to end tariffs and to move goods freely across borders. However, economic growth slowed in the 1970s. (See diagram below.) Western industries faced an oil crisis when oil-producing nations decreased production and increased prices. New competition from Japan, China, and India contributed to an economic slowdown that forced governments to cut costs.

> ### THE **BIG** IDEA
>
> Western Europe rebuilt quickly after World War II, but faced problems in the 1970s.

◼ GRAPHIC SUMMARY: *Post-World War II Economy of Western Europe*

Economic growth in the post-World War II years gave way to recession in the 1970s.

Economic Growth
1945 through 1960s

CAUSES
- Marshall Plan helps post-war rebuilding.
- Six European nations unite in the Common Market.

EFFECTS
- Governments set up welfare programs to aid the poor, the elderly, and those out of work.

Economic Decline
of the 1970s and 1980s

CAUSES
- 1973 oil crisis raises fuel prices.
- Other nations gain industrial strength and increase competition.
- Developing nations offer cheap labor; manufacturing shifts to other parts of the world.

EFFECTS
- Jobs in service industries replace jobs in manufacturing.
- Lack of funds forces cuts in welfare programs.

◼ REVIEW QUESTIONS

1. How was the Cold War a threat to peace in Europe?

2. Diagram Skills What were two causes of the economic decline of the 1970s?

THE WESTERN EUROPEAN DEMOCRACIES

◼ TEXT SUMMARY

After 1945, Western Europe joined forces through trade and military alliances. Still, difficulties existed for the nations.

Britain was economically drained by World War II. In 1945, the Labour party came into power. Labour put industries under government control and created a welfare state to care for the needy. After the economy slowed, the Conservative party returned to power in 1979. It put factories back in private hands, reduced the size of government, and cut welfare to save funds. People were out of work and general unrest resulted.

Weakened by the war, France also faced problems. In the 1950s, civil war threatened. The economy was weak, and French colonies fought to be free. France turned to Charles de Gaulle. Under President de Gaulle, Algeria and other colonies gained independence. De Gaulle worked to make France a world power once more. He supported the development of nuclear weapons and energy, held talks with communist states, and formed ties with West Germany. By the 1970s, France welcomed new power and prosperity.

Western democracies helped West Germany rebuild quickly with Allied help. However, communist East Germany did not do as well. Many Germans dreamed of living in one strong nation again. By 1989, communists had lost control. In 1990, Germans voted to reunite, but the transition proved difficult.

THE BIG IDEA

After 1945, the Western European democracies worked with increased cooperation, but each nation faced its own problems.

◼ GRAPHIC SUMMARY: *Germany Divided and Reunited*

1990	Germans vote to unite. Helmut Kohl becomes chancellor of a reunited Germany.
1989	Communism falls in Soviet Union leaving East Germany without support. Berlin Wall comes down.
1969	West German chancellor Willy Brandt tries to ease tensions with East Germany. His "eastern policy" aims to reunite Germany.
1961	East German communists divide East and West Berlin with the Berlin Wall.
1948	Soviet leader Stalin tries to force Allies out of Berlin with a blockade. Allies airlift supplies into the city.
1945	Allies divide Germany. British, American, French zones become West Germany. Russian zone becomes East Germany.

The Cold War increases tensions between East and West Germany.

In 1990, Germans reunited their divided land.

◼ REVIEW QUESTIONS

1. Why did Britain cut welfare services in the 1980s?

2. Diagram Skills What 1989 event allowed Germany to finally reunite?

NORTH AMERICAN PROSPERITY

■ TEXT SUMMARY

After World War II, the West felt threatened by communism. The United States wanted to stop that threat at home and around the world. American troops fought communism in Korea in the 1950s and in South Vietnam in the 1960s and 1970s. Economic aid helped keep communism out of developing lands. By 1990, the Cold War had ended. Still, the United States protected human rights and resolved conflicts.

In the 1950s, the United States economy boomed and social reforms changed life. Many Americans bought homes in the suburbs. Programs helped veterans, the elderly, and the poor. In the 1950s and 1960s, a civil rights movement demanded equality for African Americans. It worked to end **segregation,** the separation of people by race, in schools, jobs, and housing. Leaders organized **boycotts,** the refusal to buy goods for political reasons, and staged protest marches. As a result, Congress passed new laws to ensure rights. This movement led other minorities to call for equality.

Canada also faced challenges after World War II. Canada welcomed **immigrants,** people moving to a country permanently, because it had plenty of land and an economic boom. Yet, Canada faced unrest in its province of Quebec. French-speaking Canadians wanted to form their own nation. Today, the United States and Canada enjoy close ties. Their border is a free-trade zone, and they work together to ease pollution.

> **THE BIG IDEA**
>
> After World War II, the United States took on the role of protecting the free world and stopping the spread of communism.

■ GRAPHIC SUMMARY: *The United States After World War II*

1950s	1960s	1970s	1980s	1990s
• Economic boom • Korean War • Red (Communist) scare and McCarthy hearings • Civil rights movement		• Withdrawal from Vietnam • High fuel prices due to oil crisis		• End of the Cold War • Gulf War in Kuwait and Iraq • Restoration of democracy in Haiti through U.S. help
	• Continuing civil rights movement • Vietnam War • Increase in social services		• Cutbacks in spending on social services • Federal budget problems • Call for stricter immigration laws	

After World War II, Americans fought to protect democracy, gain civil rights, and balance the federal budget.

■ REVIEW QUESTIONS

1. What job did the United States take on after World War II?

2. Time Line Skills When did the United States send troops to fight communism in Korea?

THE SOVIET UNION: RISE AND FALL OF A SUPERPOWER

■ TEXT SUMMARY

After World War II, the Soviet Union was a superpower. Stalin still was firmly in control. He poured money into industry, science, and the military. His labor camps forced political prisoners to toil for their country.

■ GRAPHIC SUMMARY:
The Fall of the Soviet Union

CAUSES
- Leadership of Mikhail Gorbachev
- Openness to democratic ideas (glasnost)
- Reshaping of economy and government (perestroika)
- Economic problems
- Freedom movement in Eastern Europe

Fall of the Soviet Union

EFFECTS
- Loss of role as world superpower
- End of the Cold War
- Economic hardships
- Conflicts between pro-communist and pro-democratic groups
- Minority revolts and civil conflicts

By the end of 1991, the Soviet Union no longer existed.

After Stalin died in 1953, Nikita Khrushchev became the next Communist head. He allowed more freedom. Citizens enjoyed low rents, free health care, and jobs for almost everyone. However, they waited in long lines to buy goods. In 1962, Khrushchev nearly set off a war when he sent missiles to Cuba.

Under Leonid Brezhnev, Soviet life got worse. He jailed critics. He talked of limiting arms but began a military buildup. Brezhnev insisted he could send troops to any Warsaw Pact nation.

In 1985, Mikhail Gorbachev came to power. He reshaped the economy and allowed some private business in a process called **perestroika.** Soviets gained new freedom. However, new policies caused food and medicine shortages. The Gorbachev reforms sparked demands for democracy in Eastern Europe. They also led Soviet republics to seek independence. In 1991, the Soviet Union **disbanded,** or broke up. The republics formed the Commonwealth of Independent States.

The new Russian Federation faced hard times. Russia and the other republics had to deal with such problems as food shortages, massive debts and unemployment, and ethnic unrest.

THE **BIG** IDEA

Despite its early status as a super-power, the Soviet Union collapsed in the 1990s under pressure to reform.

■ REVIEW QUESTIONS

1. How was Gorbachev different from earlier Soviet leaders?

2. Diagram Skills What effect did the fall of the Soviet Union have on the Cold War?

SECTION 5 · A NEW ERA IN EASTERN EUROPE

▣ TEXT SUMMARY

In 1945, most of Eastern Europe was tied to the Soviet Union. Communists controlled government and industry. They censored the press and jailed critics.

> ### THE **BIG** IDEA
>
> **Soviet domination of Eastern Europe came to an end in 1989 and 1990.**

In 1955, the Warsaw Pact linked the Soviet Union and its satellites in a military alliance. In 1956, Hungary tried to cut the ties. Soviet troops crushed the movement. In 1968, tanks rolled in to enforce communist control in Czechoslovakia.

Communists worked hard to keep a hold on Poland. In 1980, Polish workers set up a union called Solidarity. The Communists outlawed the union and jailed its leader. However, in 1989, Gorbachev pledged to stay out of Eastern Europe. Poland held elections. Solidarity leaders won office. Soon, a freedom movement swept Eastern Europe. One by one, communist governments fell.

Under communism, **ethnic,** or racial, tensions were put down. In 1991, Yugoslavia split into several nations. Fighting broke out between the countries, but the worst was in Bosnia, where the Serbs wanted to drive out all other ethnic groups. They began attacking **civilians,** or nonmilitary people. In 1995, the Bosnian Serbs signed a peace agreement after being bombed by NATO. Then, in 1998, Serbs wanted to drive Albanians out of the region called Kosovo. Again, NATO bombed Yugoslavia in order to stop the Serbs, and Yugoslavia signed a peace agreement.

▣ GRAPHIC SUMMARY: *The Fall of Communism in Eastern Europe*

Freedom Sweeps Eastern Europe

- **Romania** Freedom protests answered with violence; dictator arrested and executed: 1989
- **Poland** Free elections: 1989
- **Hungary** Breakup of Communist party: 1989
- **East Germany** Berlin Wall opened: 1989 Free elections: 1990
- **Czechoslovakia** Free elections: 1989
- **Yugoslavia** End of Communist party control; promise of free elections: 1990
- **Bulgaria** Communist leader steps down: 1989

The fall of communism came peacefully in most nations, but in Romania there was a bloody revolution.

▣ REVIEW QUESTIONS

1. Why did war break out in Bosnia-Herzegovina?

2. Diagram Skills In what year did communism fall in most of Eastern Europe?

SURVEY CHAPTER 33
MODERN ERA CHAPTER 20 *Test*

▪ IDENTIFYING MAIN IDEAS

Write the letter of the correct answer in the blank provided. (10 points each)

____ 1. Why did the East German government build a wall through East Berlin in 1961?
  A. to stop traffic jams
  B. to stop westerners from entering
  C. to stop its citizens from fleeing to the West
  D. to stop nuclear buildup

____ 2. Which of the following best describes the European Union?
  A. weak
  B. destructive
  C. authoritarian
  D. powerful

____ 3. What caused the British to roll back the welfare state after 1979?
  A. economic prosperity
  B. a liberal government
  C. a socialist government
  D. economic hard times

____ 4. Which of the following was accomplished by Charles de Gaulle of France?
  A. winning Algeria as a colony
  B. asserting French leadership in Europe
  C. breaking off relations with West Germany
  D. ending the Cold War

____ 5. During the Cold War, the primary goal of American foreign policy was to
  A. protect human rights everywhere.
  B. encourage economic growth in communist countries.
  C. stop the spread of communism.
  D. create a world without war.

____ 6. Which of the following is the goal of separatism in Quebec?
  A. to cut ties with the United States
  B. to become an independent nation
  C. to limit immigration
  D. to quit NATO

____ 7. Which of the following did citizens enjoy under communism in the Soviet Union?
  A. abundant goods
  B. high-quality goods
  C. virtually nonexistent unemployment
  D. plentiful food

____ 8. What was one result of Gorbachev's reforms?
  A. economic stability
  B. a return to Stalinist policies
  C. independence for former Soviet republics
  D. declining unemployment

____ 9. After World War II, much of Eastern Europe was controlled by
  A. the United States.
  B. the Soviet Union.
  C. Great Britain.
  D. Poland.

____ 10. The civil war in Yugoslavia was fought
  A. between communists and anti-communists.
  B. between pro-democracy supporters and followers of Milosevic.
  C. among Serbs, Croats, and Muslims.
  D. between northern and southern Yugoslavia.

East Asia and Southeast Asia (1945–Present)

 **SECTION 1** *JAPAN BECOMES AN ECONOMIC SUPERPOWER*

◼ TEXT SUMMARY

After World War II, the bombing left Japan devastated. The job of recovery included rebuilding burned-out cities and finding food and housing for the people.

> **THE BIG IDEA**
>
> **Due to a number of favorable factors, Japan emerged as an economic superpower.**

Allied forces, led by United States General MacArthur, occupied the land. They had two goals: Stop military rebuilding and set up a democracy. In 1946, a new constitution let the Japanese elect lawmakers. It gave women equality, guarded rights, and took away the power of the emperor. In 1952, the Allied occupation ended.

By 1975, Japan had made an economic recovery. Success came from the production of exports. Japan sent steel, cars, and electronics all over the world. Why did Japan succeed? It had a large force of educated workers. New factories had modern machines. High tariffs on foreign imports encouraged people to buy local goods. Finally, little military spending meant more money for business.

Along with economic success, Japan had its problems. Global events, like the 1970s oil crisis, meant a shortage of raw materials for a country with few natural resources. Eighty percent of the population lived in crowded cities. Past success came, in part, because employees gave their lives to work. Now, some seemed less willing to give up family time.

◼ GRAPHIC SUMMARY: *The Recovery of Japan*

1945	1975
Japan occupied by Allies	Japan is ally of United States
New constitution strips emperor of power	Democracy in place
Many cities destroyed	Cities rebuilt
Japan not allowed to build up military	Japan counts on allies for defense; has more money to put into its economy
Japanese economy ruined	Japan develops high-quality exports and technology; makes foreign investments
Education only for the upper classes	Education available to all people
Few natural resources at hand	Japan exports finished goods while importing raw materials

Japan recovered from World War II and rose to economic power.

◼ REVIEW QUESTIONS

1. What were the two goals of the American forces that occupied Japan?

2. Chart Skills How did education in Japan change between 1945 and 1975?

FROM REVOLUTION TO REFORM IN CHINA

◼ TEXT SUMMARY

After World War II, conflict in China continued. Mao Zedong led the Communists to victory over the Nationalists. Communists won control for several reasons. Mao won support from peasants by promising them land. Communism valued all workers, so most women also backed Mao. Finally, Mao's army was better than the Nationalists'. In 1949, Mao united the Chinese under communism and set up the People's Republic of China.

Mao ran a totalitarian state. He put all business in party hands. He urged peasants to join lands and make larger farms. Communist ideas replaced religion. New schools taught students to praise their leader. In 1958, Mao launched a program known as the Great Leap Forward. This program called for **communes,** groups of people who live and work together, to meet production **quotas,** or shares. The program failed. In 1966, the Cultural Revolution forced people to be loyal to Mao. Red Guards made sure people followed policies.

In 1976, Mao died. New Chinese leadership brought more economic freedom, but little political change. Deng Xiaoping introduced the Four Modernizations aimed at updating farming, industry, science, and defense. In 1989, the army fiercely crushed a rally for democracy. In the 1980s and 1990s, China has tried to control its birthrate. Chinese leaders face the challenge of providing food, homes, and jobs for more than one billion people.

THE **BIG** IDEA

Communists succeeded in unifying China in 1949. They carried out reforms while building a totalitarian state.

◼ GRAPHIC SUMMARY: *Programs in Postwar China*

Leader	Mao Zedong		Deng Xiaoping
Program	The Great Leap Forward	The Cultural Revolution	The Four Modernizations
Year Begun	1958	1966	1981
Goals	• Increase farm and factory output	• Renew communist loyalties	• Reform economic system
Methods	• Communes • Production quotas	• Red Guards	• Family farms • Some private businesses • Some free-market sales
Results	• Program fails • Two years of low production and hunger	• Economy slows • China closes to outside world • People fear arrest • Civil war threatened	• Economy and standard of living improves • Gap between rich and poor widens • Foreign relations and trade improve

Postwar programs aimed to increase farm and factory output while keeping people under strict control.

◼ REVIEW QUESTIONS

1. Give three reasons why communist forces won control of China.

2. Chart Skills What was a goal of the Cultural Revolution?

THE ASIAN TIGERS

◼ TEXT SUMMARY

Taiwan, Hong Kong, Singapore, and South Korea are called the "Asian tigers" because of their strong recovery after World War II. Their locations close to China and near major ocean trading routes helped their economies to grow rapidly. All four were influenced by Confucian ideas and Chinese power. Taiwan and Hong Kong have especially strong links to China. Hong Kong reunited with China in 1997. Taiwan remains a separate land.

After 1945, the Asian tigers became economic giants and centers of trade. Their great economic success began with light industry and then moved into heavy industry as well. These countries welcomed trade with China when it was closed to the rest of the world. They thrived not only because of trade but also because of electronics, textiles, and banking. As of 1980, Singapore, the smallest Asian tiger, had the busiest port in the world.

The Korean peninsula was another area that suffered during World War II. After the war, it was divided into communist North Korea and noncommunist South Korea. In 1950, the North invaded the South. A UN force helped the South while the Chinese helped the North. A **truce,** or cease-fire, in 1953 left Korea still divided. South Korea became one of the Asian tigers. North Korea struggled under totalitarian rule and a communist economy. (See diagram below.)

> ## THE **BIG** IDEA
>
> **The nations known as the Asian tigers have combined industrialization, trade, and finance to achieve remarkable economic growth.**

◼ GRAPHIC SUMMARY: *The Two Koreas*

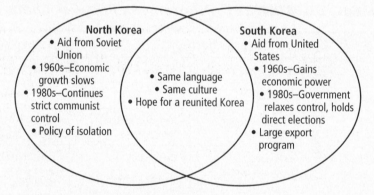

North Korea
- Aid from Soviet Union
- 1960s—Economic growth slows
- 1980s—Continues strict communist control
- Policy of isolation

- Same language
- Same culture
- Hope for a reunited Korea

South Korea
- Aid from United States
- 1960s—Gains economic power
- 1980s—Government relaxes control, holds direct elections
- Large export program

North Korea watched South Korea become an economic tiger.

◼ REVIEW QUESTIONS

1. What are two reasons for the economic strength of the "Asian tigers"?

2. **Diagram Skills** Why do you think the economy of South Korea did better than that of North Korea?

SOUTHEAST ASIA AND THE PACIFIC RIM

◾ TEXT SUMMARY

After World War II, Europe hoped to regain its colonies in Southeast Asia. However, the colonies wanted to be free. Whether freedom came easily or after years of war, the newly freed lands had problems. They had little practice with self-rule. Regional and ethnic groups fought bitterly. Modernization proved difficult.

A thirty-year period of war began in 1946 in Vietnam, a French colony. The struggle became a major Cold War conflict. In 1954, communist fighters forced out the French. The nation split into the communist North and the noncommunist South. To stop a communist invasion of the South, the United States sent aid and then troops. The Soviet Union and China aided the North. Some Americans protested the United States role in Vietnam. In 1973, United States troops began pulling out. In 1975, the communists reunited Vietnam. They later came to control Laos and Cambodia.

Asian countries in the **Pacific Rim,** or countries bordering on the Pacific Ocean, became an important market in the world economy. The whole region profited from the busy ocean trade routes on which they are located. Foreign investors brought in money. In 1967, six lands—Singapore, Malaysia, Thailand, the Philippines, Indonesia, and Brunei—formed the Association of Southeast Asian Nations (ASEAN) to increase prosperity and improve self-reliance.

> ### THE **BIG** IDEA
>
> **Following World War II, Southeast Asian nations struggled to free themselves from colonial rule.**

◾ GRAPHIC SUMMARY: *Self-rule for Southeast Asia*

Philippines
- 1946–Independence from the United States
- Political corruption and unrest
- 1986–Democratic elections

Myanmar (formerly Burma)
- 1948–Independence from Britain
- 1989–Renamed Myanmar
- 1990–Military refuses to give up power after elections

INDEPENDENCE IN SOUTHEAST ASIA

Indonesia
- 1949–Independence from the Netherlands
- 1965–Military defeat of communist revolt
- 1990–Improved standard of living through economic reform

Vietnam
- 1954–Independence from France; division of North and South Vietnam
- 1957–Communist invasion of South Vietnam
- 1975–Reunification of Vietnam by communists

Independence brought unrest to these Southeast Asian nations.

◾ REVIEW QUESTIONS

1. Why did the United States become involved in the war between North and South Vietnam?

2. Diagram Skills Name three nations that lost their holds in Southeast Asia after World War II.

SURVEY CHAPTER 34
MODERN ERA CHAPTER 21 *Test*

■ IDENTIFYING MAIN IDEAS

Write the letter of the correct answer in the blank provided. (10 points each)

____ 1. Why did the American military government disband the Japanese armed forces?
   A. to humiliate the Japanese
   B. to win World War II
   C. to destroy Japanese militarism
   D. to appease the Soviet Union

____ 2. Which of the following describes Japan's trading position by the 1970s?
   A. It had a favorable balance of trade.
   B. It suffered a huge trade deficit.
   C. It refused to trade with outsiders.
   D. It was unable to market its products.

____ 3. Which of the following contributed to Japan's economic success?
   A. low wages
   B. a trade deficit
   C. a well-educated work force
   D. high military spending

____ 4. The support of what two groups helped the Communists triumph over the Nationalists in China?
   A. Soviets and merchants
   B. teenagers and the clergy
   C. women and peasants
   D. business leaders and the nobility

____ 5. Which of the following did Mao do to rebuild the Chinese economy?
   A. decreased coal and steel output
   B. instituted free elections
   C. honored landlords
   D. placed businesses in party control

____ 6. What was Deng Xiaoping's program emphasizing agriculture, industry, science, and defense called?
   A. the Four Modernizations
   B. the Great Leap Forward
   C. the Cultural Revolution
   D. the "Little Red Book"

____ 7. Following World War II, Taiwan's economy grew
   A. slowly.
   B. quickly.
   C. sluggish.
   D. illegally.

____ 8. The Korean War was caused by
   A. the bombing of North Korea.
   B. the assassination of Kim Il Sung.
   C. North Korea's invasion of the south.
   D. MacArthur's attack of North Korea.

____ 9. South Vietnam was supported by
   A. the Soviet Union.
   B. the Chinese.
   C. the Viet Cong.
   D. the United States.

____ 10. Why is the Pacific Rim important to the global economy?
   A. Most of the world's people live in the region.
   B. It has most of the world's resources.
   C. It has most of the world's fresh water.
   D. The busy ocean trade routes provide links for trade.

South Asia and the Middle East (1945–Present)

 SECTION 1

NATIONS OF SOUTH ASIA

■ TEXT SUMMARY

After World War II, Britain agreed to free India. At the same time, riots broke out between the Hindu majority and the Muslim minority. To settle the disputes, Britain gave Muslims control of lands in eastern and western India in 1947. These became East and West Pakistan. (After other conflicts, East Pakistan became the independent nation of Bangladesh.) The **partition,** or division, of India did not bring peace. Many were killed crossing the borders between India and Pakistan.

After independence, India and Pakistan developed similar goals. All wanted a stable government. They needed technology to control nature and raise food for growing populations. Industrial and economic development was necessary to become modern nations.

Obstacles, or barriers, stood in the way of achieving these goals. (See diagram below.) Religious and ethnic battles made unity difficult. Floods and droughts ruined crops, and farms could not feed the huge populations. Few countries in the region had natural resources such as oil.

Fear and mistrust often guided relationships in South Asia. India and Pakistan fought several times for control of Kashmir, a region in the Himalayas. Both India and Pakistan developed nuclear weapons and refused to sign a treaty banning their use. In the Cold War, India signed a treaty of friendship with the U.S.S.R, but tried to remain neutral. Pakistan accepted aid from the United States.

THE **BIG** IDEA

The partition of India in 1947 created two nations— India and Pakistan.

■ GRAPHIC SUMMARY: *Obstacles to Progress in India*

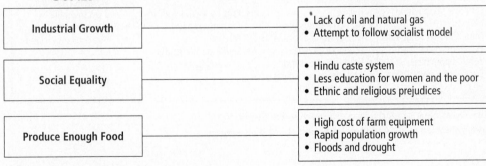

GOALS | OBSTACLES

Industrial Growth
- Lack of oil and natural gas
- Attempt to follow socialist model

Social Equality
- Hindu caste system
- Less education for women and the poor
- Ethnic and religious prejudices

Produce Enough Food
- High cost of farm equipment
- Rapid population growth
- Floods and drought

India aimed to improve life for its people, but problems got in the way.

■ REVIEW QUESTIONS

1. Why was India partitioned in 1947?

2. Diagram Skills What were two obstacles that kept India from growing enough food?

FORCES SHAPING THE MODERN MIDDLE EAST

■ TEXT SUMMARY

Diversity and nationalism have shaped the Middle East. While most of its people are Muslim, the lands are also home to Jews and Christians. People in the Middle East speak many languages and belong to different cultures. These differences have led to conflict. Likewise, nationalism caused turmoil. Europeans created borders for their Middle Eastern colonies, forcing people of different races and religions to live together. With independence, the artificial divisions led to armed clashes. At the same time, some Arabs dreamed of one unified Arab state.

Resources have had a powerful impact on the region. The discovery of oil brought power to some Middle Eastern nations, but oil resources are unevenly distributed across the region. The oil-rich nations are able to pay for their own development while those that lack oil must go without. Another precious resource, water, may soon be more important than oil. Nations argue over water rights but also work together to solve water problems.

In many countries, the laws of Islam shape every part of life from government to family to fashion. In the 1950s and 1960s, some people began to take on western styles. Muslim leaders blamed problems on the new ways. By the 1990s, a return to Islam united much of the Muslim world. While Islamic reformers often rejected westernization, they did not reject modernization.

THE BIG IDEA

Ethnic and religious diversity and an Islamic revival are some of the forces shaping the Middle East today.

■ GRAPHIC SUMMARY: *Forces Shaping the Middle East*

Religious and Ethnic Differences	Natural Resources	Governments	Islamic Traditions
• Muslims, Christians, and Jews • Different sects within religions • More than 30 languages • Religious, racial, and cultural prejudices • Desire for a united Arab state	• Largest oil fields in the world in parts of the region • Oil-rich nations gain wealth and political and economic power • Limited water supply • Arguments over dams and water rights	• Democracy in Israel and Turkey • Rule by royal family in Jordan and Saudi Arabia • Single-party dictators in Iraq and Syria	• Laws of Islam influence government, society, and personal life • Anti-western feelings • 1990s revival of Islamic traditions

These forces have created a land of unrest where people fight to claim their lands, defend their faith, and guard their wealth.

■ REVIEW QUESTIONS

1. What religion has the most influence on the way of life in the Middle East?

2. **Chart Skills** Explain how two resources have shaped the Middle East.

 **SECTION 3**

NATION BUILDING IN THE MIDDLE EAST: THREE CASE STUDIES

■ TEXT SUMMARY

Turkey, Egypt, and Iran have the largest populations in the Middle East. All are Muslim, but each has its own history.

Turkey, after years of military rule, set up a democracy in the 1920s. Then, it joined NATO in the 1950s. In the 1990s, Muslim leaders challenged the tradition of secular government. Ethnic conflicts troubled Turkey. It once aimed to stamp out the culture of the Kurds, but eventually let up. Battles over the island of Cyprus led Greeks and Turks to divide that land in the 1970s.

Since 1950, Egypt has had three strong leaders. Gamal Abdel Nasser ended foreign control and modernized Egypt. He ended British control of the Suez Canal, set up a socialist economy, and built Arab pride. Under Nasser, Egypt lost two wars with Israel. In 1970, Anwar Sadat opened doors to private and foreign business. He formed ties with the United States but angered Arabs by making peace with Israel. After Sadat was assassinated in 1981, Hosni Mubarak kept the peace with Israel and improved relations with other Arab lands.

With Western help, the **shah,** or ruler, of oil-rich Iran built industry. He gave land to peasants, granted rights to women, and removed religion from government. However, he used force to keep control. In 1979, Ayatollah Khomeini led a revolt and the shah fled to America. Khomeini died in 1989. More moderate leaders tried to build a modern Iran while staying true to Islam.

> ### THE **BIG** IDEA
>
> Turkey, Egypt, and Iran have faced similar issues, but have followed separate paths.

■ GRAPHIC SUMMARY: *Two Nations of the Middle East*

IRAN
- More ethnic groups than any country in region
- Located in Southwest Asia
- Rich in oil
- Islamic revolution in 1979
- Encouraged revolution in other Muslim countries

- Population largely Muslim
- Widespread poverty and unemployment
- Once under European control

EGYPT
- Largest population of any country in region
- Located in North Africa
- Few natural resources
- Control of Suez Canal
- Peace treaties with Israel and improved relations with United States

While Egypt and Iran share some of the same problems, each has issues of its own.

■ REVIEW QUESTIONS

1. What steps did Nasser take to end foreign control of Egypt?

2. **Diagram Skills** How do natural resources differ in Iran and in Egypt?

SECTION 4 — THE MIDDLE EAST AND THE WORLD

TEXT SUMMARY

Shipping routes and oil fields make conflicts in the Middle East global concerns. During the Cold War, the Soviet Union and the United States each had allies in the region.

In the battle over Palestine, America helped Israel and the Soviets aided the Arabs. Both Arabs and Jews saw Palestine as a **homeland,** or country of one's ancestors. Wars broke out in 1948, 1956, 1967, and 1973. Israel, the Jewish state, fought off Arab attacks, took land, and forced Palestinian Arabs from their homes. The Palestinians answered with terrorist attacks. Although Israel reached a historic agreement with the Palestinians in 1993, some Arabs and Jews accused leaders of giving up "promised lands."

Some Palestinian Muslims fled to Lebanon. There, Muslims fought Christians and Muslim sects fought each other. In 1983, a UN force pulled out after Muslim terrorists killed French and American troops. By 1990, some order returned to Lebanon.

The Persian Gulf has seen two big conflicts, each caused in part by border disputes. In 1980, an Iran-Iraq War threatened ships and oil fields. In 1987, the United States Navy went to the Gulf to protect the flow of oil. In 1990, Iraq invaded Kuwait to seize oil fields. The United States saw this action as a threat to Saudi Arabia and the oil flow. In the 1991 Gulf War, United States bombs pounded Iraq while troops freed Kuwait. The war, however, did not destroy Iraqi dictator Saddam Hussein or end Middle East tensions.

THE BIG IDEA

Global concern arises over conflicts in the Middle East because of vital shipping routes and natural resources.

GRAPHIC SUMMARY: Conflict in the Middle East: 1948–1994

The world watches as peace efforts aim to end violence in the Middle East.

REVIEW QUESTIONS

1. Explain the role the United States played in two Middle East conflicts.

2. **Time Line Skills** Which Arab nation was the first to sign a peace treaty with Israel?

SURVEY CHAPTER 35
MODERN ERA CHAPTER 22
Test

▪ IDENTIFYING MAIN IDEAS

Write the letter of the correct answer in the blank provided. (10 points each)

_____ 1. Why was the nation of Pakistan created?
   A. to allow the British to remain powerful in India
   B. to persuade the Hindus to give up territory
   C. to give Hindus and Muslims their own states
   D. to end centuries of fighting

_____ 2. Whose side did Pakistan take during the Cold War?
   A. India's
   B. no one's side
   C. the Soviet Union's
   D. that of the United States

_____ 3. The word or phrase that best describes the oil resources of the Middle East is
   A. sparse.
   B. unevenly distributed.
   C. thinly but evenly distributed.
   D. nonexistent.

_____ 4. Which is the most highly valued natural resource in the Middle East?
   A. timber
   B. sand
   C. water
   D. farmland

_____ 5. While Islamic reformers rejected westernization, they did not reject
   A. democratization.
   B. secularism.
   C. Americanization.
   D. modernization.

_____ 6. Which of the following moves by Nasser helped end foreign intervention in Egypt?
   A. undermining the authority of the military
   B. building the Aswan High Dam
   C. inviting foreign investment in Egypt
   D. seizing control of the Suez Canal

_____ 7. What action by Sadat angered Arab states?
   A. He made peace with Israel.
   B. He led two wars against Israel.
   C. He built the Aswan High Dam.
   D. He cracked down on terrorists.

_____ 8. The conflict between Palestinians and Jews in Palestine centered around
   A. differences in religion.
   B. the claim by both groups that it was their homeland.
   C. disagreements over borders.
   D. the role of the British in Palestine.

_____ 9. In 1993, a historical agreement was signed between
   A. Israel and the PLO.
   B. Hamas and the PLO.
   C. Israel and Syria.
   D. Iraq and Iran.

_____ 10. Tensions along the Persian Gulf were partially caused by
   A. border disputes.
   B. population growth.
   C. oil shortages.
   D. disinterested rulers.

Africa (1945–Present)

SECTION 1 ACHIEVING INDEPENDENCE

TEXT SUMMARY

At the end of World War II, most of Africa was under European rule. Only Ethiopia, Liberia, Egypt, and South Africa were independent. A call for freedom swept Africa after 1945.

Colonial rule left its mark on Africa. Colonial borders forced many ethnic groups into one nation. New leaders had to build unity among people of different backgrounds and customs. Yet, Africa lacked experienced, educated leaders. New nations relied on Europe as a source of goods and a market for exports. At the same time, Europeans still owned farms and mines that influenced the economy.

Colonies gained self-rule by both peaceful and violent means. Kwame Nkrumah led the Gold Coast (Ghana) to freedom from Britain. Like many African leaders, Nkrumah had gone to school in the West and had become a skilled speaker. The political party he created called for peaceful strikes and boycotts. In Kenya, Jomo Kenyatta led a nonviolent effort for independence from Britain. However, a group known as the Mau Mau used guerrilla warfare. The British jailed Kenyatta and crushed the Mau Mau rebels. Still, the struggle went on. In 1963, Kenyatta became head of free Kenya. It took a bloody war to free Algeria from France. Muslim nationalists began the fight in 1954. Thousands died before Algeria was freed in 1962.

> ### THE BIG IDEA
>
> After World War II, a tide of nationalism swept through Africa resulting in independence for many nations.

GRAPHIC SUMMARY: *The Great Liberation in Africa*

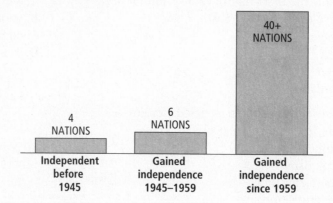

		40+ NATIONS
4 NATIONS	6 NATIONS	
Independent before 1945	Gained independence 1945–1959	Gained independence since 1959

The great liberation in Africa started slowly, then picked up speed in the 1960s.

REVIEW QUESTIONS

1. Describe the role one nationalist leader or group played in winning freedom for their African nation.

2. **Graph Skills** When did most of the African nations gain independence?

PROGRAMS FOR DEVELOPMENT

■ TEXT SUMMARY

The free nations of Africa set goals. Leaders aimed to unite their people and create stable governments. They hoped strong economies would improve the standard of living.

In most African lands, similar obstacles blocked progress. The barriers occurred in five areas: geography, population and poverty, economic dependence, economic policies, and political difficulties. Drought along with **deforestation**, or loss of vegetation, caused widespread hunger. Rapid population growth made the famine worse. Problems also arose where many ethnic groups lived in one nation. Leaders tried to replace loyalty to a culture with loyalty to a nation. When faced with trouble, many nations turned to a one-party system. Some of these one-party countries became dictatorships.

All new nations made political and economic choices to overcome the obstacles. Some nations rejected military leadership and dictators and chose to build on traditional African ways. For economic growth, nations either set up socialist state-run industries, allowed capitalist enterprise, or had **mixed economies,** economic systems with both private and state-run industries. Some states chose to grow cash crops rather than food crops. As a result, some of these countries had to import food. Many leaders helped urban industries rather than rural farms. By the 1980s, they saw food output drop and began to aid their farmers. By learning from mistakes, most states were moving forward in the 1990s.

THE **BIG** IDEA

New African nations sought unity and stability as they set up political and economic systems.

■ GRAPHIC SUMMARY: *Obstacles to Progress in Africa*

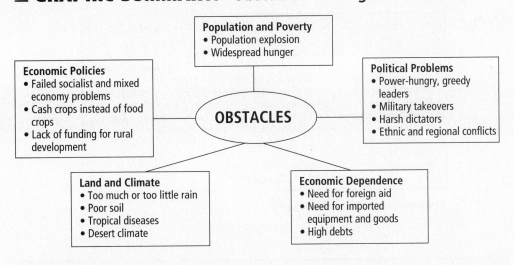

Population and Poverty
- Population explosion
- Widespread hunger

Economic Policies
- Failed socialist and mixed economy problems
- Cash crops instead of food crops
- Lack of funding for rural development

OBSTACLES

Political Problems
- Power-hungry, greedy leaders
- Military takeovers
- Harsh dictators
- Ethnic and regional conflicts

Land and Climate
- Too much or too little rain
- Poor soil
- Tropical diseases
- Desert climate

Economic Dependence
- Need for foreign aid
- Need for imported equipment and goods
- High debts

In spite of obstacles, the new nations of Africa made progress.

■ REVIEW QUESTIONS

1. What were two goals of the new African nations?

2. Diagram Skills What are two obstacles to progress caused by the land and climate?

THREE NATIONS: A CLOSER LOOK

◼ TEXT SUMMARY

Oil-rich Nigeria won its freedom in 1960. As in other new African nations, ethnic and regional quarrels led to civil war. People in the Southeast broke away in 1967. They formed a new country called Biafra. The war brought hunger and disease to Biafra. Nearly one million people died. In 1970, Biafra gave up and the war ended. The oil boom in the 1970s helped Nigeria recover from the war. Later, when oil prices fell, the country had a huge debt burden.

> **THE BIG IDEA**
>
> After independence, each African nation faced its own unique set of challenges.

Until 1960, Belgium ruled the Congo. Until 1965, the land had no clear leader. Then, Mobutu Sese Seko, a harsh military dictator, took power. He called the nation Zaire. Mobutu ran the economy into the ground and stole billions of dollars of the country's wealth. Conflicts among ethnic and regional groups sparked a war. In the late 1990s, rebels forced Mobutu from power. They renamed the country Congo.

Julius Nyerere, the first leader of Tanzania, hoped to improve rural life and do away with social classes. He wanted the country to meet all its own needs. He nationalized all banks and foreign-owned businesses. His program of African socialism set up communal farms and state-run industries. The program eventually failed. To save the economy, the next leader cut spending and allowed private business to operate. Unlike other African countries, Tanzania's food output did not decline. With foreign aid, it was also able to provide education and health care to many villages.

◼ GRAPHIC SUMMARY: A Look at Four African Nations

Nigeria Independence: 1960	Congo (Zaire) Independence: 1960	Tanzania Independence: 1961
• Rich in oil • Ethnic and regional conflicts led to civil war • Military rule • Developed cities rather than farms • Important leader: General Ibrahim Babangida	• Rich in minerals • Ethnic and regional conflicts led to civil war • Military rule • Economic decline • Military dictator: General Mobutu Sese Seko • Rebels forced Mobutu from power in 1997	• Aimed to unite people • Socialism • Emphasized agriculture • One-party rule • First president: Julius Nyerere

New nations faced years of struggle.

◼ REVIEW QUESTIONS

1. What did Tanzania try to do that Nigeria and Zaire did not?

2. **Chart Skills** What event occurred in Nigeria and Zaire, but did not occur in Tanzania?

STRUGGLES IN SOUTHERN AFRICA

▣ TEXT SUMMARY

For 342 years, Europeans ran South Africa. Whites set up a system of **apartheid,** or separation of the races, in 1948. Laws said certain races must live in certain zones. They banned mixed marriages and forced nonwhites to carry passbooks. They called for separate trains, beaches, and schools. Low wages and poor schools doomed blacks to poverty.

The African National Congress (ANC) had fought white domination since 1912. (See diagram below.) Their marches and strikes sparked violence. At a 1960 rally, police gunned down protesters. Laws then banned the ANC. The United States and others hoped **sanctions,** or actions against a nation by other nations, would force an end to apartheid. In 1990, F.W. de Klerk, president of South Africa, lifted the ANC ban. He freed its leader, Nelson Mandela, from jail. Mandela and de Klerk planned elections for 1994. Together, all races elected Mandela president of a new democratic South Africa.

Other lands in Southern Africa also struggled for independence. For 15 years, Angola and Mozambique fought wars of independence against Portugal. After gaining independence, both countries were plagued by civil wars. From 1975 to 1992, the Cold War played a role in their struggles. Americans did not trust the socialist leaders and sided with rebels in both countries. South African troops also aided the rebels. Soviets sent Cuban troops to help Angolan leaders. In 1992, foreign troops pulled out, leaving the war-torn nations to rebuild.

> ### THE **BIG** IDEA
>
> The successful struggle against apartheid in South Africa serves as a beacon of hope to other African nations.

▣ GRAPHIC SUMMARY: *Steps to the End of Apartheid*

1994	Voters of all races elect Mandela president.
1990	President de Klerk lifts ANC ban, ends apartheid, frees Mandela.
1980s	United States and other nations place sanctions on South Africa.
1964	Nelson Mandela sentenced to life in prison.
1960	Police kill 69, wound 180 at Sharpeville demonstration; government outlaws ANC.
1948	Policy of apartheid set up.

As apartheid ended, South Africa began to grant rights to all its people.

▣ REVIEW QUESTIONS

1. What were two effects of apartheid laws?

2. Diagram Skills How long was Nelson Mandela in prison?

SURVEY CHAPTER 36
MODERN ERA CHAPTER 23 *Test*

IDENTIFYING MAIN IDEAS

Write the letter of the correct answer in the blank provided. (10 points each)

___ 1. Nationalist leaders in the Gold Coast first tried to win independence from Britain using
   A. guerrilla warfare.
   B. strikes and boycotts.
   C. armed attacks.
   D. riots.

___ 2. Newly independent African nations often lacked
   A. hospitals.
   B. elementary schools.
   C. vaccines for smallpox.
   D. educated and experienced leaders.

___ 3. Why did colonial borders cause problems for new African nations?
   A. They cut them off from important resources.
   B. They created countries that were too small for their populations.
   C. They forced people together from different ethnic groups.
   D. They stopped herders from migrating with their animals.

___ 4. One problem with using land to grow cash crops is
   A. they require more water.
   B. it takes a lot of labor to grow them.
   C. the market for cash crops is small.
   D. the land isn't available to grow food.

___ 5. A mixed economy has
   A. all state-run industries.
   B. both agriculture and industry.
   C. all private industries.
   D. private and state-run industries.

___ 6. In Nigeria, conflict between ethnic groups led to
   A. permanent partition.
   B. a new democratic constitution.
   C. foreign military intervention.
   D. civil war.

___ 7. In Zaire, Mobutu Sese Seko was removed from power as a result of
   A. the economic collapse of Zaire.
   B. a civil war.
   C. a democratic election.
   D. an invasion from a neighboring country.

___ 8. What was life under apartheid like for nonwhite South Africans?
   A. open and free
   B. full of opportunities
   C. peaceful and satisfying
   D. extremely restrictive

___ 9. What happened to Angola and Mozambique after gaining independence?
   A. They became peaceful.
   B. Their economies boomed.
   C. They were torn by civil wars.
   D. They suffered under apartheid.

___ 10. In 1990, President de Klerk of South Africa
   A. tightened the ban on the ANC.
   B. freed Nelson Mandela.
   C. set up apartheid.
   D. allowed all races to vote in elections.

Latin America (1945–Present)

SECTION 1 *FORCES SHAPING MODERN LATIN AMERICA*

■ TEXT SUMMARY

Latin America has a history of inequality. A small group of people has always held most of the wealth. Others lived in poverty. In many nations, inequality, along with a rigid social class structure, a swiftly growing population, and urbanization, led to unrest.

Catholic priests and nuns started a liberation theology movement that called for social justice and an end to poverty. Most military dictators were against social reform. They said strict control would bring order. In the 1960s and 1970s, rebels fought for a socialist revolution that would bring equality.

After World War II, leaders worked to build economic development. New local industries cut the need for imported goods. However, many factories put out poor quality goods. Farming became big business. Companies grew cash crops on the best farmlands. As a result, more food had to be imported. In the 1980s, economies slowed. Governments cut spending, raised prices, and welcomed foreign business. Many economies picked up in the 1990s.

In Latin America, as in Africa, an urban migration brought change. It broke up families and weakened cultural traditions. Many city women took jobs outside the home. Some entered politics. Women became a force for social change, working for better schools and health care.

> ### THE **BIG** IDEA
>
> Social inequality, population growth, and rapid urbanization all contributed to unrest in Latin America.

■ GRAPHIC SUMMARY: *Unrest in Latin America*

Gap between Rich and Poor
- Small group controls most of wealth
- Wealthy people against reforms

Social Classes
- Upper classes descended from Europeans
- Poor majority are mestizo, Native American, and African American

Population and Poverty
- Population explosion
- Not enough land to grow food

Urban Growth
- Migration of peasants to cities
- Slums and urban shacks
- Not enough jobs

Unrest in Latin America

After World War II, inequality, poverty, and unemployment led to unrest.

■ REVIEW QUESTIONS

1. What were the answers to problems in Latin America as seen by (a) military leaders, and (b) rebels?

2. Diagram Skills Describe one reason many Latin Americans were unhappy with their lives and leaders.

LATIN AMERICA, THE UNITED STATES, AND THE WORLD

■ TEXT SUMMARY

After World War II, the United States wanted to keep communism out of the Western Hemisphere. In 1948, it joined the countries of Latin America in the Organization of American States (OAS). Members pledged to promote democracy and human rights. Each nation promised to stay out of the affairs of the others.

Before World War II, the United States and the island nation of Cuba were friendly. Then, in 1959, Fidel Castro led a communist revolt against a dictator that the United States government supported. Castro took control of Cuba and formed ties with the Soviet Union. Cold War tensions flared when the Soviets placed nuclear missiles on Cuban bases.

Castro tried to stir revolt in other lands. In response, the United States turned to a policy of **intervention**, or involvement, in Latin America. United States money, arms, and troops helped crush communist rebels. At times, the aid went to harsh noncommunist rulers. Many people spoke out against the United States policy.

Today, Latin America has links throughout the world. Venezuela joined with Arab nations to set oil prices. Brazil worked with African lands to protect coffee prices. Regions signed pacts to end tariffs and allow free trade. The Americas joined forces to control the drug trade and save the rain forests.

> ### THE **BIG** IDEA
>
> Throughout the 1900s, Latin American nations tried to limit United States influence and exercise greater independence.

■ GRAPHIC SUMMARY: *United States Intervention in Latin America*

1965 Dominican Republic
U.S. troops help fight rebel forces

1983 Grenada
U.S. troops arrive to overthrow communists

1960 — 1970 — 1980 — 1990

1973 Chile
U.S. aid helps military overthrow socialist president

1980s El Salvador
United States aids military government

1989 Panama
U.S. troops help remove dictator

United States power influenced events in these, and other, Latin American nations.

■ REVIEW QUESTIONS

1. What were two results of the revolution in Cuba?

2. **Time Line Skills** When did the United States intervene in Chile? In El Salvador?

MEXICO, CENTRAL AMERICA, AND THE CARIBBEAN

■ TEXT SUMMARY

After World War II, Mexico worked to cut foreign influence. It built the second largest economy in Latin America. What had been a farm economy became a mostly urban, industrial one. Mexico enjoyed success, but faced troubles, too. (See chart below.) In the late 1970s, new oil fields and high oil prices meant economic boom. When the 1980s brought a world **recession,** a time when business is poor, oil prices fell and Mexico went into debt. Although foreign factories were built to make use of cheap Mexican labor, there were never enough jobs. The gap between rich and poor remained.

Central America, too, had gaps between rich and poor. Leaders stole from the people and killed those who spoke out against them. Cruelty, corrupt rule, and poverty sparked civil wars in Nicaragua, Guatemala, and El Salvador. Because the United States saw most rebels as communist threats, it helped some military dictators hold power.

After a period of harsh rule, the island of Haiti held free elections in 1990. A priest, Jean-Bertrand Aristide, won the election but was exiled in a military coup. The United States helped bring Aristide back to build a democracy. It was a hard job. Haiti was the poorest nation in Latin America. The old ruling class did not care about human rights. People wondered if the new democracy could survive.

THE **BIG** IDEA

During the postwar era, several Central American countries were battered by civil wars, while Mexico had little turmoil.

■ GRAPHIC SUMMARY: *Ups and Downs of the Mexican Economy*

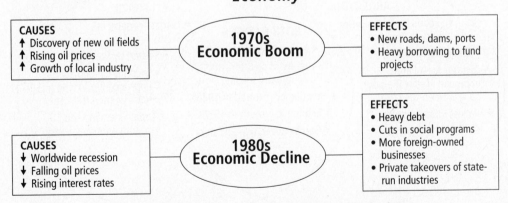

CAUSES
↑ Discovery of new oil fields
↑ Rising oil prices
↑ Growth of local industry

1970s Economic Boom

EFFECTS
• New roads, dams, ports
• Heavy borrowing to fund projects

CAUSES
↓ Worldwide recession
↓ Falling oil prices
↓ Rising interest rates

1980s Economic Decline

EFFECTS
• Heavy debt
• Cuts in social programs
• More foreign-owned businesses
• Private takeovers of state-run industries

Even during the economic boom, most Mexicans remained poor.

■ REVIEW QUESTIONS

1. Why did many Central American countries have civil wars?

2. **Chart Skills** How did global oil prices affect the economy of Mexico?

FOCUS ON ARGENTINA AND BRAZIL

■ TEXT SUMMARY

Argentina and Brazil are the largest South American nations. Each has had ups and downs while building democracy and a strong economy.

In 1946, Argentina made Juan Perón president. Nationalists liked his bans on foreign-owned business. The urban poor liked higher wages, strong labor unions, and social reforms. Perón and his wife Eva worked to be popular. Eva helped the poor, building clinics and child-care centers. To gain votes for her husband, she helped women win the vote. While Perón wooed the urban poor, he put down opposition to his strict rule. His economic policies led to huge debts, and in 1955 he lost power in a military coup.

In Brazil and Argentina, economic hard times led to military coups. Military leaders in both countries killed their critics. In the 1980s, democracy returned to Argentina and Brazil through elections. It has survived.

The 1990s also brought economic growth. Brazil had learned it could not count on exports of rubber and coffee. In the 1930s, it began to **diversify**, or make different products. The government built an inland capital. It also settled new land and pushed development in the Amazon. This spurred economic growth and helped ease crowded cities, but hurt the rain forests. In Argentina, a good economy paid for new social programs. The country soon had the highest literacy rate in Latin America. Still, wealth belonged to the few.

> ### THE **BIG** IDEA
>
> History and geography have shaped Argentina's and Brazil's efforts to develop stable governments and strong economies.

■ GRAPHIC SUMMARY: *The Giants of South America*

ARGENTINA
- Second largest country in South America
- Settled by Spain
- Dictator Juan Perón improved life for the poor; gave women the vote
- Highest literacy rate in South America

BOTH NATIONS
- Rich natural resources
- History of dictators and military rulers
- Democracy restored in 1980s
- Economic growth in 1990s
- Gap between rich and poor continues

BRAZIL
- Largest country in South America
- Settled by Portugal
- Dictator Getúlio Vargas improved life for the poor; gave women the vote
- Today is among top 10 economies in the world

A look at the people, politics, and economies of Argentina and Brazil shows that these countries have a lot in common.

■ REVIEW QUESTIONS

1. In Argentina and Brazil, what often happened to leadership during economic hard times?

2. Diagram Skills What is one way Argentina and Brazil differ from other South American countries?

SURVEY CHAPTER 37
MODERN ERA CHAPTER 24 *Test*

■ IDENTIFYING MAIN IDEAS

Write the letter of the correct answer in the blank provided. (10 points each)

____ **1.** What was the result of population growth and urbanization in Latin America?
A. a decrease in poverty
B. an increase in educated workers
C. redistribution of wealth
D. unrest and revolution

____ **2.** What did Church workers in the liberation theology movement work for?
A. increased power for the Church
B. social justice and an end to poverty
C. access to higher education
D. increased military power

____ **3.** One group in Latin America that became an effective force for social reform was
A. women.
B. military rulers.
C. Marxists.
D. the middle class.

____ **4.** What were the goals of the Organization of American States?
A. to stop the United States from taking over Latin America
B. to prevent the spread of communism
C. to overthrow Castro
D. to promote democracy and human rights

____ **5.** The United States and the Soviet Union came to the brink of nuclear war in 1962 over Soviet missile bases in
A. Brazil.
B. Colombia.
C. Cuba.
D. Haiti.

____ **6.** Which Latin American country joined Arab nations in OPEC?
A. Argentina
B. Venezuela
C. Paraguay
D. Peru

____ **7.** Despite economic successes, most Mexicans remained
A. poor.
B. wealthy.
C. in rural villages.
D. employed.

____ **8.** Which of the following terms best describes conditions in Central American countries in the past two decades?
A. democracy
B. civil war
C. prosperity
D. peace

____ **9.** Which of the following groups supported Juan Perón's government?
A. the military
B. the urban poor
C. foreign investors
D. educated people

____ **10.** Which of the following issues in Brazil provoked conflict between economic development and environmental protection?
A. destruction of the rain forest
B. illegal immigration
C. war on drugs
D. free trade zone

GLOSSARY

A

absolute ruler one who has complete authority over the government and the people he or she governs (p. 33)

acupuncture a way of treating sickness by pricking parts of the body with small needles (p. 24)

ally a country or group joined with another or others for a common purpose (p. 28)

annul to officially put an end to; to cancel (p. 77)

antisemitism prejudice against Jews; unfair or cruel treatment of Jews (p. 130)

apartheid a policy of separating the races and denying rights to those who are not white (p. 195)

appeasement policy of giving in to demands in order to keep peace (p. 166)

aqueduct in ancient Rome, bridge-like stone structure that carried water from the hills into the cities (p. 34)

archaeology study of the lives of early people through examining the things they left behind (p. 6)

archipelago chain of islands (p. 71)

aristocracy government in which an upper class has ruling power (p. 27)

armistice an agreement to stop fighting; a cease-fire before a formal peace treaty (p. 148)

artifact object made by a human being, such as a tool or weapon (p. 6)

assassination the murder of a leader or other important person (p. 146)

assembly group of people; in this case, a group that makes laws (p. 87)

astrolabe an instrument used to determine latitude by measuring the position of the stars (p. 80)

B

baroque style of art and architecture having many decorations and fancy curved designs, popular during the 1600s and 1700s (p. 98)

blitz a sudden, fierce attack meant to quickly overcome defenses (p. 167)

blitzkrieg lightning war; a method of warfare used by the Germans involving a quick, all-out attack (p. 167)

borough a town or section of a city in Great Britain that sends a member or members to Parliament (p. 128)

boycott a group refusal to buy goods or services (p. 178)

bubonic plague a deadly disease that spreads quickly and is carried to human beings by fleas from rats (p. 51)

buffer any person or thing that acts to lessen conflict between two warring forces (p. 170)

C

cabinet groups of officials who act as advisers to the ruler of a nation (p. 99)

capitalism economic system in which the land, factories, and so on used in making goods are owned and operated by individuals for profit (p. 89)

caste system a system in which people are born into social groups from which they cannot move (p. 17)

caudillo military dictator in Latin America (p. 142)

cease-fire a period of time during which both sides agree to stop fighting a war (p. 180)

censor to examine and remove or hold back anything politically or morally offensive (p. 153)

circumference the distance around something (p. 59)

civil disobedience the refusal to obey laws believed to be wrong or unfair (p. 157)

civilian a person who is not a member of the armed forces (p. 180)

civilization a highly developed and organized society; the stage of progress of human beings where they have developed the following features: cities, organized government, written language, social classes, arts and architecture, public works, job specialization, and complex religions (p. 7)

clan group of families with the same ancestor (p. 18)

Cold War a state of conflict without armed battle (p. 170)

command economy system in which the government makes all decisions for businesses and industries (p. 152)

commercial to do with buying and selling things; business (p. 45)

commune a group of people living and working closely together and sharing property and tasks (p. 183)

concentration camps prison camps for people thought to be dangerous to a ruling group (p. 168)

conquistador Spanish explorer who claimed lands in the Americas for Spain in the 1500s and 1600s (p. 85)

conservative in Europe during the 1800s, someone who wanted to preserve traditional ways (p. 113)

constitutional government a government whose power is defined and limited by law (p. 99)

corporation business owned by many people who buy shares of stock (p. 117)

corrupt changed from good to bad; dishonest (p. 33)

covenant a binding agreement (p. 14)

crusade holy or religious war (p. 49)

cultural diffusion the spread of ideas, customs, and technologies from one people to another (p. 8)

cuneiform wedge-shaped writing of the Sumerians and other ancient peoples (p. 12)

D

daimyo warrior lords directly below the shogun in Japanese feudal society (p. 72)

Daoism the teachings of Laozi that said that the best government was one that governed the least (p. 23)

decline to get worse, or to get smaller (p. 16)

deforestation loss of vegetation (p. 193)

dehydration the process of removing water from something (p. 64)

delegates those sent to speak and act for others; representatives (p. 196)

democracy government in which the people have ruling power (p. 27)

détente an easing of tensions or bad feelings between nations (p. 176)

developed nation a country with strong trade and industry and a high standard of living (p. 173)

developing nation a country with little trade and industry and a low standard of living (p. 173)

dike a high wall or dam that is used to hold back water and prevent flooding (p. 108)

direct democracy a government in which the citizens participate directly, rather than through elected representatives (p. 28)

disband to break up as a group (p. 179)

dissolve to officially end (p. 93)

diversify to expand a business or an economy by adding different kinds of products, services, and so on (p. 200)

Duma a group of officials elected to approve Russian laws (p. 126)

dynasty ruling family (p. 10)

E

empire group of states or regions controlled by one ruler or government (p. 13)

enlightened despot absolute ruler who uses his or her power to bring about reform (p. 98)

enlightenment in Buddhism, state of understanding (p. 20)

epic a long serious poem that tells the story of a hero (pp. 17, 27)

estate in feudal times, any of three social classes (p. 102)

ethnic having to do with a group of people who have the same language, culture, and so on (p. 180)

excommunicate to punish someone by taking away their right to be a member of a church (p. 44)

execute to put to death in a way that is ordered by law (p. 104)

expel to drive out (p. 77)

F

fast to give up eating for a time, often for religious reasons (p. 57)

fertile rich, able to be cultivated (p. 8)

Fertile Crescent region of good farmland around the Tigris and Euphrates rivers; home to early Sumerian civilization (p. 12)

feudalism system of government in which lords govern their own lands but give military service to a greater lord (p. 43)

fief in the Middle Ages, a piece of land given by a lord to a vassal in exchange for service (p. 43)

flapper in the United States during the 1920s, a young woman who cut her hair short and dressed in the new, short fashions (p. 162)

flying buttress arched support used in Gothic architecture (p. 50)

G

gentry wealthy landowning class (p. 68)

geography study of the Earth, including its peoples, resources, climates, and physical features (p. 6)

Gothic style of architecture common in Western Europe between the 1100s and 1500s (p. 50)

gravity the force that pulls one mass or object toward another (p. 78)

Great Depression a time during the 1930s when many people were out of work and business was poor (p. 159)

griot professional storyteller in early West Africa (p. 66)

guardian a protector (p. 91)

guilds in the Middle Ages, artisan associations that controlled particular trades (p. 45)

Guomindang in China, the Nationalist party led by Sun Yixian (p. 158)

H

haiku form of Japanese poetry that expresses a feeling, thought, or idea in three lines, or 17 syllables (p. 72)

Hellenistic a culture that blended parts of Greek, Persian, Egyptian, and Indian life (p. 30)

hereditary in a ruling family, passing power from father to son; passing a trait from parent to child (p. 47)

hieroglyphics picture writing developed by the ancient Egyptians (p. 11)

historian person who studies how people lived in the past (p. 6)

Holocaust the killing of six million Jews by Nazi Germany (p. 168)

home rule local self-government (p. 129)

homeland the country in which a person or person's ancestors were born (p. 190)

Huguenot a French Protestant (p. 92)

humanism the study of human needs and goals, rather than religious ideas (p. 74)

I

idealistic showing something in its most perfect form (p. 29)

immigrant people who come into a country foreign to them to make a new home (p. 178)

imperialism the practice of one country controlling the government and wealth of weaker countries (p. 133)

impressionism painting movement of the late 1800s and early 1900s that tried to capture the effects that objects and scenes had on the mind (p. 120)

indulgence in the Roman Catholic Church, a pardon for sins committed during a person's lifetime (p. 76)

inflation increase in the amount of money available that raises prices and wages (p. 89)

interchangeable parts pieces that are exactly alike and can be used in place of one another in manufacturing (p. 117)

intervention the act of coming in to help someone or to settle something (p. 198)

isolated apart from others; alone (p. 18)

J

joint family family in which several generations live in the same home (p. 22)

K

kabuki form of Japanese theater developed in the 1600s (p. 72)

kaiser the title of the ruler of Germany or Austria before 1918 (p. 122)

karma in Hinduism, all of the actions in a person's life that affect his or her next life (p. 22)

L

laissez faire policy allowing business to operate with little or no government interference (p. 97)

Latin the language of the Romans (p. 34)

layman person who is not in the clergy (p. 50)

Legalism the teachings of Hanfeizi that said that a good ruler should use strict laws and harsh punishments (p. 23)

liberal someone who wants political change and reform (p. 113)

limited monarchy type of government in which a constitution limits the power of the monarch (p. 93)

lineage group in which all the members claim a common ancestor (p. 66)

M

mandate after World War I, a territory that was held by an Allied power (p. 156)

Mandate of Heaven divine right to rule in ancient China (p. 18)

manor during the Middle Ages, the lord's estate, which included one or more villages and the surrounding lands (p. 43)

medieval period the Middle Ages, lasting from roughly A.D. 500 to 1450 (p. 42)

mercantilism policy by which a country tried to increase its supplies of gold and silver by selling more goods to other countries than it bought from them (p. 89)

messiah person sent by God to save the people (p. 35)

migration movement of people or animals from one place to another (p. 174)

militarism a great pride in the military and a national policy of building a strong army (p. 145)

mixed economy economic system with both private and state-run industry (p. 193)

monarchy government in which a king or queen has ruling power (p. 27)

monotheistic believing in one God (p. 14)

monsoon seasonal wind; in India, the winter monsoon brings hot dry weather and the summer monsoons brings rain (p. 16)

morale feelings of spirit and enthusiasm toward a common goal (p. 148)

mosque a building used by Muslims for worship (p. 61)

mummification way of preserving dead bodies by treating them with chemicals and wrapping them in cloth (p. 11)

N

nationalism feeling of pride in and devotion to one's country (pp. 104, 145)

nationalist a person who feels pride in his or her country (p. 113)

natural laws laws that explain why people act the way they do (p. 97)

natural rights rights that belong to all humans from birth (p. 97)

nomad person who moves from place to place in search of food (p. 7)

O

obstacle anything that gets in the way or keeps something or someone from moving ahead (p. 187)

occupation type of job (p. 17)

oligarchy a government in which a few persons have ruling power (pp. 27, 99)

Outback rugged inland region of Australia (p. 141)

P

Pacific Rim countries in Asia and America that border the Pacific Ocean (p. 185)

pagoda a temple in the form of a tower with many stories and many roofs that curve upward; in eastern religions (p. 68)

partition the act of dividing into parts (p. 187)

patrician member of the landowning upper class in ancient Rome (p. 32)

penal colony place where people convicted of crimes are sent (p. 141)

perestroika in the former Soviet Union, a policy of economic restructuring (p. 179)

pharaoh title of the ruler of ancient Egypt (p. 10)

philosopher person who studies general principles of knowledge (p. 29)

plantation large piece of land on which crops are grown, run by an owner and worked by laborers who live there (p. 86)

plebeian a member of the lower class in ancient Rome; included farmers, merchants, artisans, and traders (p. 32)

pogrom violent attack on a Jewish community (p. 126)

porcelain very thin, delicate ceramic, used for making fine dishes, vases, or ornaments (p. 68)

predestination idea that God decided long ago who would go to heaven (p. 76)

prehistory period of history before writing was invented (p. 6)

premier a chief government official; a prime minister (p. 130)

prime minister in countries with a parliament, the person in charge of the government (p. 99)

propaganda the spreading of ideas and information to make others accept something; these may be false or misleading (p. 148)

prophet a person who speaks or claims to speak for God (p. 14)

prosperity wealth (p. 21)

protectorate country with its own government but under the control of an outside power (p. 133)

province locally controlled region of a country or an empire (p. 13)

pyramid ancient Egyptian stone building where pharaohs and their kin were buried (p. 10)

Q

quota the share that is due from a person or group (p. 183)

R

rajah elected chief of an Aryan tribe in ancient India (p. 17)

ration to give out scarce items in certain shares or portions (p. 148)

realism artistic movement that aimed to show the world as it is (p. 120)

recession a period when business is poor; a mild depression (p. 199)

reform changes that correct faults or evils (p. 126)

reincarnation in Hinduism, belief that the soul is reborn after death in another body (p. 20)

Renaissance a golden age in the arts, literature, and sciences; literally means "rebirth" (p. 74)

reparations payment for war damages (p. 149)

republic a government in which the officials are chosen by the people (pp. 32, 152)

revolt to fight or rebel against a ruler or government (p. 24)

rococo style of art and architecture having many fancy designs (p. 98)

Romanesque style of architecture in Western Europe during the 1000s and 1100s using round arches, vaults, and very thick walls (p. 50)

romanticism artistic movement of the 1800s that appealed to emotion rather than reason (p. 120)

rudder a wood or metal plate use for steering a ship (p. 24)

S

samurai warrior in Japanese feudal society (p. 72)

sanctions actions taken by one nation against another for breaking international law; for example, a ban on trade (p. 195)

savanna a flat, grassy plain with few or no trees and irregular rainfall (p. 63)

scientific method a way of finding out information based on experimentation and observation (p. 78)

secede to stop being a member of some group (p. 131)

secular nonreligious (p. 44)

segregation the practice of separating people of different races (p. 178)

self-determination the right of a people to choose their own form of government (p. 149)

sepoys Indian troops (p. 136)

serf in the Middle Ages, a peasant forced to work on the land of the lord (p. 43)

shah a title used by the rulers of Iran (p. 189)

shogun in Japanese feudal society, military commander who held more power than the emperor did (p. 72)

skyscraper a very tall building (p. 118)

socialism system in which all the people, instead of private individuals, own all the property and operate all businesses (p. 111)

soviet a council of workers and soldiers set up to govern the USSR after the Russian revolution (p. 151)

sphere of influence place where an outside power claims all rights to investment or trade (p. 133)

stream of consciousness a narrative technique for exploring a character's thoughts (p. 162)

suffrage the right to vote in political elections (p. 119)

sultanate the reign of a sultan; the land ruled by a sultan (p. 60)

surrender to give up (p. 169)

Swahili an East African language (p. 65)

T

tariff a tax on imported goods (p. 129)

terrorism the deliberate use of violence to achieve political goals (p. 172)

theory an idea (p. 162)

theory of evolution idea that humans have developed to their present state over millions of years (p. 119)

total war a situation where all of a nation's resources go into the war effort (p. 148)

totalitarian state government in which a one-party dictatorship controls the lives of its people (p. 153)

tragedy in ancient Greece, a play about human suffering that usually ended in disaster (p. 29)

tributary state an independent state that has to accept that another state is more powerful and so it has to pay tribute to its ruler (p. 68)

tribute payment from a conquered people (p. 38)

truce a time when enemies agree to stop fighting (p. 184)

tsunami tidal wave (p. 71)

turnpike privately built road that charges a fee to travelers who use it (p. 109)

U

urbanization movement of people from rural areas to cities (p. 110)

utilitarianism idea that the goal of society should be to bring about the happiness of the greatest number of people (p. 111)

V

vassal in the Middle Ages, a lord who was given a piece of land in exchange for service to a greater lord (p. 43)

Vedas a collection of ancient Aryan writings (p. 17)

veto to reject; to prevent an act from taking place (p. 128)

W

welfare aid by government agencies for those who need help, for example, the poor, those out of work, and the elderly (p. 176)

Western Front during World War I, a 600-mile stretch of land from the English Channel to Switzerland, where fighting took place (p. 147)

INDEX

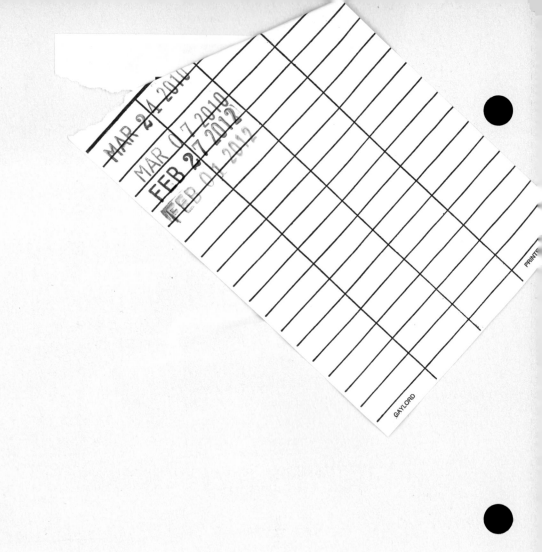